Admiral Togo

Admiral Togo

by Georges Blond

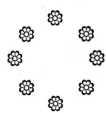

Translated by Edward Hyams

New York
The Macmillan Company
1960

This book was published originally in France under the title *L'AMIRAL TOGO: Samouraï de la Mer,* © *Librairie Arthème Fayard,* 1958.

First Printing

The Macmillan Company, New York
Brett-Macmillan Ltd., Galt, Ontario

Printed in the United States of America

Library of Congress catalog card number: 60-8592

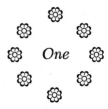 *One*

Before the First World War, the Emperor Hirohito, the present sovereign of Japan, appeared but rarely in public, and then only ceremoniously, and wearing the uniform of a grand marshal: by tradition, he is directly descended from the Sun Goddess.

After 1945 there was, at least superficially, a change. All over the world, newsreels showed the emperor wearing a business suit, and a rather shabby one at that, carrying a soft felt hat, and acknowledging greetings with an awkward, almost excessive, bow. I recall hearing audiences laugh at the spectacle; it did not, of course, occur to them that the change from ceremonial to commonplace garments had its effect on his movements, nor even that to change from a god into a constitutional monarch might be difficult.

1

In short, they had no notion of the psychological tragedy the man had been living through.

It is impossible to know what the emperor's private thoughts may have been when, yielding to pressure by the militarist caste, he signed the rescript which "unleashed the dogs of war." But we may take it that his visits to the sites of the two cities reduced to dust by atomic bombs, and to hospitals full of incurable wounded —such were the usual occasions of his public appearances— were not enjoyed as pleasure trips.

For my part, when confronted with such pictures, I often thought of another Japanese of historic importance, a man who had already aroused my interest; and certain questions came to mind: How many times a day, a week, does this defeated monarch, brave in his misfortune, think—as I do—of the man who was his first mentor—Admiral Togo? Was it what he had learned from Togo that led Hirohito to set the East on fire? Was it that same teaching which enabled him to accept the inevitable surrender realistically, whereas a majority of the men in high places shirked that responsibility by committing hara-kiri? It may well have been the same mind, and the same spirit, that inspired both decisions.

True, Togo's had not been the only voice to which the emperor had hearkened since his childhood: far from it. The victor of Tsushima had not been his tutor as the word is understood in ordinary usage. The official department concerned with the prince imperial's schooling, presided over by Admiral Togo, was composed of no less than seventeen masters. Nevertheless it is inconceivable that the long-standing fame of the victor of Tsushima, and the admiral's endearing and in some respects mysterious personality, should have failed to make an impression on his pupil.

I hope that the reasons that led me to become interested in Admiral Togo will become apparent in the course of my narrative. One of these reasons can be briefly expressed: the preceptor of the monarch of the first kingdom to be atom-bombed was, by his origins and in his youth, a medieval personage. This is not hyperbole: he

2

was a member of a feudal community living in a land more ignorant of the outside world than the France of Joan of Arc. He had done battle, sword in hand, wearing the traditional, ancestral costume bearing, five times repeated, the armorials of his family. He had rammed solid cannon balls down the muzzles of guns similar to those used in battle in the sixteenth century. But, subsequently, he had led into battle the fleet of modern battleships and cruisers that had won the victory that placed Japan among the great powers. To me this man's life has been a striking illustration of the phenomenon we rightly call the "acceleration of history."

Togo was born in the year 2508 of the imperial Japanese Era. We shall transcribe this into the terms of the Christian Era, and then glance briefly at what was happening in the world during the year in question.

1848: In Paris, a provisional government had just proclaimed the Second Republic. France possessed fifteen hundred kilometers (about a thousand miles) of railroad on which tall-funneled locomotives drew trains at twenty-five miles an hour. Men of fashion were wearing tight-waisted frock coats with silk lapels, their women bell-shaped skirts. Victor Hugo had been a member of the Chamber of Peers for two years. Balzac, at forty-nine, declared that he still had fifty novels to write in order to complete his *Comédie humaine:* he was to write two of them. The conquest of Algeria had been completed when, on December 23, 1847, Abd el-Kader had surrendered to General Lamoricière.

In Prussia, a country gentleman was preparing to leave his estate and take his seat as a member of the Constituent Assembly. The instructions that he wrote down for his bailiff were signed *Baron von Bismarck-Schönhausen.*

In Britain, Queen Victoria was in the eleventh year of her glorious reign. While all Europe was convulsed by social revolution, Free Trade Great Britain was making her fortune. Industry was developing at a frantic speed. The Peninsular and Oriental Company's steamers had already been sailing the seas for a decade. The Cunard

Line was eight years old. The Hamburg-America Line had just been founded.

On the Atlantic, a tremendous traffic was under way, and its intensity was not to diminish for half a century: in those fifty years, twenty-three million human beings were to emigrate to America.

Let us suppose ourselves aboard one of the emigrant ships. Our steamer drops anchor at Charleston: Irishmen, Germans, Englishmen, Frenchmen, Italians, Slavs pour over the gangways, all the adventurers and born pioneers of Europe, some outcast by their families, others bringing their families with them to the promised land, the land of their hopes. The more venturesome push on toward the west, traveling on horseback, in every sort of wheeled vehicle, in endless caravans across the Texan plains, the aridities of New Mexico, and still farther, to California, subject of a hundred fabulous rumors. Let us suppose that we have traveled with the boldest of these until, on the brand-new frontier between the United States and Mexico, we come to San Diego. Confronting us is the vastness of the Pacific. Launching ourselves across it, winging above its watery infinities empty of all else for days at a stretch so that a solitary whaler rotten with salt strikes us with amazement, we hold upon our course until, after six thousand nautical miles, we come at last to a halt.

We would find ourselves in a remarkable country: a country which seems alien to this century of commerce, industry, and exploration; a country closed and still; a country refractory, hostile even, to all novelty, all exchange of ideas or goods, cut off from the outside world, shut in on itself, impenetrable, impermeable. This absolute, this almost faery isolation is, however, due to no enchantment, or even physical obstacles. It is the outcome of deliberate policy, expressed once for all in the imperial edict of 1639.

"In the future, and for as long as the sun shall continue to light the world, let no man attempt to land in Japan, even as an ambassador; and let this order never be infringed, on pain of death."

The same capital punishment was laid down for any Japanese attempting to travel abroad. From 1639 to 1848: in Europe, from

4

the Thirty Years' War to Pasteur's first discoveries; in Japan, nothing. The Japan of 1848 was undeviatingly the same as the Japan of 1639; identical. And the Japan of 1639 hardly differed from twelfth century Japan.

Not one stone building: the towns were built of wood and paper. To get some idea of the crowd moving about their narrow streets, it is enough to examine the prints produced by certain eighteenth century native artists. Among them the work of Hokusai is the most interesting. No Western garment marred the bright harmony of kimono and sash, straw mantle, and hair pinned up with pins of shell or coral. The men of the laboring classes wore a kind of apron, and on their legs tight-fitting trousers, gaitered. Men of noble rank —the samurai—were recognizable by their two swords; their back hair was plaited and drawn forward in a queue erect above a carefully shaven tonsure. There were few women in the streets. The traditional costume of Japanese women has been sufficiently described, and need not detain us here. Life in the towns was animated, even crowded, as in Europe's medieval cities, and at nightfall the hawkers of warm wine began their rounds.

Japan consists of three large islands, Hokkaido, Honshu, and Kyushu, and of numerous others, smaller, some very small. Honshu, the principal island, is separated from the next by the famous Inner Sea. The south of Hokkaido is at the latitude of Vladivostok, whereas the southern extremity of the whole archipelago is one degree north of the Tropic of Cancer. Consequently the climate is not the same over the whole extent of the country.

We have, then, arrived in the Japan of 1848; braving the imperial edict, we have set foot ashore in the port of Kagoshima, at the southernmost point of the southernmost major island Kyushu. It was this island that Ninigi, grandfather of the Sun Goddess—ancestor of all the mikados—chose as his landing place, in the province of Satsuma. Togo was to be born not far from the same place, in a landscape of shady valleys between volcanic, pine-clad mountains, where rain is succeeded by bright sunshine in a clear sky. The summer is long, hot, but not excessively so, altogether agreeable.

But the day of our visit in 1848 is a winter one, and it is raining. Kagoshima appears as an extent of flat-roofed houses: not a steeple or a cupola, only tiled roofs gleaming, under the gray sky, among thatched ones.

Beyond the town a strip of sea, and beyond that again a mountain, a deeply truncated cone whose summit is veiled by clouds—Sakurajima, a volcano which is to be heard of in due course. For the time being, it is peaceful, and the whole countryside is bathed in tranquil humidity, so that there is nothing to make us suspect the hidden violence of nature in these parts, a violence which can suddenly manifest itself in catastrophic typhoons, earthquakes, tidal waves, and eruptions. At such times, the very land seems bent on reminding the world that here lies the uttermost outpost of Japanese territory where, more than once, the fate of the empire has been at stake. And among local place names which Togo, as a child, is certainly to hear often mentioned as celebrated will be that of the strait which separates Japan from continental Asia as the English Channel separates England from Europe: a legendary name, this, since it recalls the sea disaster suffered, in the thirteenth century, by Kublai Khan, who had seen his Tatar horde, one hundred and fifty thousand men of war whose like had already swallowed Asia, swallowed up in their turn as they moved against Japan: Tsushima.

The history of Japan is long, complicated, and often confused. But here there is no need to do more than sketch the social and political structure of the country at the time with which we are concerned.

The social structure was feudal. At the summit of the feudality composed by the daimios, or lords, was a sort of "mayor of the palace," the shogun, in whose hands was concentrated the executive power. Theoretically, supreme power lay with the emperor, called the mikado or tenno. But in point of fact this virtually supernatural being did not rule, but was content to reign remotely and from on high, living in the midst of his court at Kyoto, in a luxury, a refinement, and a decadent softness all beyond description.

The shogun ruled from Yedo, the city which was subsequently to be known as Tokyo. He did as he pleased, provided his vassal barons did not become too powerful, and often handed down office and power from father to son. Thus, parallel with the imperial dynasty, unchanged since its foundation by the Sun Goddess, there had been a succession of dynasties holding the shogunate: in 1848 the Tokugawa family was in power.

This had been the state of affairs since the thirteenth century. As in most primitive communities, the highest social rank was that of the warrior: the terms *warrior* and *samurai*, meaning "well born person," are synonymous. But there were degrees of rank within this nobility; and, for the lesser nobles, to fight for one's overlord was both duty and pleasure. The whole feudal society was sub-divided into clans: the Japanese word *han* signifies both the territory of a daimio and his corps of vassals. Apart from the nobility or warrior caste, the community included merchants, artisans, and peasants. It is hardly necessary to add that at all levels, from top to bottom, but notably in the nobility, the men had all the rights, the women none. A moralist of the eighteenth century, Kaibara, defined the duties of Japanese womanhood for all time in a work entitled *The Great Teaching for Women*. No Western mind could conceive of a more rigorous description of absolute—but smiling—submission. Even if her husband gives himself up to debauchery, the good wife must continue to smile, and not allow herself to feel jealous, "for jealousy would make her countenance repulsive and her voice exasperating, and she would succeed only in completely alienating her husband from herself."

It is no news that women have a way of breaking out of even the tightest theoretical bondage: it is not difficult to find instances of female slaves enslaving their masters by way of the senses, the heart, and even the mind. But examples of female emancipation have always been rare, even exceptional, in non-Christian societies. And the recognized religion in the Japan of 1848 was Shintoism salted with Buddhism. Shinto means, literally, "the way of the gods," and it was the name given to a vague mythology and the worship of ancestors and of natural forces. Shintoism has no dogma, no sacred scriptures, and no code of ethics. It might be described as an unsectarian moral philosophy, which explains how Japan had come to accept, without disturbance, both Confucianism, introduced about the beginning of the Christian era, and Buddhism, introduced toward the beginning of the seventh century after Christ. The complex metaphysic of Buddhist theology seems to have left the Japanese mind more or less indifferent, nor was it seriously affected by Confucian influences. In the course of the country's history these several tendencies—Shintoist, Confucianist, and Buddhist—were, in turn, more or less predominant. But if, impatient of such refinements, we were to ask the simple question: What, in fact, was the dominant trait of Japanese religion at the period in which we are interested? the answer would be, Ancestor worship.

This sketchy account was necessary to give the reader a rough idea of the physical and moral climate into which the child who was to become Admiral Togo was born. His mother was brought to bed on January 27, 1848, at Kajima-Machi, a village in the near neighborhood of Kagoshima. The child's father, Kichizaemon Togo, was a samurai, that is, a man of noble birth, and a highly esteemed vassal of his daimio, the lord of Satsuma Province. A distinguished swordsman and a notable man of letters, Kichizaemon Togo had been entrusted with diverse provincial offices, having been in turn comptroller of the revenue, master of the wardrobe, and district governor.

Japanese biographers of Admiral Togo tell us that his mother, Masuko, third daugher of Yosazaemon Hovi, of the same clan as her husband, "was renowned for her beauty and intelligence." As to the praise of her intelligence, no doubt it implies that she was invariably of her husband's opinion. She was thirty-six at the birth of her fourth son, our hero, who was at first given the name Nakagoro. This, according to tradition, must be his name until he attained his thirteenth year. As soon as Masuko

8

was able to leave the house, she carried her little son Nakagoro to the shrine of the Togo family divinity, and herself placed him upon the altar. And there, with samurai rites, the infant was solemnly dedicated to his country's service.

It is not impossible for us to picture the places where Nakagoro spent his childhood. First the house, surrounded by its bamboo fence: we are told that it had twelve rooms, but we must not think of it as a twelve-room Western house. A traditional Japanese house has no interior walls, but only movable frames covered with translucent paper and either set in place or stacked away out of sight, according to the season of the year and the circumstances of the household. Even the exterior walls have no permanent existence, since they consist of wooden shutters placed in position at night and stored in closets during the day. Nakagoro was accustomed to the drafts which constitute the normal ventilation of such a house from his earliest infancy. On winter's hardest days he might warm his small hands at the traditional braziers, famous alike for their low thermal efficiency and high incendiary properties. By way of comfort he was given boiling-hot baths. Old-fashioned Japanese domestic comfort has been much praised by traveling authors. One fact is certain, however: the alternation of cold drafts and very hot baths (the temperature is given as about 110 degrees Fahrenheit) had, by the nineteenth century, made a majority of Japanese martyrs to rheumatism.

The garden, rather than the house, was the center of Togo family life during the summer—a garden, however, with almost no flowers. It was, moreover, very small, and consisted largely of stones arranged with artistic carelessness and two well raked sandy paths. This was embellished on one side by a low clump of artificially dwarfed conifers—the masterpiece of Japanese arboriculture; and, on the other side, given a sacred character by the Shinto altar of the household gods. Small though it was, the enclosure included a pond and two willows.

As we have seen, Kajima-Machi was a village, so that the moment Nakagoro stepped outside the family domain he was in

9

the midst of a peasant farming community. In theory, the peasantry was next in social rank to the samurais, taking precedence of merchants, artisans, and laborers. But this exalted rank carried no moral or material advantages, and actually the peasantry was the most conservative, as it was probably the most backward, of the classes. For centuries these peasants had been cultivating the same crops—rice, barley, wheat, and millet, and a few vegetables; and using the same tools—hoe, hollow spade, scythe, a roughly made flail, and a plow comparable with primitive Egyptian models.

Neither carts nor barrows were to be seen in roads or lanes: all loads were carried on their heads or on bamboo poles by the short, wiry, muscular men. There were no pastures and no farmyards—sheep and pigs were unknown to these people, and the larger cattle scarce. Almost the whole extent of Japan is mountainous, only 12 per cent of her area being suitable for cultivation. Sloping fields made the working of the rice paddies excessively difficult. Almost everywhere mountain streams had to be dammed and canalized to retain the water and feed it, as needed, to the cultivated fields. Manure was required, and, in default of farmyards, human excrement was used. At certain seasons the transport and spreading of this manure gave the whole countryside a very peculiar odor, but no Japanese nose seemed offended by it. The cereal crops were sown in winter, while the rice paddies lay fallow. The fields, laid out in checkered squares and rising by terraces, were dark brown, almost black; but when summer arrived, and the burning heat of the sun, they turned a vivid and beautiful green. Contained between steep hills, these bright squares of cultivation filled lovely valleys broadening to the sea.

The sea divided Japan from the world, and no man knew what went on beyond the curved line of the horizon; nor, as it seemed, was anyone ever likely to know. The fishermen, whose craft could be seen at sea, were forbidden to sail beyond the fishing banks, a few miles offshore. Bold or recalcitrant spirits tempted to go beyond the limit set knew what awaited them upon their return: beheading. Nor would it serve them to plead that wind or tide had carried them away. The imperial edict of 1639 was rigid: death. Whatsoever came from the external world was anathema, as loathsome as the plague; consequently, any man who had left Japan must necessarily return contaminated, infected with the evil of foreignness, and must, therefore, die. Compared with this rigorous isolation, Great Britain's erstwhile "splendid isolation" was a mere state of mind. Never, in the history of any other people, has such an experiment in isolation been sustained with comparable rigor. We have reached the point where it will be as well to give some idea of the events which had thus led up to the maintenance of a medieval empire in the middle of the nineteenth century.

A.D. 1542: A ship carrying three Portuguese sailors, Antônio de Mota, Francisco Zeimoto, and Antônio Peixoto, and on its way from Macao to Siam, changed course for some unknown reason and put in at Tanega-shima. "These sailors," says the chronicler, "seem to have remained long enough to initiate the natives into the use of firearms." The statement throws but little light on the duration of this first incursion from the outside world: the rapidity with which firearms become first familiar and thereafter indispensable to even the most primitive peoples is well known.

At all events the example of these three pioneers was soon followed, this second exploration being much better known and documented, for Fernandez Mendez Pinto became famous with the publication of his *Discovery of Japan*. He and his two companions, Cristóvão Borcalho and Diego Zeimoto, were in the service of a pirate captain who took them aboard his ship when their own was castaway. But Pinto's accounts are marred by fantasy, he himself having admitted that he preferred "saying whatever would entertain people to establishing the truth." At least he had the merit of frankness.

During the next few years a number of Portuguese sailors visited Japan. These adventurers exchanged European and Indian merchandise—raw silk, fine fabrics, wines, drugs, and medicines—for "whatsoever of value the land had to offer." In August, 1549,

11

the first Christian evangelist set foot in the country, the Jesuit Father Francis Xavier, who was in due course to be canonized. He was accompanied by another Jesuit, Father Fernandez, and by a Japanese, one Yajiro, who had left his country in company with Mendez Pinto.

Nowadays we are likely to experience astonishment when we consider with what initial interest and subsequent fervor Japan welcomed the Catholic message. For twenty-seven months Francis Xavier met with nothing but success. "As far as I am able to judge," he wrote, "the Japanese exceed in virtue and honesty all other peoples hitherto discovered. They have a lovable nature. They are not wily and they set honor above all else." The first Christian church was built at Yalaguchi, beside the Inner Sea, on ground presented by a prince.

However, Francis Xavier was, above all, the apostle of the Indies, and never ceased thinking of the work that he had barely begun in India. It seemed to him that no spiritual conquest would present less difficulty than that of Japan. Accordingly, he reembarked for the Indies on November 30, 1551, leaving the task of evangelizing Japan to Father Torres and Father Fernandez, who were assisted by numerous native converts, one of whom was Father Laurent, the first Japanese Jesuit. And, manifestly, Heaven blessed their labors. Tens of thousands of neophytes were baptized in the island of Kyushu; a church was built at Nagasaki. At the time it was a small fishing village, but it became a town of thirty thousand inhabitants almost overnight, most of them being Christians. And during the thirty years following Francis Xavier's departure, the number of converts reached a hundred and fifty thousand.

The Jesuits numbered seventy-five—seventy-five spiritual conquerors who every day reviewed their battle plan and perfected their strategy, *ad majorem Dei gloriam*. It occurred to them that the rate of conversion of a country which, like Japan, had a feudal social structure, must depend upon their success in winning over

12

men in high places. The princes of Oruma, Bungo, and Arima were approached, converted, and baptized.

It so happened that the Jesuits' spiritual policy suited the temporal policy of the shogun, Nobunaga. This potentate, though indifferent to the Christian message, was hostile to the Buddhists, and notably to certain of their monasteries which wielded some political influence. As a result, he gave full support to the Jesuits, who were authorized to build churches at Kyoto and Azuchi. The golden age seemed to have dawned. In 1568, Father Villela was received by the man in whose hands all effectual power was concentrated, the shogun himself. In 1582 Pope Gregory XIII sent personal gifts to the converted princes.

The advantages of any policy are offset by risks. In 1587 the new shogun, Hideyoshi, began to wonder whether the great vassals of the South, with whom the Jesuits were particularly influential, might not be tempted to use their connections with the foreigners to assert themselves against the central power. Having thought this out, he published an edict ordering the Jesuits to leave the country within twenty days on pain of death.

No earthquake could have shaken the Jesuits more terribly. They had supposed themselves, if not finally triumphant, at least irremovable. One hundred and twenty of their number were assembled at Hirado for embarkation aboard the first ship outward bound.

However, their time was not yet, for, suddenly, Hideyoshi changed his mind, and restored freedom to preach to the missionaries. Whereupon twenty-three thousand people in Kyushu had themselves baptized. It was written that the West, for the first but not the last time, should itself furnish the means of its defeat.

The small peninsula thrusting out from Asia, which is called Europe and which is Christian by religion, was already busy working its own ruin and setting at nought the genius which might have placed the world at its feet; it was divided against itself even in its most Catholic heart. The Spanish Franciscans and Dominicans were jealous of the spiritual privilege accorded to the Portuguese Jesuits by Pope Gregory XIII in 1585. A number of Franciscans from Manila arranged to be allowed into Japan as envoys from the governor of the Philippines, and consecrated a church at Nagasaki. It was a mistake: numerous Japanese saw in this emulation of the Jesuits something tantamount to the competition they had observed between Spanish and Portuguese traders. A dangerous critical spirit began to stir in their minds. Thus it was a Christian indiscretion which administered the first serious check to Christian evangelization. In 1587 a Spanish ship, the *San Felipe,* arrived in Japan. Her pilot was excessively talkative, and perhaps imagined he was doing the right thing by describing, with copious detail, the might and greatness of his master, the king of Spain, and the swift expansion of his empire. And when he was asked how Spain had contrived to possess such vast territories, he replied that throughout the world the cross had opened the way for the flag. It is said that this exchange, like everything said by new arrivals, was at once reported to Hideyoshi; it is difficult to imagine what his first reaction would have been. It may, however, be noted that shortly thereafter twenty-six Christians were crucified at Nagasaki, the second warning they had received, which should have given the European settlers pause.

However, Hideyoshi died, and his successor, Iyeyasu, a tolerant man and a Buddhist, seemed to look with a favorable eye upon the preaching of Christianity. Priestly visitors began arriving in ever increasing numbers. In 1606 the beatification of Ignatius Loyola was celebrated at Nagasaki by a public procession of great splendor. Blandly indifferent to the realities, Jesuits on the one hand, Franciscans and Dominicans on the other, pressed the competition for converts ever more keenly, to the point, on occasion, of open quarreling. Iyeyasu, as watchful as he was tolerant, began to have doubts, and to lend an ear to certain Dutchmen who had also gained a footing in Japan. But, first, a brief word concerning these last.

14

The Dutch maintained a trading post in the country, having established it at Hirado. They had had some difficulty in getting admitted in the first place, owing to Portuguese hostility, but the daimio of Hirado, who had quarreled with the Jesuits, befriended them. The Dutch could not forget that Philip II had closed the port of Lisbon to their trade, and part of the increasing favor shown them by the daimio was due to the tales they told him about the Inquisition, stories for which that nobleman had a marked taste. Some of them had been retailed to Shogun Iyeyasu, who expressed a wish to hear more from the mouths of the Dutchmen themselves. Their stories gave him much to ponder upon.

Iyeyasu, moreover, had another European adviser in his entourage, a man whom we cannot omit to mention even in so brief a sketch as this. This was Will Adams,* a native of Gillingham in Kent, who had arrived in Japan in April, 1598. Adams was chief pilot to a flotilla of five Dutch merchantmen. His ship, *The Charity*, had been parted from the rest by weather or some error in navigation, and had touched at Japan, where Adams had won the shogun's good opinion, set himself up as a shipbuilder, diplomatic agent, and political adviser. This contemporary of Shakespeare ultimately married a Japanese wife and ended his life in Japan.

Though the Jesuits, and the Portuguese generally, had done their very best to put a spoke in his wheel and do him every possible injury with the shogun, they had not succeeded. Here again we have very little to go on in deciding what opinion of his enemies Adams communicated to Iyeyasu, but it seems clear that the

---

* Adams was responsible for the trading rights enjoyed by the Dutch in Japan; he also had business dealings with the Spaniards. In Nachod's *Die Beziehungen der Niederländischen Ostindischen Kompagnie zu Japan in Siebzehnten Jahrhundert* will be found a letter from Sprinckel, ·he leader of the Dutch merchants in the East Indies, to Adams, concerning Adams's efforts to obtain trading privileges for the Dutch in Japan, that is positively obsequious. Adams was also responsible for getting the British East India Company a footing in Japan. His influence was entirely due to Iyeyasu, who made Adams a nobleman and gave him a large estate. When Hidetada succeeded Iyeyasu, Adams lost his influence, though not his rank or property.—TRANS.

Jesuits would have been better advised to avoid making an enemy of the English seaman. At all events, the outcome of the shogun's thinking was an edict whereby the Christian religion was prohibited in Japan. And, six months after Iyeyasu's death, in 1616, his successor, Hidetada, promulgated a new edict making the profession of Christianity in Japan a capital crime. At the very time when mass conversions were being announced, the leading missionaries were being decapitated. The great persecution was beginning.

It was to be long and terrible: 280,000 Christians—the exact figure is doubtful but it was certainly of that order—were put to death in 1635. A profession of Buddhist faith was required of every Japanese subject. In every household all members of every family were obliged to prove that they were not Christians by trampling on an image of Christ and one of our Lady. Refractory citizens, or those suspected of concealing their true religious feelings, were denounced by official informers and put to death, often with horrible tortures. The persecution reached its highest pitch of intensity in the province of Shimabara, where an armed insurrection broke out and developed into a civil war which lasted three months or more. The rebel leader, Masuka Tokisada, hereditary enemy of the Tokugawa clan who held the shogunate, shut himself into the fortress of Amakusa with 33,000 people, of whom 13,000 were women and children. Because the Japanese cannon were not powerful enough to breach the fortifications, the shogun called in the Dutch. The chief of their trading station, one Koekerbecker, unhesitatingly responded to this appeal, and himself commanded ships and guns in the attack. Needless to say, he has been harshly judged. Koekerbecker no doubt considered himself bound to conform to the spirit of the standing orders he had received from his sovereign: "At all costs maintain our trade with Japan." He did so, at the cost of one of the greatest massacres of Christians in history. This event occurred on April 12, 1638.

In the same year, by way of reward for their devotion, the

16

Dutch were ordered to demolish their warehouse at Hirado which, being built of stone, was considered "too massive and too pleasant" by the shogun's government. They were also ordered to remove from all the buildings of their establishment the inscription giving the date of construction: it was a Christian symbol. The Hollanders' assiduity in carrying out these orders was but meagerly rewarded: as the historian Engelbert Kämpfer was, somewhat simple-mindedly, to record, "The more services we render the Japanese, the more they seem to hate and despise us." In 1641 a new residence was appointed for these trade-at-any-price gentry: the little island of De-shima in the harbor of Nagasaki. It was 220 yards long and 90 broad, and there the Dutchmen were to remain, never to leave it upon any pretext whatever excepting one day a year when they were authorized to pay their respects and make their gifts to the shogun. They were to hold no religious services, nor make the sign of the cross, nor do anything else which might remind anyone of the anathematized religion. They accommodated themselves to these humiliating conditions.

The number of ships authorized to put in at De-shima was reduced first to seven, then to one a year. Still the Dutchmen hung on. During the two centuries of isolation the brief presence of their ship was all there was to remind the Japanese that men of other nations existed beyond the horizon. Since 1621, the Japanese had been forbidden to leave their islands. In 1624 an order had been promulgated to burn all ships whose capacity exceeded 2,500 bushels, that is, of eighty-five tons' burden. Finally, in 1639 came the edict, "In the future, and for as long as the sun shall light the world . . ."

Thus, apart from a few crates of Dutch merchandise, severely restricted and accepted with insulting precautions, nothing but what was Japanese was to be found in Japan. Not even God Himself was to be looked for beyond Japan, since He was to be found at Kyoto, in the person of the mikado. The only world was Japan, and Japan filled the world. No style, no ethic, no aesthetic

17

existed or could exist but those native ones which had emerged from centuries of elaboration following their divine origin.

Such was the Japan into which Togo was born.

It is not easy to form valid judgments on certain aspects of social life in old Japan, nor even to picture them with any degree of authenticity. Thus, for example, the methods of educating boys of the samurai class have been described and their worth estimated very diversely by historians, the authors of memoirs, and travelers. We know, however, that this education was unquestionably repressive, in that it entailed a good deal of constraint, certain rules which must on no account be broken, and punishments which were in some cases harsh. But, on the other hand, it seemed to give the boys what we may perhaps call certain guarantees, just because all the rules were precise and immutable, and invariably applied in terms of a code of manners which was quite as exactly defined. There was never an unexpected blow, no shouting, and above all none of that demoralizing alternation of indulgence and harshness too frequently the lot of Western children. There were no outbursts of peevish ill temper: the scrupulous courtesy required of children was also accorded to them. When Masuko went into the room where her four sons slept, rolled in their thick padded covers laid upon mats, she would take care never to pass behind any one of them, even if they were all asleep: according to the code of manners, to do otherwise would have been rude. This, but one detail among hundreds, is by way of example. At least one advantage which samurai youth must have gained from this reciprocal politeness between parents and children is self-evident —poise.

Nor does it seem that Togo's early education, although administered according to these strict principles, was wanting in affectionate feeling. As we shall see, the constancy of his feeling for his mother, in later life, comprised much more than conventional family affection: there subsisted, unquestionably, the memory of his mother's love for him. It is a fact that Masuko played, in the lives of her husband and children, a more important part than was usual among Japanese women. And Masuko, looking upon her baby son, saw that he had a fair complexion and fine eyes. Nor was she blinded by mother love. At certain periods of his life, Togo might almost have been taken for a handsome Westerner.

Meanwhile, he was occupied with the games proper to his age: he taught himself, with notably precocious patience, to spin a top. With his mother as his first opponent, he played battledore and shuttlecock. And he flew his kite like other little boys. Moreover, he owned a pack of hounds made of strangely colored cardboard; they were his defenders against the attacks of evil spirits.

Every year, on May 5th, he went, with his brothers, to the Festival of Boys, for which ceremony the village streets were decorated with enormous paper carp, flying like flags from the tops of tall bamboo poles. The carp was the symbol of boyhood. Just as a carp swims upstream, overcoming the force of the current, so must a lad make his way through life overcoming all obstacles.

Kneeling before his mother, who also kneeled, Togo learned by heart *The Lesson of True Words* and *The Lesson of Youth*, just as we, at his age, learned *The Grasshopper and the Ant*. These *Lessons* are moral maxims supposed to have been composed by ninth century Buddhist monks, and obediently the boy repeated after his mother, "Treasures stored in a barn rot away, but treasures stored in the mind do not decay." And, "If you, being poor, enter into a rich man's house, remember that riches are more perishable than a flower stricken by frost." And again, "Human ears listen, glued to the wall; speak not evil, even in secret." And, "In Heaven there are human eyes; sin not, even in hiding." "The gods strike fools, not to kill but to chastise them; the master strikes his disciple, not in hate but to admonish him." "Of all things, be least sparing of money, for wealth undermines wisdom."

His mother also taught him the Chinese legend of the *Twenty-four Paragons or Models of Filial Piety*. Filial piety being the basic sentiment of any feudal society, its teaching is bound to be all-important. Nevertheless, some of the acts of filial virtue

19

held up by way of example to samurai youth strike us as surprising. Thus, a boy had a stepmother who treated him very badly. However, as she was very fond of fish, he lay down stark naked on the frozen surface of a pond, so that the heat of his body would melt the ice; when two carp raised their heads to breathe he caught them and took them to his stepmother. Another paragon decided to sleep without a blanket, exposing his naked body, so that the mosquitoes would concentrate their bites on him and leave his parents in peace. Another admirable son, although seventy years of age, still dressed in baby's clothes and crawled about the floor, his object being to convince his parents that, since their offspring was an infant, they must still be very young. It is impossible to know what practical conclusions were drawn by Japanese pedagogues from this instance of filial piety.

At eight years of age, Nakagoro was handed over to male teachers. He was himself by then a man in miniature, whose character was beginning to emerge. The first clear trait of that character was obstinacy: he was as obstinate as a mule. Nakagoro slipped out one day to visit his father's stables where, upon his teasing one of the horses, it bit him on top of the head. In retaliation, the boy took a stick and beat the animal. When he presented himself to have his hair dressed by his mother—this was one of the tasks she still reserved for herself—she noticed the marks of the bite. Questioned, Nakagoro at once confessed: the son of a samurai did not tell lies. Naturally he was reprimanded; and he was sensitive to reprimand. His reaction was to pay a second visit to the stable and beat the horse again—for having caused him to be punished. Clearly his early teaching had not crushed his will.

Nakagoro was sent to school. He rose at six or, in winter, at sunrise. The paper house was not yet open to the day; that is to say, the wooden shutters composing its walls had not yet been removed. As soon as they were, Nakagoro set off, with his books under his arm, toward the house of his teacher, Saigo Kichisiro. There for two hours he plied his brush, forming the ideograms of the Japanese system of writing. This calligraphy is an art. It has been said by Europeans that Japanese children waste several years of their schooling learning to write, an opinion which prevailed in the West until the day came when it became apparent that the Japanese adolescent was as intellectually advanced as his Western contemporary and that Japanese workingmen can read their newspaper or write a letter as easily as their European equivalents.

The fact is that ideograms have an educative value of their own. Moreover, according to Basil H. Chamberlain, there is an age at which the brain will absorb no matter what system of written symbols with equal ease; a great number can be learned in the same time that it takes to learn a smaller number, in the same way that the eye perceives a net made up of innumerable small meshes even as it does one of large mesh. According to this specialist, the same thing applies to spoken sounds. In early childhood any language whatsoever can be learned with equal ease; a language with complex inflections is learned by the child in precisely the same time as a very simple, monosyllabic language. I have not quoted these assertions merely because they strike me as reasonable. We shall, in due course, encounter Togo as a pupil on a Royal Navy training ship. We shall see that his early education had not handicapped him intellectually.

Meanwhile, to return to our examination of his day as a schoolboy. After his two hours of calligraphy, he returned home to join his family for the first meal of the day; rice, grilled fish, a soup made of beans, with various seasonings. This was followed by study of the Confucian Classics until noon. At noon came playtime, and Nakagoro roamed the countryside with boys of his own age, played games, and in fine weather bathed in the river. The second meal of the day was at two o'clock and was followed by his fencing lesson. One hour of swordsmanship, with a saber, at ten years of age: only those who have done it themselves will appreciate the physical effort required. But after this lesson the boy had the rest of the day to himself, to fill as he pleased with more roaming about the countryside, games, running races, battles, or hunting. In short,

21

his timetable and occupations were not very different from those of a nobleman's son in medieval France.

At eleven, Nakagoro took his place in the College of Kagoshima. There he continued to study the Confucian Classics and to perfect his calligraphy, but two new subjects were added to his curriculum: history and Japanese literature. Discussing the education of samurai youth in general, and of Togo in particular, modern historians tell us that "they were taught the principles of *Bushido*." It will therefore be as well if we try to define a term that has become a sort of vogue word and has been used in and out of season, inappropriately as often as not.

At the time when Togo was a schoolboy, Bushido did not exist: the word appears in no dictionary, Japanese or foreign, until 1900. It was coined in the twentieth century to designate nationalist morale, a composition of honor and patriotism, which Japan, having emerged from her long feudalism, decided to derive from her samurai traditions. Thus, Bushido was formed from ancient ideas, but carefully revised, and brought up to date so as to be applicable to the needs and struggles of the modern world. As regards the youthful Togo's education, then, it may properly be said that he was instructed according to the traditional principles of Japanese chivalry which were subsequently to be the foundation of modern Bushido. And it is important, in this context, and if we want to get an idea of the moral and intellectual "climate" in which our hero was reared, to bear in mind that this ancestral code of chivalry from which his teachers drew their lessons was, above all, feudal, and therefore strongly class-conscious. Thus, the word *honor* meant what we mean by it when applied to the samurai's attitude toward his daimio and toward his peers and fellow clansmen: horror of lying or any form of treachery. But in the event of war between clans, some compromise with this code of honor was admissible: for example, "all was fair in war."

Similarly, beginning in the twentieth century when the Bushido code was devised and elaborated, honorable behavior meant, or implied, honorable behavior toward the mikado as the person-

22

ification of the nation. Thus the code did not necessarily apply in Japan's relations with foreign powers. Nor should our realization of the nature of this sociological device be taken as offensive to the Japanese. A system of ethics which does not derive from a profound religious conviction is always of limited application: to the clan in the case of a feudal morality; to the nation in the case of a nationalist morality. The difference—and it is, of course, of the utmost importance—between samurai ethics and the system of ethics professed by medieval European chivalry is that the latter was not exclusive; European knights were Christians. This, of course, did not automatically turn them all into saints; still, they always knew, in their heart of hearts, that if they ill-treated the poor or behaved dishonorably in any way, even in defense of their overlord, they were sinning against the light. This may well be one of the reasons medieval Christian chivalry so quickly lost its efficacy as a military force: you cannot have it both ways—power here below *and* reward in the hereafter. The code of ethics favored by the Japanese chivalry was concerned with power here below; it was a kind of warrior's humanism. Certain moral qualities were required by the individual as attributes of his efficiency; nothing is to be expected of men who are cowardly, soft, and demoralized by the habit of lying.

To return to Nakagoro: here is an anecdote which belongs to the period of his childhood just before he entered college. The boy was traveling with his father and his three brothers. At nightfall they reached a hotel, and there Nakagoro and his brother Sokuro quarreled—we are not told what about. Sokuro, however, took his customary boiling-hot bath, which made him very thirsty. He asked his youngest brother to fetch him a drink, and Nakagoro, who could bear a grudge for as long as an elephant, revenged his injured feelings by bringing Sokuro a glass of water dosed with pepper, from which he drank a large draught. Sokuro began uttering bellows of pain which Nakagoro, concealed nearby, heard with delight. But the uproar meant that the matter could no longer remain private; the whole family, if not the whole hotel, had been startled. Kichizeamon Togo, the boys' father, no doubt secretly amused, nevertheless gravely ordered Nakagoro to beg his brother's pardon. A gentle penance, but it must be done at once; among the samurai a father's word was law. But Nakagoro refused to obey. Thereupon, everyone present became quietly attentive, and sorrowful, too, for the boy's disobedience was far more serious than his original offense. Kichizeamon pronounced sentence: ten days' banishment. During ten days Nakagoro must remain outcast from his family. Placed in charge of one of his father's subordinate officers, he was kept under close arrest, like an officer undergoing punishment. On the evening of the tenth day, his father's house was open to him again, and, humbled and silent, he took his place in the family circle. Humbled and silent, but unrepentant: he had preferred banishment to begging his brother's pardon.

A year after Togo began college, the words used by Togo's contemporaries and friends to describe him are: ingenious, conscientious, affable, reserved. It would seem that strong doses of Confucius had at least begun to make the headstrong boy easier to live with. As for his masters, their judgment was: conscientious, works well, no outstanding qualities. Later, journalists and historians, both Japanese and foreign, were frequently to ask the masters, "If a prophet had told you that you had Japan's greatest admiral among your pupils, would you have thought of Togo?" Their candid answer was to be No. Nakagoro Togo—no outstanding qualities. But there was one thing: no weakness, either. On that point his masters were equally and unanimously emphatic. On what may be regarded as his school reports, they recorded: "Intelligent. Not brilliant. Wishes to make progress in his work and applies himself with determination." In short, samurai education was turning the obstinacy of the child into the perseverance of the schoolboy and the strength of purpose which was to become legendary.

24

1860: Nakagoro was in his thirteenth year. By samurai tradition, he had attained his majority. It was an occasion to be celebrated by the whole family, the celebration being both religious and patriotic. As Roman boys of the same age put off the *toga praetexta* to assume the *toga virilis*, Nakagoro altered the style of his hairdressing; henceforth his hair would be shaved from his forehead, like a grown man's. Still more important, his given name was changed. He ceased to be Nakagoro and became Heihachiro, the meaning of which is *peaceful son*. Thus the identity that was to become famous throughout the whole world was Heihachiro Togo, and Nakagoro became only a memory of childhood. And not even that, since the name taken at a boy's majority is regarded, so to speak, as retrospective. Japanese historians thus use the first, childhood, name only once, when writing of the infant's "baptism," and thereafter use the majority name even when referring to events anterior to that majority. We, no doubt, find this singular. Japan is rich in such singularities.

"Shortly thereafter," writes a Japanese biographer, "Heihachiro Togo was appointed, despite his youth, to a post as copyist in one of the administrative offices of his clan. His monthly reward for his work was half a bushel of unpolished rice. After writing all day in his office, he did not fail to use such leisure as he had in his family's service, for example, by helping in the vegetable garden. At about the same time he made a study of artillery and became a skillful gunner. From time to time he and other boys of the same age foregathered at a vast open space near the mouth of the river Kotsuke, and there drilled and countermarched to the music of trumpets and drums."

This gracious little sketch gives an exact idea of the fate which was threatening Togo: in a word, peace. In times of peace —internal peace, of course, since the external world had no existence for the Japanese—a samurai could only vegetate. Although it is important not to think of Togo's work as a "copyist" as if it were that of a Western quill driver—the writing of ideograms being an art—it is nonetheless true that the career of more or less militarized officialdom which seemed opening to the youthful Togo was hardly an elevating one. As long as peace endured, so long as the daimio did not call his faithful samurai to his aid in some quarrel, then the samurai was simply an official in the feudal administration, either an administrator, judge, teacher, or officer-instructor. A clan war, or at least a punitive action to put down piracy, was required before a samurai found a use for the treasures of courage, address, and coolness to the acquisition of which he had brought so much fervor and so much patience. This circumstance is by no means a historical exception; it might almost be called commonplace—the circumstance, that is, of exceptional qualities finding no opportunity for expression, or, if they do, being confined throughout an entire lifetime to an absurdly exiguous stage. Thus, in the ordinary way, if Heihachiro Togo dreamed of making his name illustrious, such dreams of fame must have been confined to the province of Satsuma. We know that Togo was to be able to play his part on a vastly wider stage. Like Napoleon, Peaceful Son had the good fortune to be born at the right moment. And like the French emperor, Togo's chance was due to social change— he was ready at a moment when an old order was passing and a major transformation in the social structure of his country was being accomplished. The youth who enters college at a time of great changes, when a revolutionary period has begun, is lucky. Togo's luck—which began by looking like a disaster—was that Japan suddenly ceased to be an impregnable fortress. Under the steady battering of foreign intimidation, the wall of isolation collapsed. A revolution without precedent was about to begin: had, in a manner of speaking, already begun. And Togo was not to be an onlooker; his character was to be put to the proof in real action, not in mere drill and war games. At fifteen years of age he was to get his first whiff of powder.

The news of the Great Arrival reached Kagoshima in the second week of July, 1853. Togo was five years old. At first he did not understand why all about him seemed so excited. His father received an urgent summons to the daimio; his brothers talked excitedly together. There were callers, comings and goings, all in an atmosphere of dramatic expectation. At last the head of the family gave explicit shape to the news, and the event he announced was soon the subject of every conversation. A hundred ships, carrying a hundred thousand white men, had dropped anchor off Yedo. The terms actually used were "a hundred thousand devils with white faces." What were the events which had preceded this catastrophe?

In 1837 Kichizeamon Togo, father of Heihachiro, had, with his own eyes, seen the Stars and Stripes of the United States flying at a masthead in Kagoshima. The ship which flew this flag was a merchantman, the *Morrison*, and her mission an attempt to repatriate some Japanese seamen who had turned up in China after several shipwrecks. These unfortunate fishermen, caught in the powerful Japan Current, a sort of Pacific Ocean Gulf Stream, had been swept away to the American coast. Cast ashore near the mouth of the Columbia River, and rescued almost *in extremis* from the cruel hands of red Indian captors by some trappers, they had, after a thousand difficulties, contrived transport to China. Their tribulations had roused in them an intense yearning for their own country, and they had decided to go home, running the risk of being beheaded on their arrival. An American trader of Macao, long tempted by the idea of penetrating the mystery of Japan, seized upon the pretext of repatriating them in order to satisfy his curiosity. He even hoped to be paid a reward. He began by approaching the harbor at Yedo, but was received by a salvo from the shogun's fortress guns. It then occurred to him that he might fare better with one of the great vassal lords, preferably one of the most powerful and least dependent. By repute, the daimio of Satsuma was such a man. It was thus that the *Morrison* arrived off Kagoshima on the ninth of August, 1837.

A crowd of Japanese was massed along the shore. A cutter, sent from the foreign ship, was met by a junk, and contact was established with the seaside township. One of the prince of Satsuma's servants went aboard the barbarian vessel, where it was pointed out to him that she came unarmed. He returned ashore, and the daimio summoned his council.

Throughout the night intense but discreet activity agitated the hillsides above the sea. Afoot or mounted, messengers came and went. At dawn it could be seen that the *Morrison* was still there, motionless out in the bay. The sky paled, the sun rose, day broke, and suddenly the cannon of the fort thundered. Their cannon balls fell short by a third of the distance between the gunners and where the *Morrison* lay at anchor.

The foreign ship remained still for a short while longer, then upped her anchor and moved out of the bay, describing a gentle curve. An hour later she was no more than a smudge on the horizon. Such, then, was the only sight of the Western world ever vouchsafed to Kichizeamon Togo, and such the tale that Togo, as a child, had more than once heard told in all its detail.

As for other, earlier appearances by foreigners, the accounts of them which reached the township were listened to as if they had been legendary. Such stories were always grossly inaccurate and only very vaguely dated. The entry into Nagasaki of H.M.S. *Phaeton,* a frigate, was remembered if only because several high officials had committed *seppuku,* also called *hara-kiri,* because they had allowed her to escape. That was in 1808. Apart from that, between 1804 and 1811, a number of landings or attempts at landings, on the shores of Sakhalin and Yezo, had caused the shogun to dispatch an expeditionary force. Golovin, captain of the *Diana,* had been seized and cast into prison. To the folk who dwelt about the Gulf of Kagoshima, these events seemed very remote in time and space, beyond comparison less interesting than the arrival of the *Morrison,* which the entire population of Satsuma had been able to see for themselves.

Then there was the twice-told tale of the United States commodore who in Heihachiro's first year of life had sailed into the bay of Yedo with two ships on what he had called a "courtesy visit." He had made known his name, which, like all barbarian names, had been unpronounceable: James Biddle. Polite, but firm, the shogun's envoys, addressing themselves to this personage through the medium of a Dutch interpreter, had let it be understood that they would be glad to see him up anchor within the hour. He obliged them by doing so.

The *Preble,* Captain James Glynn, had appeared off Nagasaki two years later. Backed by the threat of his guns, James Glynn had required the release of certain shipwrecked Americans whom he knew to be held in Japan. The hills above Nagasaki were literally covered with troops, and the harbor was crowded with armed junks to prevent all contact between the foreigners and the shore. But the shipwrecked Americans had been given up.

Since then, nothing. The feudal empire continued to live according to its ancient customs; nothing was changed in the aspect of its cities and countryside, or in the character and observations of its inhabitants; or even, as regards the great majority of them, in their preoccupations. But here and there, a few realized that henceforth the integrity of Japan's isolation was threatened.

Immediately following James Glynn's successful threat, the shogun had sent to all the daimios of the coastal provinces an order which throughout history has always expressed the first, instinctive, futile reaction to a threat from the sea: they were to reinforce the harbor defenses.

Now in 1853 Kagoshima heard the news of the arrival of a hundred thousand barbarians.

A few days later the facts concerning the Great Arrival were known in more detail and with more exactitude. Commodore Matthew Calbraith Perry had cast anchor off the port of Uraga, at the entrance to Yedo Bay, not, indeed, with a hundred ships, but with four: two steam frigates, the *Susquehanna* and the *Mississippi,* and two armed corvettes, the *Plymouth* and the *Saratoga.* The crews of these ships amounted not to a hundred thousand men but to five hundred and sixty. Distance and word-of-mouth transmission of the news had multiplied their numbers, a phenomenon not unknown even in our enlightened days.

Perry bore a letter from President Fillmore, addressed to the mikado, in which the object of the visit was clearly set forth. The United States desired Japan's friendship; they wished to trade with her; they wanted humane treatment for shipwrecked seamen; and facilities for revictualing and coaling. President Fillmore made a particular point of humane treatment for shipwrecked sailors: "We take this matter very seriously," were his words.

When Perry let it be known that he had a letter to deliver to the emperor, the Shogun Iyeyoshi, with whom it lay to make a decision, was in some embarrassment. The political structure of Japan at that time has already been described. The mikado, far from ruling, could hardly even be said to reign. The fact that this foreigner was addressing himself directly to the mikado showed that the barbarians were evidently but ill informed as to the realities of the situation.

Iyeyoshi considered the United States warships and dwelt upon their manifest indifference to the artillery of his coastal defenses. The Nagasaki Dutch had thrown some light on the subject of the range and power of modern guns. He decided to call a council of feudatory princes and lay before them all he knew about this and also about Perry's purpose.

The reaction of several councilors was rather odd: "Let him," they said, "present his petition to the mikado through the Dutch at Nagasaki. The matter does not concern us."

The shogun was forced to particularize: the commodore was unwittingly—or wilfully—ignorant of the duality of powers in Japan; he considered the shogun as the mikado's first minister, and therefore the correct intermediary in transmitting a message from the American sovereign to that potentate. Perry was insisting upon delivering the letter to the shogun and to no one else—and as soon as possible. The council, disconcerted, came to no decision that day, and met again, but also to no purpose, several

30

times on the ensuing days. Perry waited patiently. Nineteenth century sailors and explorers from the West were aware that these Oriental palavers often took several days.

At the latest session of the council one of the daimios asked, "Is the court at Kyoto informed of these barbarians' arrival?"

"Yes," the shogun replied.

"What is the court's attitude?"

"The emperor has ordered prayers at all sanctuaries for a typhoon from Heaven to save our country, as in the days of our danger from the Mongols."

This was followed by a heavily charged silence. Iyeyoshi then referred once more to the corvettes' guns, and added that the American commodore's patience would not last indefinitely and that in his opinion the only solution was to allow the barbarian to land, to receive his letter, and to forward it to the emperor. The council, humiliated but seeing no alternative, agreed. This decision greatly disturbed the people when they heard of it; the country was being laid open to the foreign plague. But Perry, having delivered the letter, announced with dignity that he would return for the reply one year hence. Having said which, he raised anchor and sailed away. Nothing could have been better calculated to make an impression on the Japanese.

Exactly eight days later, Shogun Iyeyoshi died suddenly, from no apparent cause. The chauvinists, that is to say, 99 per cent of the population, had a ready explanation. "The gods have punished the shogun who allowed the barbarian to land." Alarm beacons were lit upon the hills. Nor did public feeling altogether subside during the ensuing weeks, and even months.

Perry returned as he had promised, but this time with ten ships and two thousand men. Again there were preliminary exchanges of views, and he then disembarked, setting foot on the forbidden land, preceded by two gigantic Negroes carrying the United States flag, surrounded by officers in full-dress uniform, followed by a band playing "Yankee-Doodle" and by seamen armed with unsheathed cutlasses and bearing numerous gifts. The

31

shogun, in the midst of his ministers, signed the famous Treaty of Kanagawa on March 31, 1854. The most important clauses of this document provided for hospital treatment for foreign sailors shipwrecked in Japan; authorized the provisioning, in certain conditions, of foreign ships; and opened Shimoda and Hakodate, the two worst ports in Japan, to American trade.

Japan, unable to defend her integrity against modern armaments, was at last opening her frontiers; but with a very bad grace and as slowly as possible. However, the treaty secured by Perry was rapidly followed by other, similar agreements obtained by the representatives of Great Britain, Russia, Holland, and France. The era of "penetration" had begun; and, at exactly the same time, the era of nationalist resistance. It may be of interest to show various aspects of the Japanese reaction to the imposition of relations by the Western powers, by what were, to all intents and purposes, a series of ultimatums.

At the court, in Kyoto, the only hope was in the gods, and a constant stream of prayers rose heavenward. The realistic attitude, diametrically opposed to this, was best represented by the daimio of Satsuma, Kichizeamon Togo's sovereign lord. This nobleman, Shimazu Nariakira, seems to have been one of the first to take a modern course, at least in matters military, as a result of foreign pressure on Japan. This is manifest in his behavior. In the summer of 1850, and repeatedly thereafter, the Nagasaki Dutch, always anxious to defend their monopoly, had informed the shogun's ministers that the United States and Great Britain were hardly troubling to conceal their intention of imposing their trade on Japan by force. Nariakira, having heard rumors of this, got into touch with the Dutch, learned what they could tell him, thought it over, and came to a conclusion very remarkable for a Japanese of that epoch: that Japan could not defend herself against the foreigners except by studying and adopting the new weapons and ways. He made a modest beginning by asking the shogun's permission to build a merchant ship. The shogun was suspicious, refused permission, and advised the daimio to concentrate, rather, on coastal fortifications, and set the example by building a fort near Yedo. However, by perseverance, Shimazu Nariakira at last obtained permission to operate a line of merchantmen between Yedo and Kagoshima. This in itself was a derogation of the old imperial edict whose authorization extended only to small-scale coastal fishing.

The second derogation was authorized to the same progressive daimio after the Great Arrival, when the ancient order forbidding the building of warships was abrogated. Shimazu Nariakira at once laid the keels of several large sailing vessels and three steamships. The first, the *Shohei Maru*, was ninety feet long, and as soon as she was launched the shogun came to see her. He examined her thoroughly without saying a word, and then, turning to the daimio of Satsuma, said:

"A very pretty ship. If she were offered to me as a gift, I would readily accept her."

Shimazu Nariakira was obliged to take the hint, but, refusing to be discouraged, persisted in his shipbuilding program, meanwhile issuing the following proclamation:

"The arrogance of the barbarians having become threatening, the High Authorities, bearing in mind the matter of defense against foreign ships, have made it known that they have ordered His Grace the Daimio of Satsuma to take all necessary steps for the defense of the nation and in particular to build warships and guns, today considered auxiliaries necessary to defense. Gunners have been found, but, as the warships were built only last spring, sailors are still to be found. Now, if trained sailors, and fusiliers, who are of the utmost utility in naval warfare, are not taken aboard, the building of warships will be of no help. Consequently, as His Grace is keenly desirous of enrolling sailors and fusiliers, young men who wish to serve aboard the warships should give their names to the controller in chief."

Apart from its charm as a curiosity, this document is interesting for the light it throws upon Japan's state of mind concerning the Western peoples who had begun to treat her as a colonial

33

country. Shimazu Nariakira had immortalized his name as the founder of a fleet that, eighty years later, was among the most powerful navies in the world and that was setting the Pacific and all Asia by the ears. It should, moreover, be noted, that this feudal nobleman fully realized what he was about and was acting entirely on his own initiative. For a knowledge of the historical facts reveals that the "High Authorities" from which he claimed to have orders were, in fact, at loggerheads among themselves.

First, there was the shogun's party, the realists, whose ideas can be summed up as follows: "The old Japan will inevitably perish in an unequal contest, whereas a new Japan, firmly resolved to learn from the West, may yet have a chance." This point of view had not been adopted without reservations, and even within the shogun's party there was no unanimity; but the general tendency was clear.

Another policy, or tendency, was that of the men who favored finesse, a two-faced diplomacy of yielding—as little as might be—on certain points, while preparing for a recovery as soon as possible.

The third party, called Jo-i, was composed of fanatical nationalists for whom there could be only one possible policy: the barbarians must be resisted at once and to the death.

It might be supposed that the natural arbitrator between these contending factions must be the mikado. Here, however, are the conflicting orders, issued almost simultaneously, which came from the court at Kyoto: negotiate with Perry; take steps for general mobilization; increase the volume of prayers for a typhoon; avoid ratification of the treaty signed with Perry and with the other foreign powers. A realist first minister, Li-Kamon-No-Kami, argued that this behavior was infantile, and campaigned for the ratification of the treaties. At this juncture, in 1855, the partisans of resistance acquired a new and weighty argument in the form of an earthquake followed by fire at and around Yedo, which caused a hundred thousand casualties. Tempests, floods, and an epidemic of plague were interpreted as signs of the gods' fury at barbarian effrontery. Thus, while the shogun's government was signing

34

treaties and encouraging the more realistic patriots, reactionary nationalist agitation was growing more violent.

Townsend Harris, United States consul general, authorized to reside in Japan by the Treaty of Kanagawa, had procured the opening of new ports to foreign shipping, and the abrogation of such scandalously xenophobic customs as trampling on the cross. The shogun opened schools for the teaching of foreign languages. He sent abroad for military instructors, French for the army (this was before 1870, of course), English for the navy. He was also sending students overseas to study in Western capitals. Driven by a new greed for knowledge, isolated enthusiasts were even leaving the country on their own account, in defiance of the law and at the risk of their lives. Such was the credit side of the country's awakening: the debit column was soon to be no less impressive. The Jo-i fanatics, furious in the face of a new wave of Christian evangelists, found ample material for their propaganda in the descent upon the newly opened ports of foreigners avid for gold. Persecution of Christians was renewed, and thousands of Japanese converts were seized and beheaded. The minister, Li-Kamon-No-Kami, who persisted in trying to carry out the treaties signed with Western powers, was assassinated, and his head presented on a charger to the chief of the Jo-i sect. The British legation at Yedo was twice attacked, with fatal casualties on both occasions. In 1861 the secretary of the United States legation was murdered.

The situation of foreigners in Yedo became so precarious that the representatives of Great Britain, Prussia, France, and Holland decided to withdraw to Yokohama for the time being. Order having apparently been restored, they returned to Yedo, where a member of one of the legations was promptly assassinated. The unfortunate shogun, overwhelmed by his difficulties, wrote a personal letter to Queen Victoria imploring her to consent to a postponement in opening new ports to foreign shipping and trade. Unhappily, however, the late summer of 1862 was to produce an event so serious that it was to have decisive consequences, consequences

35

which were to have a direct influence on Togo's life, for they gave rise to the event and to the line of thought which shaped his whole career.

Shimazu Nariakira, the daimio who had created the Satsuma fleet, had died in 1858. His nephew and adopted son—adoption was a common custom in Japan—had succeeded him, but because he was too young to reign, his father, Saburo Shimazu, had become regent. It was Saburo Shimazu who, on a fine summer day in 1862, happened to be on the road from Yedo to Kyoto in circumstances which gave rise to tragedy.

The mikado, under the influence of nobles belonging to the Jo-i party, had summoned the shogun to Kyoto, at the same time as the other princes of the nation, to hold conference respecting current national business, and particularly the matter of foreigners in Japan. Saburo Shimazu had offered to be the shogun's escort from Yedo to Kyoto. Upon his arrival in Yedo he met with a flat refusal: the shogun considered himself affronted by being summoned to attend the emperor at the same time as his own vassals, and had declined the invitation. Saburo could do nothing but swallow the refusal with what grace he could muster, and set out for Kyoto alone.

He had his own escort, and the party constituted a picture of the old, the strictly "medieval," Japan. At the head of the column marched heralds who, as they passed through towns and villages, called upon the inhabitants to prostrate themselves before his lordship. Immediately after the heralds came the samurai vanguard, each man armed with his two swords; then a fatigue party of porters, bearing the princely luggage slung from the ends of bamboo poles carried yokewise across their shoulders. Next came the main body of troops, in battle harness—cuirass, lance, halberd. Behind them were Saburo Shimazu in person, but altogether invisible within his ornamented palanquin, and his lordship's charger, unmounted and led by the bridle. Finally, another long column of soldiers, and the rear guard.

The incident occurred on the outskirts of the village of Nananugi,

36

at the crossing of the Yokohama road. Shimazu's party met a group of whites on horseback—three men and a woman. According to Japanese historians the whites tried to cross the road by passing through the daimio's column. The survivors of the tragedy, on the other hand, were later to swear that they had remained motionless at the side of the road. It is obviously safe to believe them: no one is silly enough to try cutting across a *military* column on the march, especially in a hostile land: the four foreigners sat their horses and watched the column pass. But the fact that they failed to dismount was considered to be not merely a case of bad manners but also a deliberate insult. The samurai rushed at the foreigners with drawn swords. The first man they reached was flung from his horse, and killed; he was an English merchant from Shanghai, Richardson by name. The other foreigners put spurs to their horses and escaped, but not without wounds; one lost an arm, and the woman, who was also English but from Hong Kong, saved her head at the price of her hair. Immediately thereafter the assailants fell back into their ranks, and the column resumed its march. For the Japanese the incident was closed. Honor was satisfied, and one fewer white in the country meant a small victory over the foreign plague.

Several months passed. Communications over long distances were much slower than they are today. But in 1862 no British citizen anywhere in the world could be molested with impunity. The Japanese were ignorant of this fact. The survivors of the "Richardson affair" had not kept silent, and Colonel Neale, the British chargé d'affaires, had sent a courier to India, where the nearest telegraphic cable was to be found. London replied to his report that Her Majesty's Government demanded a public apology, a large indemnity, and, of course, the execution of the guilty parties.

Colonel Neale conveyed this message to the shogun, who transmitted it to both Shimazu and the mikado and received the following answers: from the daimio, "The murderers? Come and get them!"; from the court at Kyoto, "Throw the impudent demands of the colonel's government in his face." The shogun, for his part at least, had not taken leave of his senses. He paid the indemnity demanded and made an official apology. The British legation thereupon sent him another message: "The incident is not closed. If the shogun is powerless to effect the punishment of the culprits, the Royal Navy will take direct action." The warning was one which, at the time, it was not generally considered wise to ignore. The shogun again transmitted this communication to Kyoto and added a word of explanation as to what direct action by the Royal Navy might be expected to entail.

The mikado's answer arrived several days later, and consisted of an edict expelling all foreigners. This was ten years after Perry's arrival and after the signature of a score of treaties with the Western powers.

Whom the gods would destroy they first make mad. The Jo-i sectaries were now in *de facto* power at Kyoto, and the most rabid of the Jo-i lords, Mori, daimio of Chosu, decided to take the initiative in his own domain, which included the Strait of Shimonoseki. This narrow strait, part of an important sea lane between the Pacific and the mainland of Asia, was declared closed, and furbished with fortresses, for the building of which thousands of peasants were conscripted. On the day fixed for the final expulsion of foreigners, when an American steamer, the *Pembroke*, appeared in the strait, she was fired upon. The same welcome was extended to a French sloop, the *Kienchang*, and a Dutch corvette, the *Medusa*. It was like the good old days, and the daimio of Chosu seemed inclined to take on the maritime powers of the entire world. Nor did a very moderate bombardment of his forts by the United States Corvette *Wyoming*, followed by the French frigate *Sémiramis* and the gunboat *Tancrède*, both commanded by Vice Admiral Jaurès, cause him to change his mind. He rebuilt and reinforced his forts and announced his intention to continue the fight. Whereupon the Western powers agreed that the time had come to administer a sharp lesson to the mikado and his turbulent vassals.

Meanwhile, however, Great Britain, less inclined than ever to consider the Richardson affair as closed until the reparations demanded had been made, followed up her threat of direct action by the Royal Navy against the daimio of Satsuma. A flotilla of ten ships commanded by Vice Admiral Kuper, R.N., arrived and dropped anchor off Kagoshima. Heihachiro Togo was fifteen and a half years old when, at twilight on August 11, 1863, he saw the ships sail in. It was almost twenty-six years to the day since his father had watched the arrival of the *Morrison*.

Early on the following morning, a sampan set out from the beach and steered for the frigate, H.M.S. *Euryalus*, which flew the vice admiral's flag at her mainmast top. The word went round that the sampan was carrying an official delegation sent by the daimio's government, with orders to discover the aim of the foreigner's visit, the probable movements of his ships, and their firepower.

The delegation returned to land sooner than had been expected, and its members had hardly disembarked when the guns of the forts fired a salvo of blanks, and signal rockets were sent up: this was to call all garrison troops to battle stations. The only answer which the daimio's envoys had been vouchsafed was as follows: "Tomorrow we shall enter the port of Kagoshima and present a letter from Her Majesty's Government to the Government of Shimazu." This answer had been delivered by Colonel Neale, the British chargé d'affaires, who was aboard the flagship.

The samurai were called to the colors. The Togo household provided four warriors, Kichizeamon Togo and three of his sons, Shirobei, Sokuro, and Heihachiro. The youngest, Shirozeamon, being a minor, could not, by samurai custom, be called upon to serve: he watched his elders put on their ceremonial garments over their kimonos. These consisted of a pair of very full trousers, almost a split skirt, called *hakema*, and a stiff surtout called *haou*, both of silk, of course, and bearing, in five different places, the Togo armorial. Their headgear consisted of a round hat bearing the family crest. Two swords were carried at the sash. Thus attired, the samurai were ready. Masuko took ceremonial leave of each in turn.

The land defenses of Kagoshima comprised ten armed forts with a total of 105 cannon. These pieces of ordnance included old siege and field guns cast on the Dutch model, not rifled, and of various calibers, firing round solid shot; a few bronze mortars; and some mortars made of stone. As for the naval force, it consisted of twelve thirty-five-foot junks and three steamers, *Seyio Maru, Tenyu Maru,* and *Hanuko Maru.*[*]

On the morning of August 13th, in conformity with Colonel Neale's message, the British squadron changed its moorings to drop anchor before the town, deliberately placing itself within range of the shore batteries. Every movement aboard the ships was closely watched by thousands of pairs of eyes. The powerful flagship was readily distinguished from the rest; the remainder of the flotilla—corvettes and gunboats—were moored astern and ahead of her on a line running from north to south.

The warriors of Satsuma had only the vaguest idea of the offensive potential represented by these ships. It was generally held that the shore defense works were indestructible and that the foreigners would be powerless in the face of Nipponese courage. All that was necessary was to employ a little guile in order to gain time in which to complete defensive preparations. It was with this intention that, as soon as the foreigners had come to their new anchorage, two of the daimio's councilors went aboard the *Euryalus* to repeat, with more authority, the questions which had already been put.

---

[*] Mr. Masaki Seo, attaché at the London embassy of Japan, has been kind enough to give me the following explanation: a widely accepted theory connects this use of the word *maru* with the same word, or *maro,* used as suffix to the names of aristocrats' sons during the feudal age. Mr. Masaki Seo compares this process of giving ships a human personality with our own use of the pronoun *she,* instead of *it,* for ships. Thus *maru* in such ship names as *Asama-maru, Hikawa-maru,* denotes an affectionate and respectful regard for the ships, just as by calling a ship *she* we, by implication, deny that the ship is a mere thing. Other theories are that *maru* can mean "all-round, full," that is, a perfectly balanced character; or that the *maru* in question derives from the *maru* used as a suffix for the names of battlements on Japanese castles. But this last theory is simply to set the argument back one term, since it can be shown that this use of *maru* for battlements implied a personification of the battlements, and thus a feeling of affectionate regard for them. As Mr. Masaki Seo says, people liked to think of the battlements as if they were strong men.—Trans.

40

Colonel Neale received them as before, and the letter addressed to the daimio was given to them. Pointing to a distant range of snow-clad mountain peaks glistening in the sun, the councilors tried to explain that the daimio was at Kirishima, where he had been informed of the British squadron's arrival. Kirishima, alas! was several days' journey from Kagoshima. Could not the colonel wait a little? Colonel Neale replied, "No. I cannot wait."

The councilors then put another question.

"Would you agree to take part in a conference ashore with the members of the daimio's council?"

"There can be no question of that," the colonel replied. "My mission is limited to the delivery of this letter. An answer is required within twenty-four hours."

The two councilors were obliged to withdraw. The general sense of the ultimatum they took with them was as follows: Richardson's murderers were immediately to be delivered up to Vice Admiral Kuper to be tried by a court-martial; and a supplementary indemnity of £25,000 was to be paid at once, by way of damages, for Richardson's family.

As soon as these conditions were known, the first plan for a surprise attack on the enemy squadron was put into operation: it had been conceived by a determined group whose members had been convinced throughout that negotiations were bound to fail.

Disguised as merchants, they set out in a swarm of small boats which gathered like flies against the sides of the ships, their occupants pleading to be allowed on board to offer their goods. The idea was to fall on the ships' officers and put them all to the sword. But the trick was a shade too obvious, even for Westerners, and the bogus merchants were firmly requested to take themselves off.

The second plan was put into operation a little later in the day. The general officer commanding the troops at Satsuma went alongside the *Euryalus*, announced that he bore the official answer to the British note, and asked leave to come aboard, accompanied by his escort. This body consisted of samurai determined not to die until they had exterminated the squadron's high command. They hoped by this means to throw the foreigners into confusion, and so demoralize them as to force them to sail away. Captain Josling, Vice Admiral Kuper's flag captain, authorized the Japanese general to come aboard, but accompanied by his two senior officers only. Thus, the second plan also broke down. Vice Admiral Kuper and Colonel Neale met the general on the quarter-deck, and received the reply to their ultimatum. The Satsuma authorities proposed a joint discussion with the shogun's government at Yedo. Colonel Neale then said bluntly that this answer was quite unsatisfactory to Her Majesty's Government. For his part, he could not see that there was anything more to be said. Negotiations were at an end. The general was not, however, detained, and the officer of the watch conducted him to the gangplank with the customary honors. Thereafter his barge was seen making for the shore as fast as she could be rowed.

The Japanese forts had been manned and the troops were at action stations. The town's streets were deserted. Every temple was crowded with people at prayer, and in every house a woman on her knees prayed before the family altar. All prayers were directed to the same end: they called for a typhoon to raise a mighty sea and sweep this alien horde away, as in the time of Kublai Khan.

Shortly after noon some of the brilliance seemed to be fading out of the daylight; a light mist began to soften distant outlines. Cirrus cloud passed high across the heavens, followed by lower, denser cloud which soon formed a complete overcast. The captains of the British warships saw the barometer fall, slowly at first, and then with remarkable speed. The atmosphere became heavy and oppressive. The roadstead surface became a sheet of small, choppy waves. Farther out, toward the darkening horizon, the waves were capped with white foam.

The Japanese were following these developments with hopeful anxiety. As night fell they saw the foreign flotilla shift its anchorage again, to get under the lee of Sakurajima. How long would they be able to remain there? The seas were beginning to rise, and in the thickening darkness the white crests of the waves could be seen racing into the harbor.

By dawn the violence of the storm had increased. A man needed to brace himself to face the furious wind, and he had to screw up his streaming eyes against the spray-charged gusts of the gale to distinguish the dark shapes of the enemy ships through a dense fog which, like the sea, was in torn and tremendous motion. Those dark shapes were moving again. It was obvious that their movement was not a withdrawal; they were sailing right into the bay where the three Japanese steamers were moored. Visibility was not good enough for the entire operation, which required most of the morning, to be observed in detail. Finally, however, it became clear that the three Japanese steamers had been captured and were being towed toward the flotilla's last anchorage. Meanwhile mounted couriers, riding furiously, were arriving at Japanese headquarters from the forts, clamoring for orders to open fire. The order was at last given a little before noon, and a few moments later the old cannon gave tongue. The samurai gunner Heihachiro Togo's battle station was in one of the forts of the northwest sector.

The gunners had to heat the cannon balls in furnaces behind their batteries; to ram loose powder down the muzzles of their antique cannon; to ram earth on top of the powder to prevent a premature explosion through contact with the red-hot cannon balls. Next came the cannon ball, and then the detonating powder was placed in the breech. The aimer aimed; the detonator was ignited; such was the method of the Satsuma artillery.

Vice Admiral Kuper did not immediately reply to the fire of the shore batteries. His first reaction was to set fire to his three prizes, and the men manning the guns of the fort saw the wind violently fanning and twisting the smoke and flames. A moment later there was a flicker of white flashes all down the line of the enemy flotilla. There followed an appalling explosion which seemed briefly to silence the storm; then the Japanese gunners felt the earth shake under them, and at the same time great geysers of soil

43

and filth spurted from the earth. The English squadron had fired its first broadside.

Japanese biographers, describing Togo's bearing during the bombardment, tell us that he was "at first surprised, then frightened, but swiftly recovered his coolness, carrying out orders without paying any attention to danger." His reaction, in short, was probably the same as that of all the other soldiers manning the forts, first yielding to the temptation to run for cover from the European shells, whose terrifying effects they had never imagined, but then returning immediately to their posts.

We are also told that, in the course of the battle, Togo suddenly caught sight of his mother who, with other samurai wives, was making a round of the forts and encampments, bringing food and drink to the soldiers. When he saw her she was seated down by the shore; a shell struck a rock face not far from her, and there was a hail of splinters. "She rose, and remained standing, doing nothing but comb her hair as she watched the enemy ships." This set piece belongs to the folklore of any country; there can be no question of historical verification, nor would anything be gained by it.

The British warships were firing their broadsides while sailing and steaming in line-ahead parallel with the coast line, led by the frigate *Euryalus*. They would sail past, all engaging one fort, then go about for the return leg. Each maneuver brought them nearer to the coast. Every salvo left a dense curtain of smoke above the sea, to be promptly rent asunder and scattered by the gale.

The storm was turning into a hurricane but, contrary to Japanese hopes, its increasing violence was to have no outcome but the destruction of Kagoshima. Despite the skill of Vice Admiral Kuper's gunners, the severe rolling of their ships was having more and more influence on their shooting. A proportion of their shells fell not on the forts but on the town—a town of wood and paper; fires broke out almost at once, to be fanned into fury by the wind. A munitions factory exploded; the town was littered with dead

44

bodies, and flames rose, roaring in the typhoon, in every quarter.

All this the Japanese gunners watched from their posts. Moreover, their ammunition was running out, while the dark shapes sailing across and across the bay seemed untouched by their cannonade. At this juncture the medieval warriors left their guns, rushed down on to the beaches and to the very edge of the sea, and stood brandishing their swords. They flung off their clothes and, naked to the waist, shouted into the gale, challenging the enemy to come and fight them man to man.

Needless to say, the enemy did no such thing. Fire continued to destroy the town, and the diabolical conical shells, never yet seen in Japan, methodically knocked the forts to pieces. Still the English sailed back and forth across the bay, increasing the devastation at each passage of the ships.

When night fell, the roar of the gale became so terrible that it was hardly possible to be sure whether the guns at sea were still firing, or had fallen silent. In point of fact, they had ceased fire. Vice Admiral Kuper had again moored his flotilla in the lee of Sakurajima. The only sound to be heard aboard the ships was that of the Marine bands, which played late into the night while across the bay fire destroyed Kagoshima.

When day dawned, after a few salvos fired at the fortifications of the islands, which had been overlooked during the battle, the British squadron withdrew. The bombardment of Kagoshima had lasted six hours. It was later learned that it had cost the English thirteen dead and sixty-three wounded. The forts of Kagoshima had been destroyed; so had five hundred houses and numerous public buildings in the town. Japanese casualties were never counted.

When the warriors of Satsuma returned to their homes, they were greeted as heroes. For the Japanese Nationalists, the battle of Kagoshima had ended in the defeat of the foreign naval squadron: the barbarians had not landed; they had withdrawn; therefore, they had been vanquished. The Jo-i proclaimed a great national victory.

The daimio of Satsuma and his ministers took a broader view; they at last began to entertain the notion of paying the indemnity which had been demanded.

The very sharp lesson of Kagoshima failed to convince the superpatriots. In the following year the daimio of Chosu mentioned before was back at his old tricks, firing at foreign shipping passing through the Strait of Shimonoseki. A bombardment carried out by a combined French-Dutch-American naval squadron destroyed the port, and the shogun's government had to pay an indemnity of three million dollars.

Heihachiro Togo was in his seventeenth year. He listened to what people were saying all about him, and doubtless reflected on what he heard. He heard obstinate men retell, for the hundredth time, the tale of the "victory" of Kagoshima. He also listened to his father, whose more open mind and whose attendance at the daimio's council meetings where something nearer to real news than legendary tales was to be heard, led him to conclusions which, although patriotic, were also realistic. In the first place, the samurai heroes, in the matter of up-to-date military techniques, had everything to learn; second—and this conclusion had a direct influence on Heihachiro Togo's future—the defense of a coast line begins at sea.

When Kichizeamon Togo told his three elder sons that he would be glad to see them enroll in the young Satsuma Navy, their acquiescence was enthusiastic. This was in 1866; Heihachiro Togo was eighteen years old.

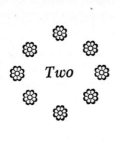

Two

At dawn on May 25, 1871, an English ship carrying passengers and a mixed cargo was steaming northwest about three miles off the Spanish coast, shortly after passing through the Strait of Gibraltar. On her bridge, the officer of the watch had just distinguished the flashing light of a lighthouse on the starboard bow. He marked the sight on the chart and, turning to the man at the wheel, said, "Keep her head so, if you please."

The sea was calm and the sky clear. Landward, the horizon was obscured by a slight mist. The passengers were still asleep in their staterooms, except for a group of strangely garbed men who were standing on the portside of the bridge staring toward the land. The officer of the watch was already well acquainted with these

47

passengers: they were Japanese, wearing their national costume. The light, at that early hour, revealed no colors, so that the group of strangers looked like ghosts.

A little later, the officer moved toward the port side of the bridge to take a bearing on the lighthouse. Several of the Japanese looked toward him. He smiled, and, pointing to the light, said, "Trafalgar."

The night before, the Japanese had asked to be called before the ship passed that famous cape. All they could now see through the mist which veiled the coast line was a light very similar to a hundred others. But that light marked a place with a very special significance for them. For these Japanese were cadets of the imperial Japanese Navy, on their way to England to be taught their profession by the Royal Navy. Heihachiro Togo was one of their number.

At twenty he looked younger than a European of the same age, albeit strong and manly. When, seated in a circle of his companions on the deck of the steamer, he sang the songs of his native land accompanied by a guitarist, he appeared, like the others, to be cheerful and carefree. At rest, or playing a game of Go, it was impossible to miss the complete self-mastery expressed in his face. In point of fact, "Cadet" Togo had nothing of the adolescent lad, new to his trade, which the word usually implies. He was a man, with several years of active and warlike naval experience behind him.

Togo had taken service in the "feudal" Satsuma Navy in 1866. Less than two years later civil war had broken out. There would be no point in trying, here, to unravel the threads of that last romantic feudal epic; no point in seeking the source of its intrigues, the origin of its secrets, lies, court treacheries; no point in describing, at length, its battles, alarums, and excursions. The detailed history of these events is of purely local interest; nothing that happened in the course of the war seems to have had any decisive influence on the course of Togo's career, the nature of his destiny, or the quality of his character.

We can however by taking a bird's-eye view get a simplified notion of what happened.

It will be recalled that since the twelfth century executive power had been wielded, from Yedo, by the shogun, or "mayor of the palace," the mikado reigning in a more or less honorary capacity in Kyoto. Since 1603 the shogunate had been in the hands of the same clan, the Tokugawa. In 1866 Iyemochi Tokugawa, died. His successor, Yoshinobo Tokugawa, also known as Keiki, by no means enthusiastic at the idea of ruling amidst the difficulties caused by penetration of the country by foreigners, decided to restore the executive power to the emperor. "That is the best course I can take" he told his supporters, "in the empire's interests."

The mikado—a boy named Mutsuhito who was later to become illustrious and to be canonized under the name of Meiji Tenno—accepted. All was going well. Or, rather, it would have been if members of the Satsuma, Choshu, and Tosa clans had not seen in this peaceful revolution an opportunity to seize the reigns of power in the new government for themselves. Needless to say, the shogun's supporters, who had either resigned with their chief or been dismissed from their posts, were furiously angry, and began a war to the death with the Sat-cho-to—as the party of the new men in office was called, the word being composed of the first syllables of the three clan names. Such was the beginning of the civil war.

The rebels were defeated on January 30, 1868, at Fushimi, after a battle lasting three days. Keiki, the former shogun, who had been obliged to put himself at the head of his partisans, surrendered. But his cause, although clearly lost, still had its defenders and its agitators, who continued the struggle for several months. The most distinguished of their number was Admiral Enamoto, who had been sent to Holland by Keiki to learn the arts of naval warfare and who felt himself bound by gratitude to the former shogun. It was against Enamoto that Togo, as a combatant in the Satsuma Navy, commanded by Genroku Atatsuka, fought his first sea battles. He was then on the emperor's side; but the foregoing

49

sketch makes it quite clear that this loyalty was fortuitous. In point
of fact, Togo was exactly what his father had been before him—
Kichizeamon Togo had been gathered to his fathers two years
before—a loyal vassal of the daimio of Satsuma.

In the course of the first part of the civil war, officers and
ratings of the Satsuma Navy did most of their fighting ashore,
for the good and sufficient reason that the embattled clans had
far more land forces than they had naval forces. The fighting was
guerrilla in character, with mounted raiding, ambushes, the hunting down of defeated detachments, and feats of surprise attack and
party vengeance. However, one fine day Togo set foot on the deck of
his first warship, in the port of Hyogo. She was the *Kasuga*, a
paddle steamer of twelve hundred tons, built of wood and with
graceful yachtlike lines, three masts, two smokestacks, her hull
painted black and her superstructure white. She was armed with
six guns. Launched at Cowes, England, in 1863, she had sailed
under the name of *Kiang-tse* before being bought, at Nagasaki,
by the progressive daimio of Satsuma. Aboard the *Kasuga*, Togo
was a gunner, as he had been at the bombardment of Kagoshima.
And it is on record that during the battle known as "the Battle of
the Awa Coast," which was fought in the Inner Sea, a shot "well
fired" by Togo carried away one of the *Kaiyo*'s masts at a range
of 1400 yards, the *Kaiyo* being the Tokugawa ship in which
Admiral Enamoto flew his flag.

Japanese historians say that this was the first naval engagement in which Japanese sailors fought a sea fight "in the Western
style." But the sailors were still wearing the kimono and their
officers still carried the two swords of a samurai. As for the
battle tactics, they were determined by the difference in the
speeds of the two principal belligerent vessels: the *Kasuga* could
steam at seventeen knots, the *Kaiyo* only twelve. There was not a
breath of wind, so that the smoke lay motionless above the sea.
It is hardly necessary to say that not even a beginning had been
made on that study of naval strategy and tactics which in due
course was to give Japan her victory over Russia. In any case

50

it is difficult to see what principles of naval warfare could have been applied by two such heterogeneous collections of vessels as composed the two Japanese fleets at this battle. While the elegant *Kasuga,* with Togo aboard, steamed along behind a singular-looking coast-guard cutter fitted with a ram, Enamoto in the *Kaiyo,* a screw steamer imported from Holland, led into action an armed paddle steamer which was a veteran of the American Civil War. About the only thing which all the embattled ships had in common was that they were built of wood. But these contingencies did nothing to limit the boldness and determination of the respective commanding officers, and old prints show us the gallant paddle steamers, smoking like factory chimneys and hammering away at each other at point-blank range. Nor were ruse and cunning out of place: one of Enamoto's ships had managed, on another occasion, by flying American colors, to steam right into one of the enemy's harbors and take the first ship hand-to-hand by grappling and boarding her.

The civil war ended with Enamoto's surrender, after his fleet had been completely destroyed. The imperial government, judging him to have fought against it only out of praiseworthy loyalty to his daimio, generously pardoned him.

Togo ended the war as an "officer of the third class" in the Satsuma Navy. But this was a sort of feudal rank, as vague as it was provisional. Togo had to begin again from the beginning, as an apprentice, when he joined the new imperial navy. Furthermore, the mikado's government had decided that apprentice officers in the navy must first know English. Togo's first task was to learn the language of Shakespeare from a Nipponese official in Yokohama, widely reputed for his learning in that tongue. Thereafter, he completed his study of the language at a school set up for the purpose. Finally, on January 31, 1871, he began his service as a midshipman in the *Ryogo,* his pay being fifteen yen a month.

In April a rumor ran round the training ship that several of the midshipmen were to be selected for a period of naval training in England. "A number of us," Togo later told a biographer, "discussed and weighed our respective chances. One of our group suggested consulting Sekiryushi, a famour seer, who lived in the Shiba quarter of Tokyo. The seer told us that we should all be chosen, with one exception, and that the latter, whom he named, must give up all hope. The unlucky one became extremely angry. But, in the event, by a curious coincidence he was not chosen." At all events, twelve young men ultimately boarded at Yokohama the French steamer which was to take them on the first part of their journey, to Hong Kong. Togo, like the rest of them, had never been out of Japan.

Hong Kong, with its teeming population, had all the air of a purely Chinese city, and the midshipmen saw hardly anything but the port. There, however, lay innumerable junks with patched sails, as decrepit, to all appearances, as China herself. Some were laden with crates and bales; others stank of fish; others were houseboats with whole families, from naked infants to mummified ancients, living aboard.

However, even at this first stage of their journey, the midshipmen were made aware of the presence of that wealthy, powerful, and even invincible nation on which their own young country was being modeled. Astern of the lean warships anchored in line ahead, holystoned, and gleaming like jewels, floated the White Ensign; and, from the poops of fat steamers moored alongside flew the red flag quartering the Union Jack which was the ensign of British maritime commerce. The Japanese travelers were to see that flag—the Red Duster—almost every day of their long sea voyage. At that time one, at least, out of every four ships afloat was British. And in every harbor of their west-bound course—Singapore, Colombo, Aden, Suez—they saw the White Ensign, protector of trade and of Great Britain's vast properties and world-wide rights. The midshipmen crossed the desert from Suez to Alexandria on camel-back. Romantic and picturesque—but it did not greatly interest them. The one thing that excited their imagination was the epic of Britain's naval greatness, subject of their most recent studies. Their hero, whose name they still had some trouble in pronouncing correctly, was Nelson. The first place name to attract their attention when they entered the Mediterranean has an ugly sound in French ears: Aboukir. The spectacle of the naval strength concentrated at Malta had astonished these young men, and filled them with admiration, and they were still talking about it among themselves on the evening of their request to be called before the ship passed Trafalgar.

The ship which carried them rounded Cape Finisterre, steamed across the vast mouth of the Bay of Biscay, rounded Ushant— in Paris the French were once again busy cutting one another's throats—entered the English Channel, and set a course for Selsey Bill. In the nineteenth century a sea voyage was still a sea voyage. All the passengers crowded up on deck to see the chalk cliffs of England lift over the horizon. Some of them turned from time to time to glance with amusement toward the young Japanese who stood grouped together, erect, motionless, their faces impassive but their eyes shining. Togo admitted years later that he, like his comrades, was deeply moved at that moment; nor was it the curiosity of tourists which excited their feelings. For them the soil of England, on which they were shortly to set foot, was, above all else, the motherland of those men whom each, in secret pride, dreamed of emulating: Rodney, Howe, Collingwood, Nelson.

Land came in sight off the port bow, like a white line growing thicker, and Togo listened to the passengers' exclamations. A little later the high hill which forms the southern extremity of the Isle of Wight could be distinguished, and a lighthouse came in sight. The ship held her course for Selsey Bill, farther east. To port, a line of pale gray cliffs slipped by, fronted by massive outcrops of rocks; beyond, at the summit of this high wall, a green and gently sloping plateau. Down beside the sea a watering place, with buildings which still seemed strange to Japanese eyes: a church, and houses built of stone. Then the land seemed to be turning about them; the ship was changing course, her head was coming round, and she was making into the middle of a deep bay. To starboard emerged the fortifications of Portsmouth. The ship began to steam more slowly. Togo was able, by virtue of his new learning, to make out the message conveyed by the first letters which England offered him, a white inscription on a huge black buoy at the entrace to the Solent: *No vessel to anchor in the fairway*.

In Spithead Roads a steam launch came out to meet the now nearly motionless vessel. The pilot came aboard, clambered up on deck, and went to the bridge. The engines began their work again, but slowly, while all over the ship the usual journey's-end bustle began. At the landward end of Southampton Water a forest of masts came in sight, and beyond them of cranes, smoking chimneys, and the impressive vastness of the red and gray city of Southampton, one of the finest ports in the kingdom.

When, in due course, their ship lay alongside, the young Japanese picked out several members of the Japanese legation waiting on the jetty. They were being met. They were taken straight to the London train and, in London, directly to a good tailor.

In 1871 there was no cinema and—in Japan—no newspapers. In other words, the newcomers had had no idea at all of what they were going to see, whereas nowadays we invariably know in advance. London was already the largest and most populous city in the world. And this immense city, its streets and houses all of masonry, was, for the Japanese midshipmen, a new world, exotic, astounding. The thing which at first made the greatest impression on them was the number and massiveness of the buildings. We should also remember, at this point, the bareness of an ordinary Japanese room. When they were shown into ordinary, comfortable hotel bedrooms, Togo and his companions were appalled. The cupboards and chairs, easy chairs and counterpaned beds, fringed curtains—in short all the furnishing of a commonplace European room seemed to them like a quite monstrous jumble of objects: How on earth were they to live in such conditions?

The sponsors to whom the legation had entrusted the midshipmen set to work at once. Their pupils were already adept at certain social rules which had been made second nature by their samurai

54

education and which were very useful to them in England: for example, calmness under all circumstances, and a complete absence of gesticulation. Dressed in European clothes, and with their hair neatly parted on one side, the young men were first taken to see the trooping of the colors by the Scots Guards in the courtyard of St. James's Palace. Thence to a meal in a restaurant, and from there to the docks. They were also taken to the theater. Gentlemen in frock coats and silk hats, and girls wearing enormous hats and red gloves were, apparently, less surprising than the displays in butchers' shop windows: it took them several days to become accustomed to such an abundance of meat.

The young Japanese were lucky. London displayed herself to them in her most attractive guise: not, that is, somber under a cloak of sooty fog, or gray under icy rain, but in the exquisite light of her brief summer: above the houses a wide, clear, pale blue sky, and her verdant parks bright with crinolines. This exotic spectacle was altogether charming. However, although the mikado's government had made provision for them to live very comfortably, they had certainly not been sent to England as tourists, simply to enjoy themselves. After several days Togo and his friends were informed that they were to be separated and that each of them was to live for some time in a good boardinghouse, where their first duty would be to perfect their English and take an intelligent interest in the mores and manners of the English people. Togo was sent to Plymouth.

The bustle and the discipline of the great harbor and naval base set the tone for the whole town. At the rising and setting of the sun, the gun salutes and trumpet calls of "Colors" rang out at one identical moment aboard the hundred warships which lay in the roads or within the harbor. Alleys and public houses were full of uniforms. The air was redolent of sea and tobacco, and frock-coated officers drove along the principal thoroughfares in their carriages. It was during this first residence at Plymouth that Togo began to have some idea of the Royal Navy's might, its degree of perfection, and its high social prestige. The mere fact that he was destined to belong to it, as an officer in training, earned him a certain special consideration in his boardinghouse.

His admission—the admission of all the Japanese—to the Royal Navy had not been obtained without difficulty, and Togo was never, in fact, to sail in any but training ships. The Japanese Government had hoped that its midshipmen would be allowed to go as cadets to the Royal Naval College,* and thereafter to serve in British warships. This was refused: the Admiralty's reply to the Japanese request was that the Royal Naval College was full. In the end, Togo was destined for the Thames Nautical Training College, which constituted a lesser, or secondary, way of reaching a Royal Navy quarter-deck. But it was enough; it meant that Togo was spared that polite want of consideration which is the fate, a priori, in England, of all that is alien. The respectable persons with whom, every day, in a conscientious effort to improve his pronunciation, he exchanged leisurely platitudes on the state of the weather, pursued such conversations with good grace and even went so far as to retail chapters of local history and advise him as to the best walks in the neighborhood. Togo thanked them with polished courtesy, but his first objective, set by himself, was that of getting to know the town and the port thoroughly, as every good sailor should. Often, leaving the small parlor where his fellow boarders were assembled after their tea or the Sunday joint, he would leave the house, walk down to the docks, and, making for a certain basin, stand in thought before a great sailing warship which lay there at anchor, and whose convex sides were pierced by numerous gun ports. She was archaic, yet, by the flag at her stern, was still to be regarded as on the strength, in service. The ship was Nelson's *Victory*.

At the end of the summer Togo left his boardinghouse to enter a naval preparatory school. Institutions of this kind had long existed at all naval bases. The one in question was presided over by a clergyman, and the subjects taught were history, mathematics,

* Presumably either Dartmouth or Osborne. The United States equivalent would be Annapolis.—TRANS.

and engineering draftsmanship. Togo applied himself to them in his usual way.

From there he went to the Thames Nautical Training College, was carried on aboard a three-masted sailing ship, H.M.S. *Worcester*, permanently moored in the river and run according to Royal Navy service regulations. Togo, a veteran of the Hakodate war, an officer of the third class in the Satsuma's Navy, and a midshipman of the mikado, went aboard the *Worcester* as a cadet in 1872. He was to spend two years in that capacity.

It might be supposed that, at least as regards the practical work, Togo, in competition with much younger boys of no seafaring experience, would, as an experienced sailor, have an advantage. He was not long in realizing, however, that his experience was of very little use to him. Naturally, when he had to go out in a boat he was not seasick. But all the work connected with drill and seamanship was new to him, despite his gunnery on the *Kasuga*. Above all, it was on his training ship that Togo was forced to accept as a fact something which since his arrival in England he had begun to suspect: he had almost everything to learn about Western *method*. This was brought home to him at almost every hour of the day, and no matter what the work in hand—holystoning the deck or solving a problem in algebra. It was in this vital point that boys whose minds were certainly less mature than his, and who were a great deal less intelligent, possessed an advantage over him: they had, as part of their birthright, what we may almost call an instinct for Western logic, whereas he, the samurai, was often baffled as to how to attack a given problem. But will power and perseverance always carry the day in the end, even when it is a question of mastering a new intellectual tool.

The months passed; there is little to tell of them: they were the uneventful months of an apprentice naval officer. There is one odd thing worth noting: Togo found a naval apprentice's rations inadequate. In his own words: "I swallowed my small rations in a moment. I formed the habit of dipping my bread in my tea and eating a great deal of it, to the surprise of my English comrades." It may be that his Far Eastern metabolism was attuned to a diet of rice, and that his body missed it; or that some other essential element was missing; or perhaps the climatic difference sharpened his appetite.

Togo's comrades called him "Johnny Chinaman." The young samurai did not like that, and on more than one occasion he put an end to such facetiousness by blows. The others soon realized that, despite his slightness, he was strong and agile and that his courage was of the highest order: thereafter, he was left in peace. But the nickname "Johnny Chinaman" stuck for a long time. His fellow students had been genuinely astonished when he first protested against being taken for a Chinese. Why on earth should the fellow want them to distinguish between China and Japan? For these young Englishmen, the notion of trying to distinguish between the nations which, apparently, claimed some sort of independent existence beyond the Channel and the protecting shadow of the Union Jack was ridiculous. Togo was a yellow man, consequently Chinese. They were a little taken aback at the end of their training, when the yellow man passed second.

Even nowadays there are to be found, in many of the world's navies, high-ranking executive officers who believe that no naval training can possibly be sound and complete unless it includes a term of service aboard a sailing ship. In nineteenth century Britain this doctrine was not even questioned. After their two years aboard the motionless *Worcester,* the cadets of the Thames Nautical Training College were posted to the training ship *Hampshire*. This vessel sailed out of the Thames, flying the White Ensign, at the end of February, 1875, and once clear of the Channel, set a southerly course. The boys off the *Worcester* were about to put into practice all they had learned concerning seamanship and astronavigation.

On April 19th, at midnight, the *Hampshire* rounded the Cape of Good Hope at sixty miles from the land. Seventy days later she dropped anchor off Melbourne, having met nothing but sharks and sea birds in her ten-week cruise. They had hardly set foot ashore when the whole ship's company, Togo included, made straight for the nearest restaurant and a meal of fresh food: sailing vessels in those days had neither iceboxes nor refrigerators. Seventy days at sea without once making land meant sixty-eight days on salted meat and ship's biscuits.

Their reward consisted in two months of virtual holiday-making at the best time of the year. The *Hampshire* remained at her moorings while her company of cadets amused themselves afloat and ashore, afoot, on horseback, in carriages, and in boats.

The Japanese have an inborn taste for nature. In the course of his two-month residence in Australia, Togo visited several atolls. He confessed that he never tired of making his way across the blue waters of a lagoon to land on one of these tiny crowns of land which seemed to float upon the waters. He observed the strange animals of the Southern continent. And, by his own account, he admired the way in which Great Britain contrived to dominate and develop a region situated at such a vast distance from her own territory.

On July 11th the *Hampshire* raised her anchor and, saluted by all the ships in the harbor and the roads, put to sea. On August 11th she rounded Cape Horn, with the land seventy miles to the north. It was on a misty morning at the end of September that she took on a Trinity House pilot at the mouth of the Thames. By the time she tied up alongside her dock, Togo had completed thirty thousand miles.

Once again he was required to do a spell ashore, giving himself up to study. This time, however, there was no question of new beginnings: his task was to master some part of the higher mathematics. His curriculum and the arrangements for it had been made in agreement with the Japanese legation in London. The legation found a suitable tutor in the person of the Reverend A. D. Capel, who received Togo into his house at Cambridge. And it was among the ancient colleges of the lovely, stone-gray university town that this samurai student of Western sciences suffered one of the most agonizing experiences of his whole life.

59

None of the biographical documents touching Togo's career gives us any specifically clinical account of the trouble which began to impair his eyesight. We are told, simply, that it began to fail and that he experienced severe pain. Togo appears to have consulted a number of oculists: their prognosis—all that we have—was that even if the disease could be checked, the patient's eyesight would be permanently subnormal. The consequence must have been distressingly clear to him: he would have to abandon any idea of being a sailor. The best he could hope for was a post ashore in the Japanese Admiralty. At twenty-seven years of age he must regard his naval career, which was to have been so brilliant, as at an end. His seafaring experience in Japan, all his patient assimilation of Western science and logic, all his years of voluntary exile were to end, not in battle on the limitless surface of the sea, but between the four walls of an office.

Here is all that is to be learned concerning Togo's disease of the eyes from the researches of both historians and journalists who set to work exploring his past after his great victory of 1905. The patient asked his medical advisers to "try everything," and some of their experiments were extremely painful. At the time only one person, apart from the doctors, was aware of Togo's condition, and even that exception was fortuitous. Togo, while discreetly undergoing successive courses of treatment, was carrying on with his mathematics and even attending the Methodist church with his tutor's family, not merely by way of courtesy but also to complete his initiation into English ways. As to his physical sufferings and his anxieties, he said not a word. However, his work was impaired by his medical treatment, and he found himself unable to leave Mr. Capel in ignorance of his condition. His tutor interviewed Togo's doctors, and it seems that it was at his insistence that Togo consented to inform the legation of his trouble. (In April, 1905, at the fall of Port Arthur, the *Strand Magazine* asked Mr. Capel for an article on his memories of his illustrious pupil. "If," he wrote, "I had not seen with my own eyes what a Japanese can suffer without complaint, I should often have been disinclined to believe many of the tales which have been told about this war. But, having observed Togo, I believe all of them.")

The legation having been informed, Togo left Cambridge for London, where he could be attended by the most eminent specialists. The Harley Street ophthalmologists saved his eyesight.

But not a moment too soon. In association with certain future events, something new was coming to pass in Japan—the birth of a national navy, and this time according to Western ideas. In 1875 the mikado's government had ordered three warships from British yards: an armored coast guard vessel of 3,700 tons, and two smaller ships of 2,250 tons each. It would be foolish to smile at these displacement figures: they were normal for the time; besides, have we any idea of the tonnage of tomorrow's atomic warships, if they are ever built? Togo had seen the news of these orders placed by his country's government, in the English press. And, like his eleven comrades, no doubt he dreamed of serving in one of these ultramodern naval craft.

The period of Togo's residence in England was coming to an end, so that when a letter arrived from the legation he supposed it would contain his repatriation orders. It did not, for a fresh decision had been reached in Tokyo. All the Japanese apprentice officers were to remain in England while the warships ordered by Japan were being built. They were appointed "inspectors" and would return to Japan on board the ships when they were finished. Togo was posted to the *Fuso*, which was under construction at Poplar, London.

It goes without saying that the title of "inspector" was honorific. "Observer" would have been more to the point. An attentive man watching a ship being built under his eyes can learn a great deal. Togo, in lodgings near the fine old Royal Naval Hospital at Greenwich, on the Thames, betook himself every morning and every afternoon to the shipyard at Poplar, kept his eyes wide open, and persisted in asking questions with a tireless politeness which soon got the better of the rather surly temper of the shipbuilding workers. At evening he wrote up his notes. In the courtyard of the Royal

61

Naval Hospital was a line of busts, representing Duncan, Howe, St. Vincent, and Nelson. This period of his life was tranquil, studious, and agreeable. Then came the news that Togo's family was in revolt: his brothers, friends and neighbors had taken up arms against the mikado.

The first news of these events to reach England was confused. All one could be sure of was that a new war had broken out. The Japanese apprentice officers were deeply disturbed. Heirs to an ancient feudal system, they were not yet emancipated from its influence. Several of them spoke of returning to Japan by the first available boat. To them, Togo said: "No. Let us finish what we have to do here. Afterwards, we shall see."

A little later it became known that the revolt had broken out over an expedition against Korea which the government had proposed to undertake and had then put off. The leader of the rebellion was Tokamuri Saigo, daimio of Satsuma. He had an army of forty thousand men. But an imperial army was marching on Kyushu. Togo's comrades, with sorrowful faces, came to condole with him. Again they asked him if he proposed to return to Japan. He replied that he did not. Then would he be sending some sort of apology for his family's behavior to the imperial government?

"No," Togo answered. "I do not feel myself under any obligation to apologize to the government because my brothers and associates have joined the rebel army. It was to be expected that they would all feel bound to follow Saigo's lead. As for me, I shall continue to do what I was sent here to do. If, later on, I am of some service to the government, that will bear witness enough to my gratitude for the great advantages they have granted me."

Supposing him to have been at home at the time, would Togo have done as his brothers did? In all probability, yes. In which case he would perhaps have died beside his elder brother who was killed in action at Shiroyama on September 27, 1877. The siege of Port Arthur and the Battle of Tsushima would, in that case, probably have had a different outcome, and Japan's subsequent history might have been very different. But this is to play the somewhat frivolous game of retrospective suppositions. It is more to the point to consider the one significant fact that emerges from this account: with a remarkable instinct, an exceptional *feeling* for the course which his destiny bade him follow, Togo refused to take any part in the last great act of Japan's feudal epic. That tragedy was like a retrospective accident in a Japan already modernized and in which he, Togo, would have a part to play. It is a distinction in men of the first order that they recognize (and avoid involvement with) what is merely contingent, for they see at a glance, and even occasionally foresee, the events that really matter.

So Togo did not leave England until the *Fuso* sailed for Japan in February, 1878.

The Sokuro Togo who was killed fighting for his liege lord at Shiroyama was the brother whose cup of water Heihachiro had once dosed with pepper. In the tragic chaos of the battlefield, his body had been hastily buried where he fell. When Masuko, true samurai mother, heard of this wretched flouting of the proper rites, she went in person to take her first-born from his poor grave. In order that no metal might touch his heroic body, she did the work with her bare hands. Thereafter he was buried in the family cemetery, there to rest in peace.

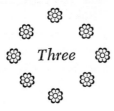 *Three*

From the bridges of the ships which were bringing them home from the West, the Japanese apprentice officers watched the coast of their fatherland rise above the horizon. This was the land they remembered, this jagged, mountainous skyline, crowned by a few white clouds, and towering above a restless gray sea. Nor did such buildings as soon became visible here and there on the hillsides seem to have changed. But when the warships reached the bar of Yokohama Harbor, the young men might have been excused for thinking that their ships had somehow steamed right round the world and brought them to some European port: for never, in their native land, had they heard the noise which greeted their coming—the bellowing of many steamships' sirens.

64

Hundreds of welcoming boats with cheering crews swarmed across the harbor waters. On brand-new jetties a waving crowd moved restlessly against a background of mighty, equally new buildings. And the uproar of ships' sirens, still persisting, seemed like the new, perhaps rather strident voice of Japan transformed. The Yokohama of 1878, with its bustle, noise, and smoke, was as little like the Yokohama of 1871—Togo had been seven years abroad—as the Yokohama of 1871 compared with the fishing village which had borne that name in 1860. For the Japan of the "Meiji era" was an express train going at full speed.

The transformation of old Japan into a powerful modern nation was not accomplished in a day, or without stumbling. Briefly and sketchily, it may be said that in the initial period of Europeanization, everything that came from the West was held to be good and wonderful, while everything that was old Japanese was thown on the scrapheap. Thus the Japanese would give European residents and travelers rare objects in gold lacquer, screens which were priceless heirlooms, and other precious treasures, in exchange for the most commonplace imported goods, without regard for price.

These first excesses were naturally followed by a reaction; then came adaptation. We shall make no attempt to follow this evolution in detail, for what interests us here, in a swiftly changing Japan, is her fighting navy, the institution that was to shape Togo's character and career, while he was to contribute to its creation. The fighting navy grew and developed without let or hindrance. Nor does the concentration of our attention on the navy entail an arbitrary choice of one of the many sectors of Japanese national development: for, as it happened, the navy was the principal and essential instrument by means of which Japan made herself a great power.

Bonaparte was commander in chief of the Army of Italy at twenty-seven; at thirty he became First Consul. At thirty, Togo was a sublieutenant in the Japanese Navy. The comparison is hardly to his advantage. But eighteen months later he was a lieutenant commander: four gold stripes, captain of a corvette, one

65

of the youngest of his rank.* Such promotion would be sensational in any navy in the world. But in the brand-new Japanese Navy, and taking Togo's antecedents into account, it was to be expected.

The Tokyo Naval School had been reinforced by an up-to-date Naval College at Tsukiji. There, thirty officers of the British Royal Navy taught their Japanese pupils the art of Nelsonian warfare, and, in addition, everything touching quick-firing naval guns, torpedoes, naval armor and electrical gear.

But Togo, on his return from England, was already tolerably well informed in all these subjects, and he and the handful of officers in like case were utilized to the utmost. The idea was to make them monitors of the new, educated Japanese naval personnel, disseminators of Western science and method. To accomplish this it was necessary to post them frequently from one ship to another. Immediately following his return, he served as a sublieutenant—second class—in the *Hiei*. He was soon posted, with the same rank, aboard the *Fuso;* in her he was promoted and, remaining on the same ship, served in her as a two-striper until posted back to the *Hiei*. On being posted again he was promoted lieutenant commander and became first lieutenant † of the *Jingei*. The *Jingei* was the imperial yacht.

It would be a mistake to envisage these successive promotions as a sort of heady, triumphal march accompanied by acclamations. Seen in close-up, Togo's life during these years was simply "the service," the usual service of an officer in peacetime, useful but obscure. Nor was it without its troubles. Those favorites of fortune who had been trained in the West enjoyed no special veneration in their ships, and were by no means listened to as if they were

* In the Royal Navy and in the United States Navy a lieutenant commander has two and a half gold stripes. Presumably the Japanese Navy ranks were differently indicated. The "captain" of a ship was not necessarily a post captain by rank, that is, commissioned as officer in command of a vessel of twenty guns or more.—TRANS.

† That is, second in command. Just as the captain of a ship need not be a post captain so the first lieutenant ("Number One," or, in the Royal Navy, "Jimmy the One") need not be a lieutenant. In a big ship he is often a commander.—TRANS.

oracles. Jealousy is not confined to our hemisphere, or envy, or even, among the most decided partisans of novelty, a certain conservatism or reserve in the face of novelty when it actually makes its appearance and cannot be denied. The Western-trained officers were put to the test more often than most. Let any difficulty manifest itself, any awkward problem appear, and it was to them, with a sardonically expectant smile, that subordinates and superiors alike turned for a solution. But Togo, who had actually seen some fighting, and was a veteran of the Hakodate war, and who was, moreover, matured by his long residence abroad, had all the advantage of experience with many kinds of men. It was difficult to surprise, intimidate, or persuade him. On one occasion a fellow officer drew his attention to the fact that he was not issuing his orders according to the traditional Japanese rules.

"The important thing is that the orders be understood," Togo said. "What counts on a modern warship is time."

As it was virtually impossible to trip him up in anything touching his seamanship and his duties, the spite, and even malevolence, of some fellow officers was powerless in the face of his impassive self-control.

If one considers Togo's conduct as first lieutenant of the *Jingei,* one would be inclined to describe it in the terms used of him by his headmaster at Kagoshima high school: "hard-working, intelligent, not brilliant, no weaknesses." The position of second in command of a ship seemed to suit him perfectly. Very few writers of sea stories have chosen, as their hero, a first mate in the merchant service or a first lieutenant in the navy. Consequently the job is one which the public knows virtually nothing about; it is, however, one of the most difficult to make a success of.

The officer in question must know all there is to know about both his ship and his ship's company. He is responsible to the captain for everything, whether it be the state of the hull, the condition of the guns, or the training and bearing of the crew. A first lieutenant must cater for his men, train them, prepare them for battle, in short, put a perfectly functioning weapon into his captain's hands. That is his job. He must have an eye on everything, boats and boat drill, the galley and messes, small arms and small-arms drill and training, sick bay, chain lockers, punishment cells, washing facilities, "heads," and the rest. Up before the morning cry of "Show a leg" and "Up and at 'em!" Number One is the last aboard to turn in, for he is perpetually on duty.

An executive officer of the *Jingei*, noted for his conscientiousness, once said that in rough weather it was his habit, whether the ship was at sea or at anchor, to get up three times during the night (whether it was his watch or not), and make the rounds. On every occasion he had invariably found Togo up and correctly dressed. In the morning, when the men were swabbing decks, Togo was there, feet bare and trousers rolled up. Apparently the mikado never made use of the yacht during Togo's term aboard her. But when the *Jingei*—she was a wooden ship with two funnels and two masts, and a swan-necked prow, a very pretty vessel—was carrying someone of consequence, Togo stood beside her captain, in full-dress uniform, making sure that the honors were done in style, and the ship gleaming like a jewel.

However, Togo was only one officer among many others. By all accounts he showed no outward sign of exceptional talent. There was just the fact that any commanding officer could be certain that any task entrusted to him would be carried out to perfection. Months passed. The *Jingei* cruised on various missions among the islands of the Rising Sun. And it was in the course of his service aboard the imperial yacht that Togo married.

His betrothed, Tetsuko, was nineteen. Although she was the daughter of a noble samurai of Satsuma, Togo had never met her before the ceremony which is called Mi-Aï, that is to say, "Mutual Sighting." This ceremony had, as was customary, been arranged long in advance, and after careful negotiations, by a family friend. Theoretically, the ceremony is meant to enable the young couple to decide whether they are likely to suit each other. In practice, everything has been decided before it takes place, and it may be

68

noted that, in 1881, no case was on record of a girl having refused to marry the man chosen by her family, after the Mi-Aï.

Gifts having been exchanged, a lucky day was chosen according to ancient rites, and Tetsuko was attired in white, the color of mourning, which signified not only that she would henceforth be dead to her own family but also that she would not leave her husband's house until she did so as a corpse. As soon as she had taken leave of her own people, her father's house was ritually swept from top to bottom, as a symbol of purification.

The marriage ceremony proper consisted in a feast which took place as soon as Tetsuko had passed into the house of Masuko, Togo's mother, and changed her white gown for a new one, the gift of her husband-to-be. The bride and bridegroom each drank three times from three goblets of wine of different sizes, or rather touched the wine with their lips. Then Tetsuko changed her dress a third time, putting on one which she had brought with her from her parents' house, while Togo also changed his clothes, in another room. When the feast was over, the bridal pair were conducted to the nuptial chamber and once again exchanged vows over nine goblets of wine. But whereas at the beginning of the ceremony Tetsuko, being a guest, was the first to drink, on this second occasion it was Togo who drank first: for he was now her husband, that is to say, her lord and master.

Three days later the bridal pair paid a ceremonial visit to Tetsuko's parents. Meanwhile, the municipal authorities had been informed of the wedding, the only legal formality which was required. All Togo's friends sent their congratulations, and his superiors were satisfied by the traditional and honorable way in which he had taken a wife.

Apparently their respect for traditional forms did not put happiness out of the question for Togo and his wife. It is even quite possible that their union was as happy as if he had married the object of a grand passion—incidentally a ridiculous hypothesis at that time and for a man in his position. As is well known, the marriage of a Japanese might later be, as it were, supplemented by the taking of one or two official concubines. But Togo was dedicated to his profession as a sailor. As to his treatment of his young wife, he considered it his duty to be courteous, kind, and tender to her, and invariably was so. She, for her part, found it natural (as well as obligatory) to satisfy him in all respects, which she never failed to do. This recipe for a happy marriage is, perhaps, not a bad one.

Shortly after their wedding, Togo went back to sea and Tetsuko went to live with her mother-in-law, which was also traditional. A year later the young couple bought a house in Tokyo. They had it enlarged in 1905, and lived there for the rest of their lives.

After two years as first lieutenant of the *Jingei*, Togo was posted, again as first lieutenant, to another ship, the *Amagi*. The *Amagi* was one of the oldest and weakest units of the Japanese Navy: six hundred tons, and of wooden construction. So that Togo's posting was the reverse of glorious, and even looked rather like a demotion. Togo does not seem to have been depressed by it. Under his first lieutenancy the old tub began to shine like a new pin, and both the ship's company and the gear began to give of their best. Meanwhile, things were beginning to happen in the world of Asia.

Toward the end of July, 1882, the *Amagi* was at Shimonoseki. Togo as usual was busy seeing that the ship and her crew were carrying out their duties, when he was sent for by his captain, who said: "It looks as if there may be a war. Read this note which I have received from Tokyo."

The substance of the letter was as follows: His Excellency Hanabusa, Japanese Minister to Korea, had just arrived at Nagasaki aboard a British warship, the *Flying Fish*. This ship had picked up the diplomat, and some members of his suite, in a state of almost total exhaustion, a few miles from Chemulpo, on the beach of a small island. The Japanese legation in Seoul had been attacked by Korean civilians and soldiers. A number of Japanese had been murdered. The minister and the other survivors had managed to escape to Chemulpo, and from there put to sea in a junk.

"The insult," said the *Amagi's* captain, "is an intolerable one. We can presumably expect a punitive expedition to start at once."

"As far as we are concerned," Togo replied, "the ship is ready."

Three days passed. The officers of the warships which lay anchored at Shimonoseki did not conceal their hope that war would be declared. It was the general opinion that the violence offered to their minister at Seoul was really due to China: China was behind it all, and it was Li Hung-chang's agents with Li Hung-chang's gold who were stirring up the Koreans.

Li Hung-chang was chief minister to the old Empress Dowager Tzu Hsi. In 1882 Korea offered the typical spectacle of a weak country at the end of its tether: its unstable nationalist movement was, inevitably, being exploited by interested foreigners—the last phase before total loss of sovereignty. From time immemorial Korea had been a vassal state of either China or Japan. Despite these political vicissitudes, it had developed a peaceful national culture until the arrival, at the end of the sixteenth century, of Hideyoshi's invading army. Hideyoshi, often called the Japanese Napoleon by the historians of his country, died at the time of the invasion, and the Japanese Army withdrew. Strangely enough, Korea did not recover from what must have seemed a providential liberation. The political climate remained one of anarchy and violent disturbances; the national culture declined; and a sort of totalitarian xenophobia developed. During the same time the nationalist slogan most effective in rousing the mob in the Land of Morning Calm was "Death to the Europeans!" And as insufficient ammunition was available for shooting all Christians, an ingenious craftsman invented a guillotine which could behead twenty people at a time.

In 1876, twenty-three years after Perry's ultimatum to Japan, Japan called upon Korea to lay herself open without delay or reservation to the benefits of civilization. Korea gave way in the face of Japanese pressure with about as much good grace and enthusiasm as Japan had manifested in giving way to pressure by the Western powers. The same violently nationalist demonstrations followed the signature of the treaty between the two countries.

In the year (1882) of the incident in Seoul, the United States and Great Britain, following Japan's lead, had persuaded Korea to open her ports to their trade. Japan, who had insisted that the Treaty of 1876 proclaimed Korea's "complete independence," maintained in Seoul not only a legation but also an "instructor" whose mission was to create the nucleus of a modern Korean army. In short, Japan was extending a protective hand over the tender independence of Korea. Korean nationalists foamed at the mouth with rage, just as the Jo-i had done in Japan. China, while showing no overt interest, allowed a certain amount of money and a small supply of weapons to be slipped into nationalist hands.

The violent events of 1882 had their origin in the weather. The year—and it happened to be the one in which Korean ports had just been thrown open to foreigners—was remarkable for an extreme drought, and the rice harvest was a total failure. While the king, I-Hyong, was on his knees before an altar in the palace gardens, praying for rain, a group of starving and furious soldiers attacked the palace with the intention of killing both him and his ministers who had "sold out to the Japanese and the Occidentals." The king escaped by a miracle from the attack which had been instigated by his own brother, Tai Won-kun. As for the queen, she owed her life to the devotion of a lady-in-waiting who took her place and pretended to be her royal mistress. The Japanese minister, Hanabusa, and his followers had retreated, fighting. Such were the facts.

Four days later the Japanese Government issued sailing orders to eight of the warships which lay at Shimonoseki; one of the eight was the *Amagi*. The task force was commanded by Vice Admiral Nire, whose orders were to reinstate the Japanese minister, if necessary by force, and to obtain apologies and an indemnity.

If this small squadron were to be shown on a modern newsreel, it would no doubt appear ridiculous to an audience accustomed

72

to huge task forces composed of aircraft carriers piloted by radar. But it must be remembered that the very want of modern navigation aids meant that nineteenth century sailors had frequently to solve problems which a seaman of today would find difficult. When Vice Admiral Nire arrived off Chemulpo, he not only had no radar: he had no pilotage charts of the harbor, and he could hardly signal for a Korean pilot. Rather than risk running one of his ships aground, Nire decided to wait for a local vessel to appear, and to follow her in. The first ship to appear, however, came not from the open sea, but out of the harbor, a Chinese vessel of considerable displacement. All the officers of the watch in the Japanese squadron carefully observed her course, and she was hardly over the bar before they were steaming in, in line ahead, over the same course in reverse.

The Japanese had barely dropped anchor when three Chinese warships made their appearance. The Japanese ships' companies were immediately piped to action stations. A boat put off from one of the three Chinese ships—she flew an admiral's flag—and rowed across to hail the Japanese flagship. She bore a message from the commanding officer of the Celestial flotilla to the effect that the Chinese, like the Japanese, were there to "restore order." The Chinese admiral was Ting Ju-chang and he was, in reality, the naval officer commanding the whole of China's Northern Fleet.

Togo learned these details only incidentally. He could not know that he was to be the Chinese admiral's most formidable adversary and eventual conqueror.

The Japanese squadron put ashore a landing force which immediately marched on Seoul. Each ship's contingent was, according to the custom obtaining in all navies at the time, placed under the command of the ship's first lieutenant. Thus, Togo led the *Amagi's* company.

There was no resistance. Seoul was entered without a shot being fired, and the king reinstated on his throne. The Japanese minister returned to his legation. However, the negotiations concerning the reparations to be paid to Japan for the wound to her

73

pride dragged on for a long time. Hanabusa, whose orders were clear and definite, did not hesitate; he broke off the talks, returned to Chemulpo, and went on board a Japanese ship.

Since all the Japanese ships remained in the harbor, their crews were again piped to action stations. The gunners began to train their guns on the town. There were, in Korea, many people who had heard of, and remembered, the events of Kagoshima, and Shimonoseki, for accounts of them had been disseminated throughout the Far East. The Japanese demands were agreed to in full.

But after the Chinese squadron had steamed out of the port, it was learned that Tai Won-kun, the king's brother and leader of the nationalist faction of agitators, had left Korea aboard the flagship.

The mikado's government, wishing to do all in its power to ensure Korean independence, left its naval task force at Chemulpo for six months. During this time the *Amagi* was sent to show the flag and made a survey up the river Taedong, going seventy miles upstream. Togo made soundings, drew charts, noted outstanding features and peculiarities of the region. In Seoul, thereafter, he was thrown by chance into the company of a very singular individual, a Chinese official on duty who was only twenty-three years old.

"What a pity it is," said this young man, "that your country favors Western penetration of Korea! Believe me, the white man's influence is pernicious. I very much fear that even Japan will feel the truth of this before very long." And he went on to develop his theme in more detail and for considerable time. Togo listened to him politely and attentively, but said nothing. The man in question—and Heaven knows what his real opinions were at the time and what he was thinking as he carried out his task as a counterpropagandist—was Yüan Shih-k'ai. Togo's interlocutor, in short, was one of the most remarkable political adventurers in all Asia, and was, in due course, to succeed Sun Yat-sen as President of the Chinese Republic, at that time an inconceivable political entity.

74

In February, 1883, Korea having been pacified and furnished with several Japanese "advisers," the naval squadron left Chemulpo and returned to Shimonoseki. It was shortly after their return that Lieutenant Commander Togo, while his ship lay at the naval station of Bakan, revealed, in a rather odd demonstration, the persistence of certain traits of character first apparent in the schoolboy Heihachiro Togo at Kajima-Machi. The *Amagi's* captain was on leave when a British warship dropped anchor in the roads. Having inspected the flag at her masthead, Togo had what he considered the requisite salute fired by the *Amagi's* guns. It seems that he made a mistake. Without going into details of naval etiquette, and the subtle difficulties presented by the case of a post-captain-acting-commodore, it will be enough to say that the British commanding officer let it be known that the salute accorded had been inadequate. Togo admitted this, and had another series of blank rounds fired by his guns. "Still too few," signaled the Englishman. "Even fewer than the first salute." Togo's signal in reply read, "If you will be good enough to add the two salutes together, you will find the number correct."

The English captain at once telegraphed a signal of protest to the Japanese Admiralty. The matter was serious, since the appointed vessel was one of Her Majesty's ships. Togo was not without advocates who maintained that there was nothing in the regulations to say that the number of discharges in a salute must all be fired in one salvo; it followed that a salute could be "completed," as the *Amagi's* Number One now claimed. This point of view did not prevail, and Togo was informed by telephone that he would have to fire the salute again.

To the general stupefaction, he insisted that he was right, and refused. It is difficult not to feel the same surprise as the Japanese naval authorities at this obstinacy. Looking back, it has about it the kind of childishness which might make one suspect some psychological "complex." As we shall see, this was not the last instance of frankly inexplicable conduct in Togo's life.

Some days later, the *Amagi's* first lieutenant was urgently sum-

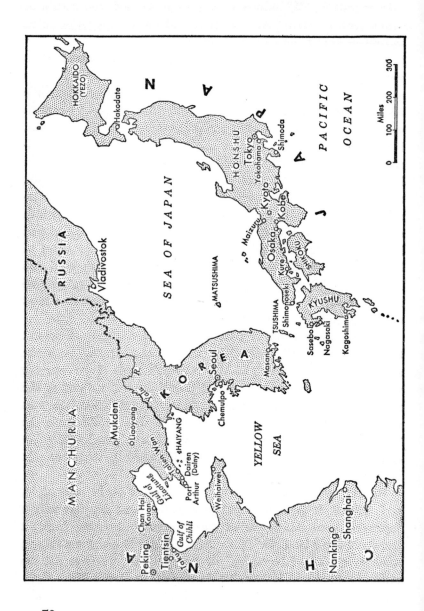

moned to Tokyo. Impassive as ever, he presented himself at naval headquarters. General opinion among the officers who knew of the incident was that things looked bad for him.

It is at this point that the story takes what we can only call a peculiarly Asiatic turn. Not a word was said to Togo about the saluting incident by his superiors. He had been sent for to receive official intimation of the emperor's satisfaction with his service in Korea. He returned to Shimonoseki and there, a few days later, received another signal: he was posted to the command of the imperial navy's ship *Daini Teihu.*

"Sole master aboard under God" is an expression no longer much heard. And, indeed, it is no longer, or very rarely and exceptionally, applicable to a modern ship's captain. The perfecting of means of communication has had the result of making the captain on his bridge, and even an admiral commanding a fleet, dependent on his base or Admiralty. Still, something remains of the ancient splendor of the office, a moral element much feared, alas! by the mass of latter-day men, but still very attractive to certain men of parts and strong mind: its name is responsibility. Responsibility for whatever may happen and without regard to what may have been the failings of one's subordinates.

At the time when Togo was posted to the command of the *Daini Teihu,* the command of a ship was still, however, a thrilling and absorbing task, certainly among the most satisfying a man of spirit could aspire to. It mattered hardly at all that the *Daini Teihu* was an even smaller ship than the *Amagi,* in fact a very small ship indeed; 125 tons' displacement, and only 135 feet from stem to stem. But for Togo she was *his* ship. Her duty, for a year, apart from one or two training cruises, was to keep watch on the coast in the neighborhood of Kure and Sasebo, where the Admiralty proposed to build important naval bases. But in May, 1884, Togo was once again summoned to Tokyo, where he learned that he had been posted to the command of his last ship, the *Amagi,* and that he was to join her at Nagasaki and sail as soon as possible.

"You will join the Middle Fleet at Shanghai."

The Japanese Middle Fleet was commanded by Rear Admiral Matsumura. The orders which that officer had just received were such as could not fail to be of the utmost interest to any Japanese naval officer: "On the suggestion of Her Britannic Majesty's Government, the Imperial Government has decided to join the British, United States, and German governments in sending warships into Chinese waters to protect the lives and property of citizens of neutral States in the event of war between China and France. You will therefore act in concert with the officers commanding the fleets of the three powers named above. In the event of war you will observe strict neutrality." Thus, only twenty years after the bombardment of Kagoshima, a Japanese admiral was receiving orders to act in concert with the naval high commands of three great powers. There was, of course, no question of any comparison of naval strength with that of the Western fleets. But Japan was there, acting as an equal with the Western powers. The Rising Sun was rising indeed!

These orders were not the only ones Matsumura received: secret instructions urged him to lose no opportunity of observing the personnel, equipment, and methods of the three fleets with which his own would be cooperating.

Immemorial China, the China of the last Manchu emperors, inert, immense, anarchic amidst the swift current of the first industrial century, China changeless yet stirring and grumbling with revolt,* had just signed the Convention of Tientsin with France. This convention envisaged the opening of talks on the subject of Tonkin. But an apparent agreement deceived no one. It was well known that since the murder of the French Captain Rivière, perpetrated by members of the Black Flag Society a year before, at Hanoi, war had been likely. Jules Ferry, ridiculed in France under the nickname of "The Tonkinese," and paralyzed by op-

---

* The Moslem uprising in Yunnan and Kansu between 1862 and 1877 had cost millions of lives.

78

position in the Senate, was doing his best to ensure France's position in Annam and Tonkin by forcing China's hand with very inadequate military resources and without declaring war. China, according to her ancient usage, was gaining time. Corruption of vassals, subsidies for pirates, secret supplies of arms—such were the methods which, in May, 1884, were typical of Chinese policy and which could not fail to attract the interested attention of a man like Togo. It was with great satisfaction that, very shortly after his arrival in Shanghai, he received orders to steam up the Yangtze River as far as his ship would go, showing the flag and charting the river.

The Blue River did not, it is true, look like a great artery leading into the heart of the country, but, rather, like some mean, interminable slum in a Chinese city, an immense and wretched ribbon-like development of junks overcrowded with a teeming and miserable population. These junks, painted in glaring colors and decorated on each side of the prow with a staring, painted eye, were moored side by side for miles, and in places composed veritable floating cities; and it was among archipelagoes of such stinking, reeking artificial islands that Togo had to pilot his ship against the current of turgid, yellow waters thick with dead animals and uprooted trees. The *Amagi* steamed upriver as far as Hankow, six hundred miles in the interior. No ship of her size had ever been seen so far from the sea. Togo brought her back to Shanghai at the end of June, to be greeted with the news that Chinese-French tension had increased.

On June 23, 1884, Admiral Ting Ju-chang (to be known from now on by the simpler name of Admiral Ting) had arrived with his fleet at Chefoo to pay his respects to Admiral Lespès. A grand regatta, or maritime gala, had been held. But on the same day six hundred French soldiers on their way to occupy Langson according to the terms of the Tientsin Convention, were attacked at Bac-Le by ten thousand Chinese regulars.

France immediately addressed to the Chinese government a note demanding an apology and an indemnity of 250 million francs * and the right to occupy Nankin and Fuchow. To this there was no reply. Some days later it was learned that Vice Admiral Courbet —the great Cu-Pa, as he was called by the Chinese—had sent a squadron of several warships up the river Min, and it now lay at anchor off the Chinese naval base at Fuchow. On July 18th, the French government presented an ultimatum to Peking which expired at noon on August 2nd.

The officers of the foreign "observation" fleets based on Shanghai, and the Far Eastern correspondents of European newspapers, felt some of the excitement of the spectators at a football game just before the kickoff. Here, as a matter of interest, and followed by an account of what actually happened, is the most favored prognostication of these naval and journalistic pundits:

China would ignore the French ultimatum. France would attack her, but would be unable to overcome Chinese resistance.

This view was particularly popular among the English and American officers, who were being kept informed by their fellow officers stationed at Fuchow. They gave it as their opinion that not one of the French warships would ever get out of the trap they had entered when they steamed up the river Min. Courbet had committed ten of his ships to this venture: the cruisers *Volta, Duguay-Trouin, Villars,* and *d'Estaing;* three gunboats; two torpedo boats—the tiny nameless but numbered torpedo boats of the time were ninety feet long and had a ten-foot beam; and the heavy cruiser *Triomphante.* The Chinese naval force at Fuchow consisted of eleven diverse ships—cruisers, transports, gunboats; twelve armed junks; and various torpedo-firing launches and fire ships.

"The Chinese ships aren't up to much," pointed out the few prophets who favored French chances; "their armament is not comparable with that of the French."

* Gold francs: that is, about 62 million gold dollars; the modern equivalent would be about 250 million.—TRANS.

"Perfectly true," said China's backers, "but the shore batteries of the base were made by Krupp and are up to date. Moreover, the most dangerous enemy Courbet has to reckon with is the river itself. It is cluttered up with sandbanks, channels, and tidal currents. Only a few days ago one of the French cruisers went aground, had great difficulty in getting off, and nearly broke her back doing it. And don't forget that the Chinese have ten thousand troops armed with modern rifles, entrenched ashore."

Togo was occasionally present at such discussions: in the presence of foreigners he did not care to express an opinion, but to his Japanese fellow officers he said:

"Most of the Chinese ships have their guns pointing forward and they are not reversible. But that is not their worst handicap. You've only to look at the deck of any Chinese warship to see that the gear is neglected. That means—low morale. The French will win."

Nothing happened during the afternoon of August 2nd, or on the third, or on the fourth. The first shell did not explode until August 5th, and then not in the river Min, but at Keelung on the coast of Formosa. This was fired by the battleship *La Galissonnière*, Rear Admiral Lespès's flagship. Details of the operation came in a little later. In one hour, and despite a return fire which was well aimed and accurate, the Chinese forts at Keelung had been reduced to silence. Thereafter the battleship had landed a shore party of two hundred men with the object of seizing the coaling station. This part of the operation had been a failure. Threatened with encirclement by three thousand well armed Chinese, the French marines were obliged to fall back on their ship.

Attention was now concentrated on Fuchow, where it was evident that the second half of the game was to be played. On August 12th, France sent her second ultimatum to China, and the third on August 19th which was to expire within forty-eight hours. The Chinese replied by simply turning over his passports to the French *chargé d'affaires*. Almost at the same time Admiral Courbet received orders from Paris to open fire. The neighboring forts were deliberately dismantled by gunfire during the following days. The French

81

losses amounted to ten dead and forty-eight wounded. As for the Chinese, some thousands of bodies floated downstream like flotsam, or were drawn by eddies into the banks of the river.

Togo was able to see these results of the French punitive expedition with his own eyes: sent as an observer, his *Amagi* arrived at the scene of the action on September 1st. Togo collected all the information he could, sent it to his admiral, and then set a course for Hong Kong in the French fleet's wake. At the beginning of October the French ships steamed out of Hong Kong on their way to the Strait of Formosa, and once again, after a few days, the *Amagi* followed them. Her captain's reports on the crews, gear, and methods of the Western navies were very highly valued by the Japanese Admiralty.

Courbet was anxious to seize some Chinese territory by way of pledge, in Formosa. His objectives were Keelung and Tanshui, two ports on the island's northern coast. His plan was to capture Keelung by main force, disembark, and attack Tanshui simultaneously by land and sea. The first part of this plan was carried out successfully, but not the second: Lespès, arriving off Tanshui with three ships, landed six hundred men, who were attacked by three thousand Chinese. The French were forced to retreat to their ships, while the column marching to join forces with them from Keelung was intercepted by the Chinese in force. Formosa was saved from conquest, but Courbet decided to blockade the island.

Togo, having watched the operations at Tanshui, dropped anchor in Keelung. Naval etiquette required him to pay a ceremonial call on Courbet, aboard the *Volta*. Like everyone else, he wondered why the Frenchman had chosen that 1,200-ton wooden cruiser as his flagship instead of, for example, the *Duguay-Trouin*. But nobody would have dreamed of questioning the admiral, a harsh, cold man, and certainly not Togo. Courbet received him in his cabin with the utmost politeness. Togo asked if he might see a copy of the report on the action at Keelung, and was provided with one. He also asked if he could have permission to visit the Chinese military works ashore, and that, too, was granted. So the *Amagi*'s captain and several of her officers went ashore and inspected the demolished forts and what remained of their guns, taking copious notes in great detail. Togo also took notes of the gun emplacements and the configuration of the ground. They might one day be useful to a Japanese officer commanding an assault. A young French infantry officer of the colonial service had been placed at his disposal by way of guide, and had introduced himself: his name was Joffre.

On October 23rd the *Amagi* returned to Shanghai, and Togo delivered his notes to Admiral Matsumura. A few uneventful weeks followed, while the *Amagi* served as duty ship at Shanghai. At the end of the year she was recalled to Japan, and on January 14, 1886, Togo, pacing his forebridge, brought her into Nagasaki. He was particularly happy to be home, for Tetsuko was expecting a baby in February: their first child, a girl, had been stillborn. There was compensation in the birth of the second, a lusty boy. A few days later, as a reward for his distinguished service, Togo was invited to a banquet given by the mikado: it was a notable honor.

China, feeling herself threatened on all sides, and anxious to bring her armament up to date, did so in the simplest possible way: she bought weapons ready-made abroad. Japan, however, was determined to teach herself to manufacture all she needed at home, as soon as possible. The keels of three warships were laid down at Onahama. The engines were made at the Yokosuka dockyards, where the workshops had been founded and given their start by a Frenchman, Emile Bertin. The guns, by Krupp and Nordenfelts, were imported, but in parts that were assembled by Japanese workmen. Japanese engineers, draftsmen, industrial operatives, skilled and unskilled, must be trained, a tradition of industrial craftsmanship built up, in shipbuilding as in every other domain. Few Japanese naval officers were as well informed concerning Western techniques as Togo, who had watched over the building of the *Fuso* in the British shipyard. It was for this reason that, promoted commander on June 20, 1885, he was sent to Onahama to supervise the building of the *Yamato,* one of the first three warships to be built in Japan. And when she was launched it seemed logical to give him command of her for her maiden cruise, since he knew the ship better than anyone else. He was posted to his command in May of 1886. In July of the same year he was again promoted. He was a post captain at less than thirty-nine years of age, and it was with both envy and admiration that his brother officers forecast a brilliant future for Captain Togo.

Two months later his career was at an end; or so, reasonably enough, it must have seemed, even to his best friends. Picture the scene: The *Yamato* is at sea, her prow breasting the long Pacific swell; the Rising Sun streams gaily at her masthead; but the officer in command on her forebridge is not Togo. He, the captain, is stretched on a mat in his quarters. Paralyzed. Togo's first victor was no foreign naval commander, but, most unromantically, the notorious Japanese version of rheumatism.

The *Yamato's* commanding officer was relieved of duty in September, 1886. A year later he was still more or less bedridden, and had only left his house two or three times during brief periods of ephemeral relief from pain. The reflections which tormented him as he lay surrounded by every comfort his wife's sympathetic tact could suggest were even blacker than when he was first stricken down.

In August his last surviving brother, Shirobei, had died; of the four samurai knights whom Matsuko had welcomed back to the house after their "combat" with the British naval squadron, three were dead; and the brother who had been too young to fight that day was also dead. In Togo's hands alone lay the honor and reputation of his family: and he was a helpless invalid, a haunter of medicinal watering places. Hot water baths were tried. His health would improve; he would write to the Admiralty; the Admiralty, taking note of his report, would convert his sick leave to convalescent leave. And the convalescent would become a very sick man again, and once more begin the struggle.

The sounds of the city reached him through the open side of his bedroom. When the humidity was high, a new smell came with them, a smell which nobody was yet quite used to: factory smoke. From newspapers and the talk of such friends as called on him, Togo learned that while he lay motionless, immobilized, Japan was marching forward more swiftly than ever. A Constitution had been promulgated. The telegraph was being installed everywhere; railways were being built; and ships.

Ships: from time to time Togo would stop reading, or listening to his friends' talk, and his face would become mortally sad.

Time passed. To a sick man who has no vocation for sickness (and there is such a vocation), a year is interminable: 1887, 1888— two full years. At the end of them Togo was not cured, physically at least. But there came a change in his expression. He was no longer sad. And the pile of books and reviews beside his bed grew taller and taller, while he read from dawn till dusk. What manner of literature did he read? Textbooks of international law, works which he devoured with fabulous industry and without wasting an hour, as if he were going to have need of all this legal erudition at any moment. Was he thinking of adopting a new career? By no means. He explained his reasons to such brother officers as called to see him:

"Nothing can be more useful to a man in command of a warship than a knowledge of diplomacy. The captain of a ship can easily find himself in a situation such that he may of his own accord, and without recourse to advice, be obliged to take a decision of international significance."

Those who heard this explanation approved his opinion while wondering how Togo could possibly suppose that he would ever command a warship again. But Togo did suppose so; and he was right. Moreover, this dictum concerning the value to a naval officer of being learned in international law was shortly, as we shall see, to be vindicated in his own experience. How remarkable is that quality of foresight in all that touches upon their purpose, which is invariably to be found in men of Togo's stature! When, in England, he had heard the news that his kinsmen, faithful to their feudal duty, were in revolt against the emperor's government, he

85

had never for a moment wavered in his own allegiance, the allegiance which served his purpose. And now, again, in sickness, his instinct was as sound as ever. And if instinct is not quite the right word, the attribute is almost as deep-rooted, a sort of "success wish" peculiar to great men of action, and much rarer than its antithesis, the all too common "failure wish" that drives a man to seek out what will defeat his own ends.

And, of course, Togo's "instinct," offspring of his will, was not at fault. At the beginning of 1890 he recovered his health. Slowly at first, and with relapses reminiscent of earlier but temporary recoveries, he got better. The weight that had borne him down was lifted, and this time for good. By mid-May of 1890 Togo was back on duty as chief of staff to Vice Admiral Nakamuta, commanding the naval base at Kure. The unhappy interlude was over.

The Chinese of the Old Empire were, as is sufficiently well known, great sticklers for good manners. That, perhaps, was why the Japanese Government was not particularly surprised when Admiral Ting, commanding the Chinese Northern Fleet, asked permission for his ships, which were at sea for maneuvers, to enter the port of Yokohama on a courtesy visit. The substance, if not perhaps the terms of their reply, was, "By all means! It will be a pleasure!"

Subsequently it became clear that Admiral Ting's principal purpose was to show the Japanese two units of his fleet which, to his mind, could not fail to awe them into respectful behavior. There were the *Ting Yuen* and the *Chen Yuen*. Both ships, built in Germany, displaced 7,430 tons, were armored, with heavy steel plate, and carried four 12 inch guns in two double turrets. Ting showed the flag in one Japanese harbor after another and everywhere entertained in style. The officer commanding the base at Kure was invited, together with his chief of staff and other staff officers, on board the Chinese flagship. Impassive as ever, Togo drank his ceremonial cup of tea. After the reception, when they were once again ashore, the Japanese admitted to each other that the armament of the two Germano-Chinese or Sino-German warships was impressive. Asked his opinion, Togo gave it: "We should need to know a little more about it."

A few days later one of the two ships which were to have made the Japanese respectful put into the shipyard at Kure to undergo a minor refit—some repairs which, albeit trifling, might suggest to an experienced sailor that certain gear made in Germany was being utilized by hands not remarkable for their skill. During the Chinese ship's short term in drydock, no one paid any attention to a commonplace-looking man in plain clothes who was hanging about or moving around all day long, appearing and disappearing among the bustle of engineers and workmen; and who, from time to time, jotted down a note with the most casual air in the world. The man was Togo.

It is nowhere recorded that Togo thereafter addressed a report in form to whom it most concerned; but that he did so is more than likely. We do know that when a brother officer again mentioned those disturbing 12 inch guns, Togo replied placidly, "Nothing to be afraid of."

And to those who raised astounded eyebrows at this assurance, he explained that a dirty gun which was used as a clothesline for drying the crews' washing was likely, in battle, to be served by gunners of questionable worth. He was not mistaken; and his argument is still valid.

Togo's service at Kure, together with a cruise aboard a ship installing underwater defenses in the Strait of Shimonoseki, enabled the Admiralty to feel tolerably sure that the former invalid was indeed restored to health. Togo was given command of a ship greatly superior to anything that had hitherto come his way. New, British-built, all steel, her displacement was 3,800 tons, and she was armed with two Krupp 10 inch guns, six 6 inch guns and six torpedo tubes. Such was the *Naniwa*, with a speed of eighteen knots. Under Togo's command she was to become famous. Coupled with his own, her name was to make the cables hum even in European and American capitals.

Togo began by taking the *Naniwa* on a hydrographic survey of the Chinese Sea about the Ryukyu Islands, and thereafter off the shores of the great Japanese island of Honshu. Objects—instruction and training of the ship's company, and practical seamanship. Togo was not impatient; he was back in his element. He lay at anchor in Yokohama, having just taken his ship to the relief of a ship in distress, when he received orders to sail at once for Hawaii. Revolution had broken out in the islands. His orders were to protect the lives and property of 22,000 Japanese citizens.

Togo's interlude at Hawaii was to be a sort of final pause before his career as a warrior began. Its cause, the Hawaiian revolution, reads nowadays rather like the script of a motion-picture comedy.

First, the heroine: Queen Liliuokalani was a fair-skinned half-caste, formerly Mrs. Lydia Dominis. She was the widow of a Bostonian. She had succeeded to the throne in place of her brother Kalakaua, who had been driven out in the course of an earlier revolution and had died in San Francisco. Liliuokalani was fifty, a philanthropist, much traveled, a poet and a composer of songs. She was full of verve and life and an enemy to any kind of constraint, or even restraint. To infuriate the missionaries she had authorized the unrestricted importing of opium into her territories; and, in her private life, took a great deal of freedom in affairs of the heart. In short, Liliuokalani would seem to have been just the right monarch for the popular conception of Hawaii, merry kingdom of the *upa-upa*.

She had, however, been a guest at the Jubilee celebrations in London in 1882, and had since been inclined to fancy herself a Queen Victoria, intolerant of contradiction. Whence, on occasion, arose certain difficulties with her subjects. As a rule however such difficulties were easily smoothed over, ending in a feast and a dance. On the whole, the state of the kingdom was satisfactory.

88

The queen's misfortune, or rather the origin of her misfortunes, was her kingdom's great strategic importance in the Pacific Ocean. And one might hesitate to swear that there was no connection between that strategic importance and the fact that for some time certain gentlemen from the United States had been busily endeavoring to convince the Hawaiian sugar-cane planters that their lot under the yoke of the tyrant Liliuokalani was an atrociously hard one. "Only a great democracy," insisted these conscientious agents, "is capable of ensuring that you, in common with the rest of the population, shall live in a manner worthy of such enlightened citizens as yourselves."

Such language is apt to find the weak points in the best of armor, and to set up a sort of social inflammation. In no time at all the planters were organizing meetings and mass demonstrations. The queen, irritated, set her police on them. The situation became tense and the mob began to growl. It was at this juncture that the United States minister to Hawaii sent the State Department a coded cable which, though I cannot claim to have read it, must have expressed a simple idea that can be summed up in four words: "The pineapple is ripe."

In the next few days the United States guard ship landed a small force: needless to say, this was to ensure order. The American Marines pitched their camp near the Ministry of the Interior, while a "Hawaiian Committee of Public Safety," conveniently appearing on the scene, took possession of the Ministry building, proclaimed the abolition of the monarchy, and the constitution of a provisional government to deal with current business. This was to be in office "pending the arrangement and approval of terms and means of union with the United States of America by the new legislative body."

Such was the film script subsequently called the Hawaiian revolution. Nor would it be appropriate for its historian to become excited about it: search the annals of the world's peoples for a revolution which has occurred without the slightest shove from any foreigners whatsoever, and you will search for a long time.

Japan did not send a ship to Hawaii in order to dispute United States ownership of that key to the Pacific. Not yet. Her purpose was confined to showing the flag, putting in an appearance, and gathering information. A growing nation is bound to consider its future objectives very far in advance. Togo was well aware of all that. He had received precise orders, and his new learning in international law was fresh in his memory when, on February 23rd, after steaming thirty-four hundred miles, he brought the *Naniwa* into the wonderfully blue waters of the Kaiwi Channel, steering a course for Mauna Kaala, the highest peak of Oahu. Land came in sight, brilliant, gleaming, fringed with the green of coconut palms. The *Naniwa* slipped between coral reefs, steamed parallel with that seaside Garden of Eden called Waikiki, and lost way as she came level with the jetties. At half an hour after noon the anchor chain ran out with a clatter into translucent water, the Hawaiian flag was hoisted to the mainmast top, and the *Naniwa* fired a twenty-one-gun salute—whereby the revolutionaries were informed that Japan had nothing to say to their revolution and did not recognize the provisional government.

Having thereafter saluted the flag of Rear Admiral Skerret, the United States senior naval officer who had three ships outside the port, with the regulation thirteen-gun salute, Togo took the *Naniwa* into the harbor and by a little after two o'clock lay moored alongside.

There was another Japanese vessel, the training-ship *Kongo*, in harbor, on her way from San Francisco to Japan. Her captain went aboard the *Naniwa,* accompanied by the Japanese consul, and Togo was brought up to date as to the situation in the islands. He then went ashore, visiting the consulate to obtain further information—this time in writing. As soon as he returned on board his ship, he sent for his officers and had the whole ship's company piped to lay aft, where he addressed them as follows:

"By our presence here we render the imperial government present in these islands. Our responsibility is a heavy one. We must not lose sight of the fact that, whether there is disorder in this country or not, whatever we do will have an ineffaceable effect on the empire's reputation. Consequently we must be careful to do nothing without consideration. At the same time I desire that, when the time comes to go into action, you all show, resolutely and without hesitation, the true spirit of Japanese warriors."

Which may seem in retrospect rather more solemn than their situation, under the bright sunshine of Hawaii and confronted with a musical-comedy revolution, warranted. But it is not a naval officer's business to appreciate the comic aspect of a political situation; his duty is to consider any such situation as serious. Togo issued precise orders to his crew, and to the consulate staff, as to their conduct should fighting break out. He then paid Rear Admiral Skerret a visit of ceremony aboard the U.S.S. *Mohican,* and paid the same compliment to H.M.S. *Garnet,* also present in Hawaii. Everything being in order, Togo could wait upon events.

There were none: nothing whatever happened. Togo sent the *Kongo* back to Japan, and time passed. There were a few very trifling incidents. On one occasion a number of Hawaiian political personalities were taking their glass or two of rum at a small saloon beside the sea, when a launch made her way across the waters of the harbor.

"Look at her flag!" exclaimed the local politicians. "It's our President! See, the warships are saluting him!"

And, indeed, the British and American ships fired the salute due to a Chief of State. But no smoke belched from the *Naniwa's* guns, which remained mute. There was an outcry from the Hawaiians. This was an insult! The President should not tolerate it! We have omitted to mention that the provisional president of Hawaii was a bearded gentleman named Sanford B. Dole.

On another occasion a Japanese prisoner escaped from the prison in Honolulu. Pursued by Hawaiian police officers, he nevertheless contrived to reach the harbor and, having jumped into the sea, swam desperately toward the Rising Sun flag that hung from the *Naniwa's* stern. The Japanese naval ratings dragged him aboard

91

before the Hawaiian police could catch up with him. Togo refused to give him up to the authorities.

"I am here," he said, "to protect all my fellow countrymen, without distinction."

Two official *démarches* failed to move him. The incident provided excellent copy for the two newspapers which represented two different shades of Hawaiian pro-American nationalism. One leader put the case as follows: "If the captain of the *Naniwa* persists in his refusal to hand over the criminal, the officer commanding the forces of a certain power might well send troops aboard the Japanese ship to remove him by force." This article was shown to Togo, who smiled and said nothing. Two days later the vice president of the provisional government, a pure-bred Hawaiian, asked to see the *Naniwa's* captain. Togo received him. This worthy, after assuring Togo that his government had no connection with the author of the article, asked him not to get a false idea of the Hawaiian provisional government's attitude to Japan. A warning had already been sent to the newspaper's editor. Togo bowed. The vice president went on to say that he would, however, be vastly obliged to Togo if he would be so kind as to give up the Japanese convict. Togo bowed again; and refused.

A few days later, however, a cable from Tokyo ordered Togo to give way. Whereupon he handed over his prisoner not to the Hawaiian authorities, but to the Japanese consul. "I am bound to obey orders," he told that official, "but on the other hand I cannot refuse a Japanese subject my protection. I will not, therefore, hand the man over to the representatives of this government, which in any case is merely a government *de facto;* but to you, another representative of Japan. If you decide to hand him over, I do not wish to witness or have anything to do with it."

The *Naniwa* remained another two months in Hawaii, and then, since the situation did not change, was recalled to Japan.

The name of the Siberian port of Vladivostok means Domination of the Orient. Situated in the same latitude as Marseilles, it is closed

92

by ice for a third part of every year. In the month of August, 1893, its livid waters already reflected autumnal skies. Dark clouds driven by a cold wind clung to the hills surrounding the bay called after Peter the Great. A Japanese naval squadron lay in the harbor, paying an official visit. Togo, standing on the bridge of his own ship, was carefully comparing the chart spread open before him with the place itself. Buildings that were not accounted for on any map were visible farther along the coast. Some of them were new. And it occurred to him to wonder why the Russians should go to so much trouble to build so great a port in that harsh country, a port without a hinterland, placed at an enormous distance from the country's vital centers, far from all aid in an emergency.

The official visit over, the squadron cruised off the coasts of Hokkaido, the northernmost of the Japanese islands. Togo was able to revisit the places where he had fought against Enamoto, during the Hakodate campaign in 1869. Japan—and Togo—had traveled a great way since then. Nevertheless, progress in this part of the country had clearly been much less swift than in central and southern Japan. The Hokkaido which Togo was seeing for the second time remained almost exactly like the old Japan.

On November 11th the *Naniwa* steamed into Tokyo Bay. Three days later—such is a sailor's life—she was crossing the bar again, outward bound for the vast Pacific. Disturbances had again broken out in Hawaii.

There is nothing to record of this second Hawaiian interlude, which lasted from December until April. There were more American warships there this time, and they were more modern and better armed. It was Christmas, and very hot. Togo had grown a short, close beard; he wore a white cap and white trousers. On the anniversary of the establishment of the provisional government, he refused to fire a salute and refused to dress his ship, as imperturbably as he had done the year before—which, this time, surprised no one.

In March, Togo had the satisfaction of seeing the *Takachiho* arrive off Honolulu. She had come to relieve the *Naniwa*, her

93

sister ship. Her commanding officer was Captain Namura, with whom Togo had studied English at Mitsukuri. Their careers had kept almost consistently in step both in the Admiralty lists and in life. Namura had become famous for a somewhat unusual order issued to his ship's company when the ship he was commanding had been caught in a typhoon and all but castaway: "Let all prepare for death." The order had caused all the more surprise in naval circles in that Namura belonged to a type which is rare in Japan: the laughing, cheerful samurai. Tall, loud of voice and garrulous, his laughter was a great roar of pleasure, accompanied by a violent slapping of his thighs. This merry giant, and the slight, laconic Togo, were united in an ideal friendship. The two ships' captains had time for a few sessions of happy reminiscences of the good old days; then the *Naniwa* sailed for Japan.

Hawaii—we have already said it—was the last interlude.

A week after his arrival in Japan, Togo was no longer on the *Naniwa's* bridge, but ensconced in an office at the heart of a large building: commanding officer of the naval training establishment at the Kure base. It was promotion, but also, in a measure, it was disappointing, for the rumors in circulation were particularly exciting for naval officers burning to do great deeds on active service.

Korea was in the news again, but not, this time, alone. The Korean Government, unable to put down the disturbances in their own country, disturbances provoked and maintained by China, had recently appealed for help to—well, naturally, China.

A few days passed, and then the mikado's government received a note of information from Li Hung-chang's Ministry: China considered it "a matter of duty" to go to Korea's aid. To "restore order," of course. Three divisions were already on their way. Three divisions were a serious matter. But there was something even more serious, and that was an expression used in the Chinese note to the Japanese Government, an expression which implied a wish to abandon all cautious reserve in the matter of Korea: Korea was described as *a tributary state of China*. Officially; in a diplomatic communication.

The dilemma was self-evident: the Japanese Government could either accept the expression *tributary state of China* without protest, and by so doing accept the ultimate consequences of its implications; or they could protest and prepare for war.

According to the new constitution, only one person in the land could make the final decision—war or peace—the mikado. But it is apparent that it was not the emperor's business to study the situation himself and weigh the pros and cons. It was the prime minister's duty to place, as it were, at the mikado's feet the conclusions elaborated by his government, whereupon the mikado would utter the one, deciding word.

The prime minister's name was Ito. The conclusion resulting from his deliberations with his ministers and the service chiefs was clear: there could be no question of allowing Korea to become Chinese: better to go to war with China.

At the very moment, however, when this conclusion was about to be placed before the mikado, the foreign minister handed Ito a cable which had just been decoded. It was from St. Petersburg and was signed by Nishi, the Japanese minister in the Russian capital: "In the event of war, it is probable that the Russian Pacific fleet will support the Chinese fleet."

To take the risk of war with China was not madness despite her numerical superiority on land and sea. The Japanese Government was not, in theory, wrong to consider that this superiority would be more than offset by the more warlike spirit of the Japanese fighting man. But to run the risk of war with Russia was unreasonable. Russia was a great power. On paper, at least, the Japanese fleet had no chance against the Chinese fleet and the Russian Pacific fleet acting in concert.

The real decision was made by two men: Ito, after reading Nishi's cable, sent for the service chiefs, and left them together, saying, "Examine the situation and tell me what you think of it."

All the senior army and navy officers present at this conference were determined fighters. Their fanatical ardor once war was declared was never in question. But the responsibility thus thrust upon them left them in some perplexity. The very existence of Japan was at stake. It was at this juncture—Oriental reactions are notoriously difficult for us to foresee—that two officers, General Kawakami and Admiral Kakayama, burst out laughing. Together, they rose. The general spoke: "Is it possible, gentlemen, that we should discuss this project without hope of victory?"

Thereupon both left the conference and went to call on the prime minister.

"We have been sent by the chiefs of the army and navy to tell you that, after examining the question, they approve, unanimously, the decision to go to war, without fear of the consequences even if the Russian fleet intervenes."

Ito thanked them and summoned a secretary. The diplomatic machine was set in motion toward war.

On the same day Togo received an official letter marked *Urgent*. Mobilization was beginning. The *Naniwa*, which had undergone a refit, was his again; Captain Togo was to join her and take command immediately and without delay.

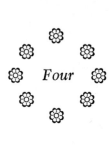

Four

At the beginning of July, 1894 almost the whole Japanese fleet was concentrated at Sasebo, a naval base situated on the western promontory of Kyushu, the southernmost of the Japanese islands. Information received from China was to the effect that the Chinese northern fleet was gathering at Weihaiwei, at the eastern extremity of Shantung.

War had not been declared. But for several weeks both China and Japan had been landing troops in Korea, with the avowed object of restoring order. The Japanese were landing their forces at Chemulpo on the west coast; the Chinese, at Asan, also on the west coast, but a little farther south. The two armies had not yet met. In theory, order should by now have been restored very

97

thoroughly indeed in Korea. Both nations had warships at sea, escorting their transports.

On July 23rd the Japanese fleet put to sea, at eleven o'clock of a fine, still morning, with the sea like a polished mirror. The fleet was accompanied by an auxiliary vessel, the *Takasogo Maru*, carrying Admiral Kabayama, naval chief of staff, the same man who had burst out laughing at the idea of Japan hesitating to take the risk of fighting a Sino-Russian alliance. For some hours the *Takasogo Maru* kept company with the fleet, and then put about, hoisting a signal which was read at once on every bridge: "Add to the fame of the imperial navy."

Shortly thereafter, a part of the fleet commanded by Rear Admiral Tusboï, comprising the armored cruisers *Yoshino, Akitsushima,* and *Naniwa,* parted from the main body of the fleet and steered directly for Asan. Its object was to carry out an advanced reconnaissance and at the same time to intercept any transports carrying Chinese troops for Korea. The three cruisers arrived in the area of their destination during the morning of July 25th.

The weather was still fine, although there was some mist despite a light breeze. At about seven o'clock two ships were sighted steaming out of the Asan Strait. They were soon identified as the *Chi Yuen,* an all-steel cruiser of 2,300 tons, and the *Kuang-I,* a 1,200-ton gunboat. The two Chinese ships made straight for the Japanese squadron—it will never be known why, since a few minutes later the Japanese opened fire at a range of 3,300 yards.

Japanese accounts say that the first round was fired by the *Chi Yuen;* the official Chinese account says the *Naniwa.* It was inevitable that, sooner or later, a Japanese officer would make up his mind to "add to the fame of the imperial navy." It may very well have been Togo; for a man's notion of international law is apt to be modified by an order from a superior in his hierarchy.

The engagement was brief. The *Chi Yuen,* caught by converging salvos from all three Japanese, caught fire. Her secondary armament was silent. But she still came on toward the Japanese cruisers.

98

Meanwhile a gathering overcast, and smoke from the guns combining with the mist, was rapidly reducing visibility until the Chinese ships gradually faded out of sight. Togo, on his bridge with the glasses to his eyes, was looking for the two enemy phantoms. Suddenly he saw the *Kuang-I* emerging, ahead and to port, out of the fog. All the *Naniwa*'s guns instantly opened on her, whereafter the wretched *Kuang-I* was seen to be maneuvering with difficulty, like a punch-drunk boxer, until she went suddenly about and steered straight for the land. Then the *Chi Yuen* reappeared: she too had gone about, but onto a course due west, and was making full speed ahead. At this juncture a string of flags fluttered out from the Japanese flagship's signal halyard: "Freedom of maneuver." Togo instantly decided to go after the bigger ship.

Accompanied by the *Yoshino,* the *Naniwa* made all speed in pursuit of the *Chi Yuen.* Her bow clove the sea; her deck vibrated as the engines gave of their best; and beneath his feet as he paced his bridge Togo could feel his good ship throb with life in a way that rejoiced his heart. First battle, first victory: the campaign was beginning well. Togo kept his glasses to his eyes. Suddenly his officers saw his impassive face light up: a white flag had been run up to the mainmast top of the Chinese ship; the *Chi Yuen* was surrendering. Victory, indeed!

But was it? The *Chi Yuen* had shown a white flag, but Togo soon realized that her speed had not diminished. And she was already beginning to fade into the fog thickening above a rising sea. Even the outline of the other pursuing ship, the *Yoshino,* was becoming indistinct.

At this moment the *Naniwa*'s lookouts signaled two other ships in sight, coming from the west. Attention was at once diverted to them: one was a small Chinese sloop, the *Tsao-Kiang.* The other was a large merchantman flying the Red Ensign of the British merchant service. Togo steered toward this singular convoy. It was 9:00 A.M.

From the *Naniwa*'s bridge, Togo was able to see that the *Tsao-*

Kiang, which had changed course a point or two, was exchanging signals with the fleeing *Chi Yuen* and that after this exchange she went about and steered due west in the wake of the other Chinese ship. The British merchant ship held her course, alone, and presently her name became visible: she was the *Kowshing*.

She came on steadily, manifestly aware of the invulnerability which, even at the scene of a naval battle, was conferred on her by the Red Ensign at her peak. Any ship, even the most wretched of tramps, that could fly that flag could afford a certain insolence on any sea in the world: for there was not a sailor afloat but knew that behind every Red Ensign was the White Ensign of the Royal Navy, dominant and invincible. Thus, without any attempt at concealment, the *Kowshing* held on her way to Asan, her decks swarming with Chinese soldiers. Such was her good pleasure. It was eight minutes past ten.

At this moment the *Naniwa*'s guns fired two blank rounds, and two flags of the international signal code were run up to her signal halyard: J. W.—*Heave to immediately.* Meanwhile the *Naniwa* had changed course to approach the *Kowshing*, and her guns had been kept bearing on her. The *Kowshing* began to lose way, and stopped. Togo gave an order, and two more signal flags fluttered aloft: L. P.—*Drop your anchor.* A few seconds later came the splash of her anchor and a rattle of anchor chain. The *Kowshing*, for all her Red Ensign, was obeying orders.

Togo's intention was to pursue the *Tsao-Kiang* first, and then deal with the transport. As the *Naniwa* began to go ahead, the *Kowshing*, clearly unaware of the seriousness of the situation, hoisted a signal of her own: *Can I proceed?* The answering signal read, *Remain at anchor, or proceed at your own risk.* The *Kowshing*'s bridge could take a hint. A few minutes later Togo realized that the *Tsao-Kiang* was going to run within range of the *Akitsushima*'s guns. One ship was quite enough for so exiguous an adversary. The *Naniwa* went about again and returned to the British merchantman, and steamed round her several times, as if smelling her out. The Chinese soldiery ran from one side to the other, watching the warship, and emitting a curious chattering noise for all the world like the clamor of sea gulls. At 10:40 Togo decided to board and make a thorough investigation.

One of the *Naniwa's* boats was lowered away, and Lieutenant Hitomi took his place in her. She was rowed across to the cargo ship and made fast to a ladder that had been put over her side. All the Chinese crowded to the side, and their chatter became shriller than ever.

A little later the *Naniwa's* boat put off from the *Kowshing* and returned to her own ship. Lieutenant Hitomi went to the bridge to make his report, glancing from time to time at his notes and stumbling over the English names:

"The *Kowshing* belongs to Jardine, Matheson and Co., Agents for the Indo-Chinese Steamship Company of London. Chartered by the Chinese Government, she is carrying 1,100 Chinese soldiers, fourteen guns, and other weapons, from Tahu to Asan. Her master's name is Thomas Ryder Galsworthy. She also carries a German major, Constantin von Hanneken. Captain Galsworthy wishes me to convey to you an official protest for stopping a British ship, in peacetime, in non-Japanese waters."

"Thank you very much indeed," Togo said, and gave an order to his signals officer. Another string of flags went aloft: *Raise your anchor and follow me.* Instead of doing so, the *Kowshing* made a signal: *The captain wishes to consult you in a matter of importance and requests you to send him a boat.*

The boat that had taken Hitomi to the *Kowshing* was still in the water. Togo's orders to his lieutenant were as follows: "If the Chinese are unwilling to follow out the *Naniwa's* orders, find out the intentions of the captain and the English officers. If they want to come aboard the *Naniwa,* bring them with you." Lieutenant Hitomi set off on his second visit.

This trip took longer than the first, but in due course the lieutenant returned to make his report: "The Chinese are preventing the *Kowshing's* captain from carrying out the *Naniwa's* orders. They threaten to shoot him or to cut his head off. The situation on board is out of hand." Togo gave another order, and the yeoman of signals sent another string of flags aloft: *Crew of Kowshing to abandon ship*. The reply read off by the *Naniwa's* officer of the watch was—*Send your boats*.

The situation was deteriorating: the excitement among the Chinese was visible, and it seemed likely that if the *Naniwa* sent her boats across she might never recover them. Togo had his signal repeated with an addition: it was impossible to send any boats. In any case the *Kowshing* had enough, clearly visible, slung from their davits, to bring over both crew and afterguard. The fact that they were not being lowered away meant that Captain Galsworthy was no longer master aboard his ship. And, in fact, a new signal hauled down almost as soon as it reached the masthead confirmed this: *Neither captain nor crew are allowed to leave ship*.

Togo's signal was left flying: in addition, he had a red flag hoisted to the masthead: it meant that he was going to open fire.

The sea was empty: the mist hid both coast and horizon, so that the two ships were isolated, as if alone on some alien planet. The dark hull of the merchantman tugged at her anchor chain, as she rolled gently to the Pacific swell. The Chinese soldiers still swarmed on her deck. Togo could even see some of the men, half naked, excitedly brandishing their swords at the *Naniwa*.

The *Naniwa*, a long, low shape with a plume of smoke at her funnel, was drifting gently. From time to time the officer of the watch telegraphed slow-ahead to the engine room, to hold her in place. It was the only sound aboard the silent ship. Gunnery and torpedo ratings were at action stations. The whole ship's company waited for orders.

The laborious flag dialogue had occupied two hours. At one in the afternoon Togo was still watching the *Kowshing* through his glasses: her bridge seemed to be deserted and she was making no more signals; the *Kowshing* had said all she had to say. Time was passing; the Chinese fleet must be cruising somewhere in the vicinity. If the wind rose enough to clear the mist, there was

102

serious danger of the intercourse between the *Kowshing* and the *Naniwa* being suddenly interrupted. Five past one. A decision was imperative. Let the troops and weapons pass; or open fire on the British flag? Togo doubtless recalled what he had said when, a sick man, he had used his leisure to read international law: "A naval officer may often be placed in such circumstances that he must take decisions on his own accord which . . ." Must he decide to fire on the Red Ensign? What of the consequences? It was a very long time since any ship of any nation had taken such a risk. On the other hand, if he shrank from doing so would not all Europe consider it a sign of weakness? Was it not essential to make it clear to everyone—even to wave-ruling Britannia—that no one could help an enemy of Japan with impunity? At ten past one Togo lowered his glasses, turned to the officer of the watch, and said, "Open fire."

In a moment, the excitement reigning on the *Kowshing's* deck was turned into wild panic. The Chinese, in their mad rush to jump overboard, began fighting among themselves. At one-fifteen the *Kowshing* began to settle by the stern.

Examining all the evidence collected after the event, the following conclusion may be drawn: the *Kowshing* went down in the midst of a furious, chaotic, and abject outburst of killing on board. The Chinese who remained on deck began shooting at those who took to the water and at the boats which some had managed to lower away. The men in the boats fired back at them. As the ship sank, her captain and officers were picked up by the *Naniwa's* boats.

Questioned by Japanese officers at the Sasebo naval base, Captain Galsworthy later told the following story: there was a Chinese general aboard the *Kowshing* who had forbidden him to carry out the *Naniwa's* orders. The unfortunate Englishman had pointed out that he could not possibly fight the warship: she could sink him with a single shot from one of her guns. "Better to die than be taken!" the general exclaimed, and went on, "Besides, I have eleven hundred brave men with me, and they cannot be more than four hundred over there: we can attack them!" To which Galsworthy had replied that if the general really proposed to fight, he and his officers would leave the ship. "If you attempt to do so, I shall have you shot," was the general's answer.

Chinese survivors accused Togo of having had boats and swimmers from the *Kowshing* machine-gunned. But their evidence was confused and often contradictory. One Cantonese stoker asserted that the Japanese were firing their machine guns *from the cruiser's masts,* which is, to put it mildly, highly improbable.

Hanneken, the German major, managed to swim ashore, and sent a written account of his experience to the British vice consul at Chemulpo: "I saw a Japanese boat put into the water, full of armed men. I thought that it was coming to pick up survivors. But the men in the boat opened fire on the men who had remained on board the sinking ship." But as the men remaining in the *Kowshing* were shooting indiscriminately at Chinese and Japanese boats alike, the confusion may be imagined.

The *Kowshing*'s first mate was kept apart from his captain until both had been interrogated at Nagasaki. He said that he had been picked up by one of the *Naniwa*'s boats, and very well treated on board. "Two volleys were fired from the *Kowshing*," he said, "to sink two lifeboats full of Chinese. The Japanese made no attempt to save any of the Chinese."

Long and violently was Togo reproached by the Chinese and those partial to their cause for his failure to rescue survivors. But was it possible for him to have saved any, and if so, would it have been wise? He did what seemed to him his duty: having taken the Europeans, except the German major, on board, he cruised about the scene of the sinking during the afternoon, then set a course for the Japanese base in Korea, reporting to Admiral Ito the following morning. Before doing so, he must have wondered whether his fate would be congratulations or a court-martial.

The first British reaction was a peremptory note from Admiral Freemantle, commanding the Royal Navy's Far Eastern Fleet, to Vice Admiral Ito, forbidding the Japanese Navy to stop any British ship on the high seas. A few days later, cables having been exchanged, it was known that Lord Kimberley, Secretary of State for Foreign Affairs, had sent for the Japanese minister in London and handed him a note protesting against the *Naniwa*'s action. The Japanese Government was held responsible for damage caused to the lives and property of British subjects by officers of the Japanese Navy. At the same time a cable in cipher from their minister gave the Japanese Government an idea of the state of public opinion in England. The action was being described as an act of piracy and an insult to the flag. Japan was said to have behaved "like a hostile power." Such, at all events, were typical newspaper headlines. For the first time Togo's name was printed in newspapers all over the world—generally accompanied by unflattering comments.

In Japan, public opinion, and opinion in official circles, were also hostile to the *Naniwa*'s captain. It was felt that he had overplayed his hand or staked too much. However, Togo was not reprimanded by his superiors. Nothing whatever, official or unofficial, was said to him about his conduct by any of them. It was almost as if secret orders had been issued that the affair was to be passed over in silence. Togo himself, of course, held his tongue.

Japanese opinion, meanwhile, began to change when it appeared that Great Britain's indignation was dying down and that there were to be no evil consequences, and especially when it was learned that English voices were being raised not, indeed, in Togo's defense, but to point out that his action against the *Kowshing* could not be regarded simply as an act of piracy. The famous jurist Thomas Erskine Holland, writing in *The Times*, pointed out that the *Kowshing* had been carrying troops and arms destined to be used against the Japanese and that no operation of that order could be carried out without risk. Declaring that he was deliberately confining his remarks to the juridical aspect of the matter and that he would leave the task of judging the Japanese captain from the humane point of view to others, Holland concluded that neutral rights had *not* been infringed. In this finding he was supported by another expert, Professor Westlake,

105

and by J. B. Moore who, writing in the *Digest of International Law*, expressed his approval of the two jurists for having stated their opinion "in the teeth of popular excitement."

Japan, thereafter, began at last to talk of Togo: he became the first national hero in the war against China. This was not officially declared by the Empire of Japan until August 1st, two days after General Oshima had attacked the Chinese at Asan and after the Chinese, deprived of the *Kowshing's* reinforcements, had suffered defeat.

The first naval battle of the Sino-Japanese War was fought six weeks after the outbreak of hostilities. It is of interest not only because it was the first of that series of engagements by means of which Japan, with ever growing determination, was to win for herself the status of a great power, but also because historians consider it to be the first great *modern* naval battle. A brief gloss on this opinion will not be out of place.

The first great sea fight in which armored ships were engaged on both sides was the battle of Vis, fought between the Italian and Austrian fleets in 1866. At the beginning of the battle the Austrian Admiral von Tegetthoff made the following signal: *Iron-clads will ram and sink the enemy.* And victory was, in fact, obtained by the Austrians with the help of ramming. Whereupon, throughout the world's navies, prows were strengthened and provided with rams. Some years had to pass before it was realized that a ramming contest, a new version of the ancient tactics employed by war galleys, could only be very exceptional between warships carrying guns and torpedo tubes with a range of several miles. And, in point of fact, no such battle was ever fought after Vis. But what is more, there were no naval battles in any of the wars of the period—the American Civil War, the Franco-Prussian War of 1870, the Russo-Turkish War of 1878. For more than thirty years steel armor, naval guns, and torpedo mechanism were constantly improved upon, but could not be put to the test. Dozens of "ironclads" were built, became obsolete, and were broken up

106

without having seen a shot fired in anger. Strategists and technicians theorized about the proper use of new weapons, and their theories were tested in the course of maneuvers. But none of them received the only really valid test: battle.

So that, according to the historians, the first real test of new naval tactics and techniques can be dated September 17, 1894, the day of what, in the East, is called the Battle of the Yellow Sea, and in the West the Battle of the Yalu.

On the morning of September 17, then, the Japanese fleet was cruising off the island of Haiyang, in the bay of Korea, making for the anchorage at Talu Island. A little before half-past eleven, lookouts in the cruiser *Yoshino*, leading the line ahead of the First Light Flotilla, sighted smoke to the east-northeast: before the invention of airplanes most modern naval battles began with a plume of smoke above the horizon. Admiral Tsuboï, commanding the fleet, gave orders to change course and steer east-northeast.

A few seconds later another plume of smoke appeared, then a third and fourth. Shortly, there were at least twelve of those thin black columns drawn parallel against the clear blue of the sky above the horizon. A few moments later a signal was made by the Japanese flagship: *Enemy fleet in sight*. The time was eleven-thirty. The Chinese fleet was steaming in line-abreast. One minute after the admiral's signal, the imperial standard, red with a golden chrysanthemum in the center, broke out at the mainmast top of the flagship, the *Matsushima*, which led the main fleet. All ships were piped to action stations.

Before, in retrospect, we watch this battle—in some respects surprising to eyes accustomed to subsequent and very different sea fights—it will be well to glance at such documents as establish a theoretical comparison between the two fleets. It will be of use in helping us to understand the action.

The Chinese had five ironclads, seven unarmored ships, four torpedo boats,* and three small gunboats. Among the ironclads

* The ancestor of the destroyer.—TRANS.

107

were the two 7,430-ton battleships bought in Germany, to which the reader has already been introduced.

The Japanese had seven up-to-date "ironclad" cruisers, one small and partly armored cruiser, two "old" ships, both armored—which Togo had watched building in England, launched in 1878—a gunboat, and an auxiliary cruiser, in fact an armed passenger steamer. Twelve ships in all.

The Chinese fleet was the better protected: in particular, the sides of the two coast-guard battleships were very heavily armored. On the other hand, the Japanese had the advantage in striking power: they carried seventy big guns against the fifty-five of the Chinese. The Chinese had nothing to compare with the long 8 inch breech-loading French guns, made by Canet, carried by four of the Japanese cruisers. The Japanese also had 128 quick-firing guns of the latest pattern, some of large caliber: these were a sensational technical novelty at the time, since their recoil was made to operate a mechanism which automatically returned the guns to the loading position.

It is not difficult to picture the Japanese fleet steaming into battle: the sky was blue, the sea was blue—in short, the weather was perfect. A sea as flat and round as a plate, with twelve Japanese warships moving across it in line-ahead. First, the four ships of the light flotilla, Togo's *Naniwa* lying astern. Next, separated by a larger interval, the main fleet, six ships led by the flagship. Astern of these, and a little to one side, the two auxiliary ships. What did the ships look like? From a distance, like yachts, since they were all painted white, and their prows decorated with a painting of the golden chrysanthemum. At every mainmast top fluttered the national flag, a red sun with red rays on a white ground. A festive rather than a warlike spectacle, as if they were all setting out for a regatta. This impression is strengthened by the relative smallness of the ships compared with the giants of 30,000 tons and more which we are accustomed to thinking of as composing a line of battle. The largest of the Japanese ships displaced little more than four thousand tons. We may

108

visualize them as miniatures of our own battleships and cruisers, but painted white.

Admiral Ito, commander in chief, knew that the fleet with which he was seeking to bring the enemy to battle would have to encounter the two German-built battleships among the Chinese warships. Moreover, his intelligence service had informed him that there were European officers on several enemy forebridges. The German major, von Hanneken, a *Kowshing* survivor, was aboard the enemy flagship *Ting Yuen*. The nominal captain of the *Chen Yuen* was a Chinese officer, but the actual captain was Commander Philo Norton McGiffin, a former United States naval officer. Other Chinese ships carried English engineer and gunnery officers, some of them one-time warrant officers in the Royal Navy. The Mandarin Ting, commander in chief of the Chinese fleet, was a soldier rather than a sailor, "but he had some experience of the sea and a great deal of courage."

By 11:40 all the officers in the Japanese fleet could distinguish the enemy clearly with the help of their glasses: ten ships in line-abreast. In the center were the *Chen Yuen* and the *Ting Yuen*. The Japanese fleet was steaming straight toward that center.

As the distance between the fleets diminished, Admiral Ito realized that the enemy formation was not strict line-abreast. The ships were steaming in echelon, forming a convex crescent, rather as if they had been sailing ships. And it seemed to him that this want of rigidity was a good omen.

All the Japanese guns were at maximum elevation, and bearing on the enemy. The fleet was at about six miles from the Chinese center when Admiral Ito ordered a change of course to port. When this had been carried out, the Japanese line-ahead was no longer steering toward the Chinese center, but toward the Chinese right wing. It is possible to explain the significance of this maneuver to the reader without requiring him to enter into tedious strategical and tactical considerations.

A fleet steaming toward an enemy in line-abreast can bring

109

only its forward guns to bear on him; its other guns therefore serve no purpose. The correct placing of a fleet for a gunnery duel is, therefore, line-ahead, the enemy being kept as nearly as possible abeam. Thus all the ships can bring their maximum firepower into action. The ideal plan for such a battle is as follows:

Approaching the point at which they will come within range of

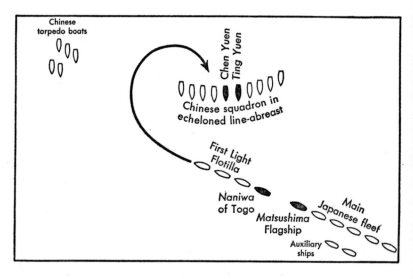

Battle of the Yalu

each other, each fleet may be in any formation whatever. Line-abreast is by no means excluded, being, indeed, a good "probing" formation. But it is advisable, when the enemy comes in sight, to change formation and for the ships to take up stations in, for example, line-ahead, in order to bring both forward and aft guns to bear. The two lines-ahead then steam toward each other and, as they pass, bombard each other.

But, of course, it is self-evident that the real problem is to maneuver to such purpose that the enemy is placed in an inferior position. A good solution of this problem consists in changing

110

course so as to pass astern of the enemy line and at right angles to it: this is called "crossing the T." If it succeeds, the enemy's line-ahead can only bring the after guns to bear on you, whereas you still have your whole "broadside" at your disposal, an advantage which can decide the final outcome. Obviously, the enemy will try to avoid being placed at such a disadvantage and will probably attempt to "cross the T" on his own account. If the two lines are steaming at the same rate of speed, they will be chasing each other's tails in a circle. But if one is faster, it is quite likely to succeed in "crossing the T." There is an alternative: supposing your enemy's course to be parallel with your own, and his direction the same, you can attempt to "cross the T" ahead instead of astern of his line—always provided, of course, that your speed is sufficiently greater. At all events, "crossing the T" was the maneuver that dominated naval tactics at the time. But at the beginning of the Battle of the Yalu, this operation was only sketchily attempted, for reasons which will be apparent hereafter.

Admiral Ito, seeing the enemy fleet advancing in line-abreast, would be inclined to suppose that Admiral Ting was going to carry out a sudden change of formation, and, by ordering all his ships to make a ninety-degree turn, place them in line-ahead. It is probable that Ito's maneuver—that is, changing his course to steer for the Chinese right wing instead of their center, was intended to enable him to choose his own combat distance and to "cross the T" when the Chinese changed formation. But as it happened, Ting had remembered only a part of the lessons he had received from his European instructors: he continued to advance in line-abreast.

The Chinese ships were now clearly visible. Most of them had kept in their superstructures a quantity of art objects in carved wood, gilt or lacquered in vivid colors. In addition to which the *Ting Yuen* was flaunting, by way of admiral's flag, an immense yellow dragon. The ships' hulls were painted black; they were slowly drawing nearer to the white hulls of the Japanese fleet.

The sea was like polished metal under the brilliant sunshine.

111

McGiffin, the *Chen Yuen's* American officer, wrote of the spectacle presented by the two fleets: "Fresh and dainty in their bright colors, and gay with the flags and signals flying from their mastheads, the ships had such a festive air that they seemed to be meeting for the purpose of a friendly visit."

At 12:50 the centers of the two fleets were about six thousand yards apart. The Chinese were steaming at six knots, the Japanese at twelve. It was at this moment that a red flash lit the gun muzzles of the *Ting Yuen's* forward turret. There was a puff of smoke and, some seconds later, the detonation was heard. Then the whole Chinese line of battle began to "volley and thunder," and fountains of water spurted up from the sea. The *Yoshino* made a signal to increase speed to fourteen knots. The gunlayers on every ship in the Japanese line kept their sights fixed on rapidly growing targets; every officer of the watch had his glasses turned on the *Yoshino,* alert for the next signal—"Open fire"; but the Japanese fleet continued to advance in perfect formation without firing a single shot.

Seconds, then minutes passed. The Chinese shells were still churning the sea into geysers. Aboard the Japanese ships nothing was to be heard but the regular throb of the engines and snoring of forced draughts. The distance between the fleets grew less and less. The decks of the Chinese ships could be seen clearly with the naked eye, and, presently, the gun muzzles.

At five past one and at a distance of about four thousand yards, the *Yoshino,* followed by all the ships of the Light Flotilla, opened fire. Togo directed the *Naniwa's* salvos against his obvious targets, that is, at the *Ching Yuen, Ch'ing Yuen, Chao Yung,* and *Yang Wei,* the four ships of the Chinese right wing, in succession.

A word in passing: there is no need for the reader to exhaust his attention in trying to remember these names. We have only to consider a few of them—*Ting Yuen, Chen Yuen, Lai Yuen, Ching Yuen, Ch'ing Yuen,* and so on, to realize that these words are simply rough approximations to Chinese names which we can neither pronounce nor, in Latin letters, spell. All we need to remember is that the *Ting Yuen* and *Chen Yuen* were the two battleships steaming in the middle of the Chinese line.

Steaming obliquely across the course of the Chinese line-abreast, the Japanese line-ahead returned the Chinese fire with their 128 quick-firing guns. The gunners did not have the range at first, and their shells fell short. Even so, the Chinese were appalled at the rate and weight of fire, inconceivable to men accustomed only to older types of naval guns. The sea ahead of the Chinese fleet was transformed into a seething caldron of foam, and the Chinese ratings and officers stationed forward were drenched by huge waterspouts. A few seconds later, this hail of explosives was no longer striking the sea, but the superstructures of the Chinese fleet, and some of the Chinese ships were losing formation, so that the crescent became a semicircle and several of the ships had their guns masked by other ships of their own fleet.

The Japanese, on the other hand, kept perfect station. A new signal was run up aboard the *Matsushima*, which the *Yoshino* promptly acknowledged, and, changing her course still farther to port, led the Light Flotilla toward a point beyond the Chinese right to carry out the fresh order—to envelop the enemy's right wing. Ito was taking advantage of the fact that Ting was maintaining the line-abreast formation. The Japanese maneuver was carried out calmly, perfectly, as if the flotilla were on maneuvers and the enemy an imaginary one.

From his bridge Togo could hear the range finders calling the range of the nearest target: 2800—2600—2500. He could foresee the exact moment when Admiral Ting would begin to pay the bitter price for his unorthodox formation.

The Japanese maneuver placed the ships of the Chinese right wing—unfortunately they were the weakest—under a cross fire from the Light Flotilla, which was working round behind them, and the main fleet, which was steering obliquely across their course. Moreover, the Chinese ships were now so stationed as to mask many of each other's guns. They could do nothing but fire

113

at the last ships of the Japanese line with their forward guns.

The two ships of the Chinese right wing which were between two fires, the *Chao Yung* and the *Yang Wei*, seemed to be advancing with difficulty under the hail of shells. Their guns were firing regularly but slowly. Amidships of each vessel part of the upper works could be seen, with a gangway above and, in the bulwarks, rectangles which were, in fact, stateroom doors, painted, varnished, and gleaming in the sunshine. The Chinese were accustomed to polish all the painted and varnished wood in their ships with an oil rag. Suddenly, part of this woodwork aboard the *Yang Wei* burst into flames. In a few minutes the whole deck was on fire. Some minutes later—it was 1:10—a similar fire broke out aboard the *Chao Yung*. The gun turrets of the two blazing ships ceased fire. The *Yang Wei* broke station, left the line, hesitated, and then steered for Talu Island. The first of Ito's adversaries was *hors de combat*. A second soon followed, for at 1:20 P.M. the *Chao Yung* took a sharp list to port and a moment later sank beneath the surface of the sea like a torch extinguished.

The Chinese left wing, meanwhile, had not taken much punishment. Nevertheless, Ting was to lose two ships from that quarter, owing to the cowardice of their captains. The ship on the extreme left was the *Chi Yuen*, which Togo had already set on fire—not seriously—by gunfire during the preliminary engagement on July 23rd. Her captain evidently had painful memories of that encounter, for, without apparent reason, he left his station and steamed away from the battle at full speed, giving the Japanese fleet as wide a berth as possible, although the Japanese cruiser *Chiyoda* managed to hit her at least once. Arrived at Port Arthur, the *Chi Yuen*'s captain asserted that he had borne the heat and burden of the day, and had not left his post until nightfall. But his crew bore witness against him and he was beheaded. The other deserting ship was wrecked on the coast and castaway with nearly all hands. A majority of the other Chinese ships fought bravely.

The leading Japanese division, having completely turned the

114

enemy's right wing, changed course again, to port, in order to avoid coming under the fire of their own main division, which was now directly in front of the Chinese line, and still in line-ahead, all guns bearing and firing. The big Japanese cruisers kept station impeccably, but the older, slower ships lagged a little, and the Chinese battleships were shelling them. The *Fuso* came very near to being run down, and the *Hiei*, too far astern of the fleet, had to run a slow gantlet of Chinese shells. Her captain decided on an all-or-nothing maneuver, made a sharp turn to starboard, and steamed right through the Chinese line. The Chinese guns flamed at him from both quarters, and torpedoes could actually be seen jumping from wave to wave, but the *Hiei* got through undamaged and joined the Light Flotilla behind the Chinese fleet.

From the start of the battle the *Naniwa's* navigation officer had followed his leader, the *Akitsushima*, with admirable exactitude. Togo could see that his flotilla, veering to port once again, was being led back toward the heart of the battle where the little 615-ton gunboat *Akagi* had become a target for several of the Chinese ships and seemed to be in trouble. At this moment the auxiliary cruiser *Saikyo Maru* came up on the port bow of the *Naniwa*, as if to cut right across her course. Admiral Ito had signaled to her, and to the *Akagi*, that they were free to withdraw from the battle, but samurai tradition put any such behavior out of the question. The *Saikyo Maru* steamed straight ahead, flying the signal *My steering has gone*, and pursued by several Chinese ships. A shell had burst some of her steampipes, and the servo-motor controlling her rudder was no longer working. Deliberately, Togo hove to to let her pass ahead of him. As a result the *Naniwa* was soon parted from the rest of the division, and under sudden attack. The spouts of water caused by shells hitting the sea were now very close, and there was a clatter of shell splinters falling on the deck. Togo, on his bridge, remained impassive as ever, and his ship's company followed his example. At the height of the uproar a lookout sighted several Chinese torpedo boats approach-

115

ing through the smoke. Togo steered for them, swept their decks with machine-gun fire, and drove them off. The *Naniwa* set out to regain station astern of the *Akitsushima,* the waterspouts falling behind as she put on speed.

The *Saikyo Maru,* which had already escaped her pursuers, came near destruction a second time. Attacked by two cruisers and four torpedo boats, she fought off the big ships, turned the small ones by threatening to run foul of them, and thereafter made for the shore. A parting shot in the shape of a torpedo was fired at her at a range of forty yards and by a miracle passed clear under her keel.

It was not yet three o'clock in the afternoon, and Admiral Ting had lost four cruisers: the two which had caught fire on the right wing, and the two deserters from the left. Admiral Ito had withdrawn three of his ships from the battle: the auxiliary cruiser *Saikyo Maru,* the gunboat *Akagi,* and the *Hiei.*

The second phase of the battle consisted of a long gunnery duel at a range of some three thousand yards. Ito's superiority in speed enabled him to choose his own range and position, and the thorough training of his crews enabled him to concentrate his full firepower on one enemy ship after another. His high-explosive shells decimated the Chinese crews with shrapnel and splinters, and started fires in the ships. As to the superiority of Japanese tactics and maneuver, the entire battle bears witness of it. Thus, the Chinese ships were driven remorselessly into a huddle while the Japanese steamed round and round them like a hunting pack, shelling them without remission.

The cruiser *Chih Yuen*—not to be confused with the *Chi Yuen*—had fought gallantly under the command of her English engineer officer, Purvis, and her captain, Tang. Attacked from both quarters, riddled with holes, barely able to steer, the ship seemed on the point of sinking. Tang was determined to try ramming at least one enemy ship before going down. He steered for the *Yoshino,* but the damage he had sustained was too serious. Caught in the concentrated fire of the whole Japanese Light Flotilla, his ship

116

was literally hammered to pieces. Her prow plunged into the sea; her screw, still turning, reared heavenward; a moment later she was gone, leaving nothing on the surface but flotsam. Among the wreckage Tang himself appeared, clinging to an oar, his big dog swimming beside him. Then the Japanese saw the dog clamber onto his master's shoulders, and a moment later both went down together.

Another Chinese cruiser, the *Lai Yuen*, burst into flames. More than half the Chinese fleet had by now either been destroyed or put to flight, while the main Japanese fleet had still suffered no losses. Ito was able to concentrate his fire on the two Chinese battleships.

At 3:26 there was a violent explosion aboard the *Matsushima*, the Japanese flagship. She had been hit by a shell from one of the Chinese battleships. According to Ito's report the shell came from the *Ting Yuen*, but the *Chen Yuen*'s gunners subsequently claimed the credit for it. They also claimed that it had been the last 8 inch explosive shell in their locker—out of the three which they had possessed at the beginning of the battle! (Their other shells had been so-called "armor-piercing" shells, solid projectiles but quite ineffective.) The hit caused serious damage aboard the *Matsushima*. The official Japanese casualty figures gave it as forty-six men killed or seriously wounded, but the unofficial figure was much higher. One officer was blown to pieces. A fire broke out on board, and for some minutes the ship seemed all but lost.

However, the *Matsushima*'s company fought the fire with one hand while continuing to fight the enemy with the other, and the ship's bandsmen took the dead gunners' places. Fire was raging between decks, immediately above one of the magazines, and the deck-head protecting the magazine began to gape. The warrant officer and ratings responsible for the magazine used their clothes to stuff the gaps, protecting the explosives until the fire was got in hand.

A signal had been run up to the flagship's masthead: *Ships of*

117

the main fleet are free to break formation and pursue the enemy.
Shortly thereafter Admiral Ito's flag fluttered out at the *Hashidate*'s
mainmast halyards. The Japanese fleet was still circling the enemy
and firing with all their guns. The enemy soon consisted of no
more than the two battleships and one torpedo boat—the other
Chinese ships were either in flight, sunk, or on fire. Of the two
battleships, one, the flagship *Ting Yuen,* was on fire. Her mast
and yards had been shot away so that Admiral Ting, himself
wounded, could no longer signal. Since the start of the battle
the *Chen Yuen*'s crew had extinguished eight fires on board. Everything not made of metal on both ships had been smashed or burned.
But the two German-built ships were still fighting.

The ships of the Japanese fleet, still firing, continued to
steam round these two floating fortresses. Admiral Tsuboi's light
cruisers were away in pursuit of retreating enemy vessels. The
Chinese ammunition was practically exhausted; but Japanese
magazines were not in much better case: the quick-firing guns
had consumed an impressive quantity of shells.

Furthermore, the light was beginning to fail. Like Jellicoe twenty
years later, when he saw the mist beginning to settle down over
the North Sea, Admiral Ito had to consider his position. The
destruction of the Chinese cruisers must have seemed to him an
adequate result, and he had no wish to spend the night off the
mouth of the Yalu, within range of Chinese torpedo boats. At
5:30 P.M. he broke off the engagement.

The *Ting Yuen* and the *Chin Yuen,* followed by a remnant of
the dispersed Chinese fleet—a few smoking hulls still half on
fire in the gloaming—steamed slowly away on a southerly course.
"I supposed," Ito wrote in his report, "that they were making
for Weihaiwei, the Chinese base in the Shantung Peninsula. Having
reassembled my fleet, I steered a course parallel to the enemy's
presumed course, intending to resume contact with him on the
following morning."

At dawn, however, there was no sign of a single Chinese
ship. Ting, and his surviving handful, had taken advantage of

the darkness to seek refuge not in Weihaiwei, to the south, but in Port Arthur, to the north. The Japanese fleet set a course for their provisional base at the mouth of the Taedong River.

Upon arrival in Port Arthur, Ting announced that he had beaten the Japanese fleet. It is highly probable that he really believed this. Not all the guns in the Japanese fleet had succeeded in sinking his two battleships. That, however, was really the only consolation the Chinese could look to. Five Chinese ships had been lost, and the others had suffered very serious damage, necessitating a long refit. Something like a thousand Chinese had lost their lives in battle, fire, and shipwreck.

Of the Japanese ships, the *Matsushima* had suffered most. The others damaged, the *Akagi*, the *Saikyo Maru*, and the *Hiei*, were vessels of no great naval value, at least as regards their hulls, engines, and gear. Official Japanese casualty figures were ninety killed, and two hundred and four wounded. Nine enemy shells had hit the *Naniwa*, but no member of her company was either killed or wounded.

In a single afternoon the imperial Japanese fleet had won mastery of the Yellow Sea. And the Russian Pacific Fleet had not intervened.

Not yet.

Five

The war that Japan had declared on China lasted less than a year. It consisted in a series of Japanese victories, and is interesting chiefly because it offers several examples of strategical and tactical skill on the part of the naval and military leaders of a country which less than twenty years earlier had still been sunk in medieval feudalism, barely open to Western penetration, and torn by civil wars. To us, of course, the war is interesting because it was Togo's opportunity, enabling him to rise both in rank and reputation. There were battles on land and at sea. The simplest plan will be to give a brief sketch of the war—a glance at the map will help here—and then to return and study in detail those parts of it which are germane to our subject.

It will be remembered that the Japanese had political and

120

military control of Seoul, the Korean capital. Marching northwest from Seoul, they crushed a Chinese army at Pyongyang, on the 15th and 16th of September, 1894. On October 24th they crossed the Yalu, the river which divides Korea from Manchuria. On November 21st they seized the important fortress of Port Arthur, which dominates both the entrance to the Pohai Wan, with its access to Tientsin and Peking, and the Dairen Peninsula of southern Manchuria. In February, a landing force reduced Weihaiwei, the fortified port on the north coast of the Shantung Peninsula and forced it to capitulate. The Japanese fleet had been blockading the place, and was able to liquidate the Chinese fleet which had taken refuge there. Another Japanese army was still advancing in Manchuria. A Japanese expeditionary force had landed in Formosa. At this juncture the Chinese sued for peace, which was signed on April 17, 1895.

The first detail to engage our attention belongs, in point of time, to the period just before the war; the place is southern Manchuria. It was nothing striking, nothing apparent, even: the miserable and laborious life of the southern Manchurian peasantry and artisans went on its immemorial way; no one could possibly have realized that a number of these peasants and craftsmen were, in fact, not what they seemed to be; or that their trades were really nothing but a front.

Manchus, northern Chinese, Japanese—the racial "types" are not so very different; and the swarming bustle of China created favorable conditions for the activities of Japanese agents. By them were noted and recorded details of the roads of Korea and the neighboring provinces; the strategic points and water sources were mapped, as were ferries and fords. This intelligence work was carried out with amazing thoroughness. The timber necessary for the crossing of rivers by bodies of troops was actually felled and stacked in advance at predetermined points. Long before Admiral Kabayama had hoisted the fateful signal, *Add to the reputation of the imperial navy*, the officers who would command the landing parties which were to "maintain order" in Korea, had the results of this patient

121

espionage among their papers. There is no point in doing things by halves: either you prepare for war or you do not.

November, 1894: Japan, since the naval victory off the mouth of the Yalu, was mistress of the Yellow Sea. Her troop transports were free to steam across it unhampered. In Manchuria two armies were marching on Port Arthur. Kinchow fell, and in the dispatches describing that operation appeared a name worth bearing in mind —Nogi, General Nogi.

November 6th: The imperial fleet arrived off Talien Wan, the last Chinese strong point before Port Arthur. Since the Yalu battle the *Naniwa* had been cruising off the Chinese ports of the Yellow Sea, her task being reconnaissance and exploration. The attack on Talien Wan from the sea was to take place on the morning of the 7th.

November 7th: six o'clock in the morning. Taking season and latitude into account, it was still more or less dark. Five small Japanese ships swept the approaches to the port—presumed to be mined—to clear a channel for the fleet. The sky lightened, the sun rose, and the fortifications surrounding the port became visible. The first shot, fired by one of the ships in the van of the fleet, shattered the tranquillity of the morning. The guns of the whole fleet were bearing on the port, ready for the answering salvo. None came.

Nine o'clock: Admiral Ito ordered his fleet into the bay. Still nothing stirred. Talien Wan—or the bay of death.

As the distance diminished, the officers who were watching the shore through their glasses were able to make out small, antlike figures bustling about the earthworks. Presently some of them unbelievingly polished their lenses and took another look: the ants in question were wearing Japanese uniforms. Even as the fleet watched, a flag was broken out on the flagstaff above one of the forts: the banner of the Rising Sun. Meeting with almost no resistance, the army had seized the strong point at dawn. Talien Wan had become a Japanese advanced position.

November 21st: The imperial fleet, including the *Naniwa*, arrived off Port Arthur at daybreak. The place is worth a quick glance; it was to count for a great deal in Togo's life.

From the sea it appears only as a range of high, stony hills, a barren and melancholy land. On the high point to the north called Golden Mountain sits a fort, apparently a massive one. On the summit of the central peak, a tower. On the sloping face of another hill, to the south, a lighthouse. Below that, a pagoda; then a complex of formless buildings. The shore line seems unbroken; no breach is visible in that stony barrier. Only from much nearer to the land does a narrow gut of sea, not 350 yards wide, appear: it is the entrance to the harbor. The valleys between the hills are shut off by redoubts. Port Arthur, if attacked only from the sea, would seem to be impregnable.

Which was why the army, not the navy, was to bear the brunt of the operation, the fleet confining itself to bombarding the forts from a point beyond their range. On the evening before, the land forces had attacked the outermost hills of the natural fortress, and taken them by assault. At dawn the Japanese siege guns began to snap and growl from beyond the nearer hills. Then the infantry went in. By noon all the fortifications round the town were in Japanese hands. The ground was sodden and slippery; gun-carriage wheels sank in and became bogged down, and the mud sucked at the men's boots. But nothing could stop them. By nightfall the city was theirs.

The taking of Port Arthur by the Japanese caused much surprise in the West. Europeans and Americans were still accustomed to comparing China and Japan in terms of their relative importance in an atlas. Hardly anyone had realized the speed at which the Japanese military machine had developed. And no one could even have conceived of the patient, insectlike sapping by Japanese agents which had prepared the way for every military move. This was only known—and even then not well known—much later.

The war continued. December 19, 1894: Admiral Ito, his fleet at moorings in Talien Wan, received the following order from imperial General Staff Headquarters:

"First: as the enemy fleet has taken refuge in Weihaiwei, refusing to respond to our challenge, it may become an obstacle to our operations when we land our troops at the entrance to the Gulf of Pohai. To eliminate this danger, we are obliged to send a military and naval force to take possession of Weihaiwei.

"Second: You will convoy the Second Army's landing force, and, acting in concert with it, you will take possession of Weihaiwei and destroy the enemy fleet."

Weihaiwei is a natural harbor, a semicircular bay open to the northeast. On the cord of its arc a high, rocky island towers out of the sea; it is called Liukung, and it was fortified. There were forts to both east and west of the town. The Chinese fleet lay at anchor in the bay. The most obvious solution to the problem of seizing the place was to attack it directly, exposing the fleet to the combined fire of forts and fleet. This was as stupid as it was obvious and the Japanese tacticians had a better plan. Their papers contained all the information they required concerning a place called Chefoo, on the north coast of the Shantung Peninsula, about seventy miles west of Weihaiwei: mark well—*west*.

On the afternoon of January 18, 1895, the people of Chefoo— some ten thousand souls, a very trifling matter in all the hordes of China—were very far from thinking about the war with Japan. Many of them hardly knew that any such country existed. Snow covered the ground, and a storm was raging at sea. Streets and waterfront were deserted by all but a few hurrying figures covered with the traditional straw cloak. Daylight, under that overcast sky, would be of brief duration.

3:45 P.M.: Gunfire. Stupefaction. Such Chinese as ran down toward the sea saw, quite close, three warships such as they had never seen, their gun muzzles flaming. To us the three ships are by now familiar: *Naniwa, Akitsushima, Yoshino*. They were bombarding the forts, which were answering their fire.

The officers commanding the forts sent mounted messengers galloping over the snow to the provincial governor: "The Japanese are upon us." From the military capital of the province the

124

telegraph warned Peking: "The Japanese are upon us. The Japanese are about to land at Chefoo."

Nightfall put an end to the Japanese bombardment. But the alarm had been given. Chinese troops were on the move, by forced marches, to Chefoo. Chefoo had no sleep that night and, in the morning, as soon as a rift appeared in the veil of whirling snow which masked the sea, Chefoo heard the guns again, and, in their thunder, seemed to hear the marching of the enemy's advance guard. The alarm was repeated; fresh forces were warned and diverted to the place by the Chinese authorities. As they began to arrive, the defense was organized on the beaches before the town.

On the following day the Japanese Army landed at Yung-Cheng, about fifty miles *east* of Weihaiwei. The feint had succeeded perfectly.

Nor was Yung-Cheng chosen without care as the real bridgehead. Its garrison of some three hundred soldiers, could be—and was—dealt with by a few bursts of machine-gun fire, after which all the invaders had to do was to march along the coast to Weihaiwei, using the maps prepared by their intelligence agents. The agents, however, had made no mention of snow, mud, or an icy wind. The temperature fell to nine above zero; the soldiers' breath hung in clouds before their faces. But they did not halt.

Weihaiwei came in sight; and was attacked, beginning with the forts defending its eastern approaches. In vain the Chinese warships at anchor opened fire on the Japanese ashore. The eastern forts were taken by assault. As soon as the Rising Sun flew above them, the Chinese ships opened on the forts. During the following days the Chinese fleet was likewise to bombard their own western forts—which also fell into the invaders' hands. There remained the central strong point.

It was attacked on January 30th. The bombardment of the forts guarding the entrance to the harbor was entrusted to the *Naniwa*, the *Akitsushima*, and the *Katsuragi*. Note the order: the officer commanding the three ships was Togo. Togo's guns fought a duel with Ting's. The port ammunition depot exploded.

February began with atrocious weather. The sea raged furiously; the rivers were frozen; a bitter wind cut though sailors' and soldiers' uniforms. The bulk of the Japanese fleet sought haven in the bay of Yung-Cheng, while the army tightened its grip on Weihaiwei. It was important, however, to ensure that Ting's ships did not take advantage of the conditions to escape: the *Naniwa* and her two sister ships of the First Light Flotilla patrolled outside the harbor. It was a task of importance, a position of trust.

From a distance the three small ships, tempest tossed and covered by the waves, seemed certain to be sunk. Visibility was almost nil, and the seas grew hourly steeper and more violent. They could be seen breaking on the reefs in fountains of white foam; yet the ships could not withdraw to safety, for the entrance to the harbor was not to be lost sight of for a moment. Since it was at night that this proximity to the coast was most dangerous, it was at night that the closest watch had to be maintained. Day and night, without remission, Togo, tortured by renewed attacks of rheumatism from the weather, was on his wave-swept bridge.

Meanwhile, in his stateroom aboard the *Ting Yuen,* in the midst of his fleet of ships condemned to die, Admiral Ting reread the letter that Admiral Ito had sent him before the final attack, by the good offices of a British merchantman's master—she was the *Severn* and lay off Weihaiwei at the time. For reasons which will appear hereafter, this letter deserves to be quoted in full:

"I have the honor to address this letter to Admiral Ting. Regrettable circumstances have made us adversaries, but wars are conflicts between nations, not personal quarrels, therefore my friendship for you remains unimpaired. I request that you will not regard this letter as an attempt to persuade you to surrender, but to believe that it is inspired by a deep anxiety for yourself.

"There are, unquestionably, diverse reasons for the successive defeats suffered by your army and navy, but there is also a principal cause, easy to discover if the question be considered impartially and which, therefore, cannot have escaped so clearsighted a man as yourself.

126

"The present condition of your country is not due to the faults of a few leaders, but is beyond question the outcome of your system of government. You appoint a man to office in consideration, solely, of his literary erudition, which is an immemorial custom. Those in power are all accomplished men of letters. I do not argue that this system is altogether bad: and no doubt it was good for just so long as your country remained in isolation; but it is now archaic. Moreover, in the present condition of the world it is not possible for any country to live in isolation.

"You are well aware of the difficult situation in which the Japanese Empire found itself thirty years ago, and of the manner in which we have undertaken to overcome the troubles which press upon us by rejecting our ancient system and adopting the new one. Your country should likewise adopt this new way of living. If it does so, all will go well; if not, it can only perish sooner or later. Such is the logical fate which awaits your country.

"Whosoever desires to serve his country loyally and honestly must not be willing to be swept away by the great tide which threatens to drown that country. He would do better to reform the most ancient empire on earth, an empire with immense territories and a glorious history, and thus render it for ever indestructible. When fate is against a man and the times unfavorable, the surrender of a fleet is an event of little weight compared with the resurgence or the fall of a great nation. I therefore request you to come to my country and there to await the moment when your country will call upon your help in its work of reformation. Hearken to the advice of a sincere friend, offered with that sense of honor which the whole world associates with the name of samurai.

"I need not remind you that the history of several countries contains numerous instances of men who patiently accepted a passing disgrace, later to render eminent services to the State. In France, for example, Marshal MacMahon surrendered to the enemy, and remained with the enemy, and, when the time was ripe, returned to France and took part in the reform of her government.

127

So little dishonored by his surrender did his fellow countrymen consider him, that they elected him president of the Republic. Likewise the Turk, Osman Pasha, gave himself up at Plevna and was made prisoner, but when he returned to his country it was to be made Minister of War, in which office he showed himself capable in reforming his country's military organization. If you agree to come to Japan, I will guarantee the clemency of our emperor. His Majesty not only pardoned those of his subjects who raised the banner of revolt in the War of Restoration, but several of them, notably Admiral Enamoto and Privy Councilor Otori were appointed to very important offices. In the case of a foreigner, and especially of a man of high repute such as yourself, there cannot be the smallest doubt that his conduct to you will be infinitely more generous.

"In short, two courses are open to you and you must choose between them. One consists in sharing the fate of your country which, by reason of its obstinate attachment to the old system, is running into the greatest dangers. The other, to husband your energies for future services.

"It has ever been the custom of your country's warriors to reply with boasting to letters from enemy chiefs, and to make a parade of strength to conceal their weakness. But I know you to be too intelligent to follow such examples. This letter is written in the sincerity of true friendship and not inspired by the need of the moment. I ask you to rest assured that should you accept the proposal made in this letter, I will, with your permission, submit suggestions touching the means of carrying out our intentions."

Why have I thought this letter worth quoting in full? It is obvious that the "sincere friend" who is writing to Ting "with the sense of honor which the whole world associates with the name of samurai" would have been horrified at the very idea of himself yielding to the arguments he was putting forward. The conclusion to be drawn can only be that the Japanese High Command, already well informed in the matter of modern strategy and tactics, and far from ignorant of the science of military intelligence, here proved itself equally adept at what is now called psychological warfare. Ito's very clever letter, dealing as it did with realities which could not be denied, was a tract designed to demoralize the enemy.

It goes without saying that Ting knew perfectly well that he could not hold out for long against a Japanese attack. The part of Weihaiwei that still remained in Chinese hands consisted only of a small island called Yih, Liukung Island, and the ships sheltering behind it. The area in question was smashed beneath the weight of shells both from the captured forts and from the Japanese fleet; during nine days the thunder of the bombardment had never ceased. Ting, meanwhile, had shown Ito's letter to his officers and told them that while, for his part, he could not forget his duty to his country, they were at liberty, if they did not want to go on fighting, to give themselves up to the enemy, and that he would not blame them. To which they replied, to a man, that they would rather die with him.

February 3rd: the storm began to slacken and visibility to improve. Admiral Ito had the following message delivered to the officers commanding his three flotillas of torpedo boats: "Your orders are to sink the enemy ships in the harbor forthwith. No such operation has ever hitherto been undertaken by any navy in the world. I am asking you to sacrifice your lives for your country and to earn undying fame for yourselves."

The Japanese torpedo boats were tiny shells of 150 tons; life aboard them was hell in anything but perfect weather. In every one of them—as soon as the admiral's orders were known—everything was done strictly according to rule. Their captains burned their ships' papers—codes and signal books. Officers and men changed into clean clothes, and one hour was set aside so that all could prepare mind and spirit for death. Immediately this respite was over, all ships' companies set about carrying out their orders. That same evening, with the storm still raging, torpedo boat Number Six succeeded in breaching the boom which closed the harbor.

129

February 5th, three o'clock in the morning: Four torpedo boats made an impetuous attack on the western entrance. It was a diversionary attack, however. By reason of the high seas and the near-by reefs, the task was a dangerous one; moreover, its whole object was to attract the offensive attention of the Chinese fleet. Admiral Ito had entrusted the command of this operation to the man he considered to have the coolest head and the best knowledge of Chinese coastal waters among all his officers: Togo. The operation was perfectly successful and entailed no casualties or losses whatsoever.

At the moment of this attack ten torpedo boats moved quietly in toward the east entrance to the harbor. The decks and guns were covered with ice; their torpedoes were frozen into the tubes; and in the gigantic swell the tiny warships rocked like so many kayaks. Two were hurled onto the rocks. Eight found the breach in the boom and made their way through it, thereupon darting at full speed at their target—the Chinese fleet.

The alarm was sounded; searchlights began to probe the darkness, and guns to thunder. Three of the torpedo boats were hit and limped out of the battle; a fourth could not free its torpedoes from the ice in the tubes. Four fired their torpedoes. The *Ting Yuen* was hit and ran aground on the rocks.

February 6th, same time: five Japanese torpedo boats again got through the boom and sank three Chinese warships. One of them, the *Lai Yuen,* turned turtle completely, imprisoning a number of her crew alive. For days the men could be heard frantically knocking on the inside of the hull. When, at last, it was possible to go to their rescue, it was too late.

The death throes of Weihaiwei began. On February 7th the sea was calmer. Action stations was sounded by the buglers aboard the whole Japanese fleet. Presently, in line-ahead, Admiral Ito's ships got under way, their bows breaking the skin of ice, thin as glass, that covered the surface. Each ship fired in turn, as its guns were brought to bear, as if on maneuvers. The sinister yellow smoke

130

of exploding shells hung darkly above the harbor; at sea, the smoke from Ito's guns dimmed the light of the sun.

In the course of this murderous merry-go-round, the last twelve Chinese torpedo boats made a desperate sortie. They were hardly across the harbor bar when Ito unleashed his light cruisers. Of the twelve, only two escaped: the others were either sunk, driven aground on the rocks, or captured.

February 8th, 9th, 10th, 11th: the bombardment of Liukung Island and of the remaining Chinese warships continued. Nearly all Ting's ships were sunk; the survivors huddled at the western extremity of the harbor. Ashore, only one fort, Huang-Tao, was still firing. Then came the final attack: *Naniwa* and *Akitsushima,* the ships that had fired the first shots in the battle of Weihaiwei, engaged this last strongpoint all through one moonlit night until dawn.

Daybreak. Dark clouds hid the sun, and a slight breeze had swept the smoke of battle from the silent harbor. A Chinese gunboat issued from the east entrance, flying a flag of truce. As she made slowly for the Japanese flagship, a signal was hoisted to Ito's signal halyards: *Cease fire.*

"It was my intention to fight to a finish, desisting only when all my ships were sunk and all my men dead. But I cannot bring myself to cause the death of thousands more. I surrender to your forces one warship, the island of Liukung, the forts and their armament. I ask you most earnestly to put an end to the fighting and to let soldiers, sailors, and the local inhabitants return to their homes and live in peace. If you accept these conditions, the commander of the British squadron * will guarantee my good faith." Such was Ting's message. While Ito was drawing up his answer, the two Chinese envoys collapsed and slept in the ward-room chairs: they had not slept for ten days.

---

* It is not clear which. Ting may have meant the British Far Eastern Fleet. —Trans.

131

"I am agreeable to all your proposals. When all arms have been handed over, my ships will take you and yours under their protection, and will escort you to whatever destination suits you best. But, as I suggested the other day, the best solution for the future well-being of your country would be for you to come to mine and there await the end of the war. Nevertheless, if such be not your wish, I have no desire to force such a decision. It is entirely unnecessary for you to ask the commander of the British squadron to stand your guarantor. As one seaman to another, I have every confidence in your word."

With this message, and a gift of cakes and a case of champagne, Ito sent the Chinese envoys back to his conquered adversary; their gunboat flying the white flag made its way back to the harbor. It reappeared the following morning, carrying one of the two Chinese officers with a new message for Admiral Ito.

"I have received your message and, in the name of my men, thank you from the bottom of my heart. I regret my inability to accept the gift you so kindly sent me and I beg you to consent to receive it back, with this message, and my thanks for your excellent intention."

When Admiral Ito had finished reading, the Chinese officer spoke:

"Our admiral was grateful for your kindness and declared that he now had nothing more to regret. He then turned toward Peking and, having swallowed poison, died."

The mortal remains of Admiral Ting were placed aboard a transport lent by Admiral Ito to carry them to China. The transport steamed past the Japanese fleet. Flags were flown at half-mast, and the guns, sounding at long intervals, fired the regulation salute.

So ended the Chinese fleet. In Peking the senior officers whom Ito had left at liberty were put to death.

Meanwhile, a Japanese army continued to advance in Manchuria. The Chinese, ill fed, poorly led, and unwarlike by nature, were not very formidable opponents. The cold was much more redoubtable. The infantry were marching in two feet of snow. In one battle, at Taiping Chan, casualties were fifteen hundred cases of pneumonia. But nothing stopped the Japanese, and the medical and commissariat corps carried out their tasks to perfection, in the heart of a poor country and in the most unfavorable weather conditions. Their organization surprised European observers as much as, indeed more than, the fighting spirit of the Japanese troops.

The Chinese, still retreating, found themselves brought up with their backs to the river Liao, beyond the southern peninsula of Manchuria. Moreover, the Chinese high command learned from its agents—the Japanese were not the only ones with an intelligence service, and it must not be forgotten that they were now an "army of occupation"—that another expeditionary force had been mustered at Port Arthur, its purpose being a landing at Shanhaikwan. Shanhaikwan is on the Gulf of Liaotung, at one end of the Great Wall. Its distance from Peking is 175 miles—in China, nothing. The government in Peking lost its nerve and seized the opportunity of the first Western offer of good offices to send a negotiator to Japan. Japan had won her war.

After the Second World War, historians and commentators drew attention to the military courage of Japanese soldiers, sailors, and airmen. The quality of the Japanese troops was just as apparent, perhaps even more so, during the time of their retreat as during their conquest of the Pacific. It was this fighting retreat which witnessed the prowess of the *kamikazes*, and saw Japanese infantrymen, hung with grenades, throwing themselves under American tanks. Today it seems that this fanatical self-dedication, which had been fostered and developed by the militarists in power during the years which preceded the war, is on the decline; and that Japan is now tending to give expression to her dynamism, even expansionism, in the industrial and scientific fields. The warlike temper of a people has its ups and downs; and there can be no doubt that in 1895 the Japanese offensive spirit was at a peak.

What does appear surprising is the swiftness with which army and navy assimilated Western methods. No military expert of

133

world-wide fame was responsible for the building of this very efficient war machine. For the army, the mikado's government had called in a number of French military attachés, subsequently replaced by Germans. For the navy British instructors, plus a handful of men who, like Togo, had acquired a smattering of Western naval technique, but who were certainly no Nelsons.

One element which unquestionably counted was the absolute devotion to their profession on the part of all Japanese officers. Japanese soldiers and sailors were obliged to suffer the strictest discipline, and they led a hard, even an ascetic, life. But the officers imposed upon themselves an even harsher discipline and led an even more ascetic life. They despised comfort and pleasures, slept, like their men, on a straw mat, ate the same food, slept shorter hours, and exposed themselves more to danger. As a consequence, they could make great demands on their men—ask all, and receive all. In so far as it is possible to recapture the feeling in the services at that time, the relationship between officers and men was "frank and free from arrogance." Such, at least, are the words to be found in contemporary documents.

The diplomats now had the floor. But the government of a victorious power, so long as no armistice has been signed, has the right, one might almost say the duty, to capture as many trump cards as possible. On the very day that Li Hung-chang, the Chinese plenipotentiary, left Tientsin for Shimonoseki, where he was to confer with Count Ito, a large part of the Japanese fleet set sail for Sasebo. The new objective was Formosa.

The Portuguese, when they made their landfall on the east coast of that much coveted island, had discovered an impressive landscape of high mountains towering above vegetation of extraordinary luxuriance—whence the name, *Ilha formosa,* Beautiful Island. For the Chinese, Formosa was, above all, the terraced rice fields of the west coast—Taiwan, Bay of Terraces. In point of fact, Formosa was an island with a trying climate, infested by mosquitos and malaria, and inhabited by natives reputed ferocious. It was held, more or less, by a few weak Chinese garrisons. To reinforce

134

these regulars, China had recently, for cash on the nail, hired the services of Lu Yung-fu and his mercenaries, and sent them to Formosa. Lu Yung-fu was the leader of the Black Flags who had distinguished himself in the fighting against France in Annam. China wanted to hang on to Formosa as an important strategic position. Japan wanted to conquer it for the same reason. The chiefs of the imperial General Staff decided: "The naval squadron and the landing forces will first seize the Pescadores Islands. Formosa will then be attacked." Their offensive spirit was in no wise disturbed by the current diplomatic negotiations.

March 15, 1895: the people crowding the jetties at Sasebo watched the fleet sail. At the head of the line was the flagship *Matsushima;* in her wake the main squadron—*Ikutsushima, Hashnidate, Chiyoda*—screened by torpedo boats, and followed by seven transports carrying troops, arms, equipment, provisions, in short everything necessary to the expeditionary force, including coffins. As usual, the fast cruiser *Yoshino* led the First Light Flotilla: *Naniwa, Takachino, Akitsushima.* Aboard the *Naniwa,* the ship's company had a new voice to obey. A new captain paced her bridge. Nevertheless, she was still under her old captain's orders: the flag that fluttered at the *Yoshino*'s masthead—a Rising Sun underlined and surmounted by horizontal bars—was no longer Tsboï's. It was Togo's: he had been made rear admiral in January, 1895. Heihachiro Togo had acquired the title by which he was to be known for the rest of his life: Admiral Togo.

The sea was rough and the heat of the sun torrid. The soldiers suffered from seasickness. As soon as Formosa was sighted, Admiral Ito sent the cruisers forward. He had a good reason for doing so. Of all his subordinate officers, few were acquainted with these waters. But Togo knew them, and even had some acquaintance with the island itself: apparently certain excursions he had made in the vicinity of the Chinese fortifications of Keelung, in the company of a young French Lieutenant named Joffre, were going to be useful.

While the main body of the fleet, and the transports, were making for a provisional base, Togo cruised parallel to the east coast of

Formosa and rounded its southernmost cape. On the following day the Pescadores were in sight: low rocks with a thin cover of soil and a few reefs. As for the climate, there are torrential rains which hold off just long enough, every year, to enable the inhabitants—the *pescadores*—to dry their fish. Add to these amenities the fact that the tides between the small islands are such as to cause violent and incalculable currents. Even today, for a captain provided with up-to-date charts, these waters are dangerous. In 1895, only exceptional luck could get a seaman through them, in anything bigger than a fishing boat, without shipwreck. Togo was all the more preoccupied by this problem of pilotage because a total overcast had prevented the taking of bearings for several days, and he had been navigating by dead reckoning. Fortunately, the sky cleared as he was due to make his landfall, and the Pescadores appeared on the horizon. The first bearing taken on a point of land revealed an error of twenty-eight miles in the dead reckoning. The change in the weather had come none too soon.

Admiral Ito had entrusted the task of choosing a landing place to Togo, and the point he selected was accepted by the admiral without hesitation. There was a fortified position in the Pescadores: the cruisers shelled it, and the expeditionary force occupied the islands.

April 1st: the admiral received a signal informing him that an armistice had been signed between Japan and China. He was to remain where he was, and wait. While the fleet and the army waited, they were attacked by an enemy unfamiliar to Japanese troops: cholera. The cholera bacillus killed many more Japanese soldiers than did the Chinese guns. At last, on April 28th, came the order to return to Japan. At dawn on May 5th the imperial fleet dropped anchor in Sasebo harbor once more.

Peace had been signed on April 17th. It was a victorious peace, but a bitter disappointment throughout Japan.

In the first place, the peace treaty was not what had been hoped for at the beginning of the negotiations. This was due to a stupid manifestation of superannuated nationalism. We have al-

136

ready mentioned the fanatical Jo-i nationalist movement. In 1895 it was not extinct, and one of its members had fired a pistol shot at the Chinese plenipotentiary Li Hung-chang while he was on his way to a session of the peace conference at Shimonoseki. The impression made by this attempt at assassination was all the more unfortunate in that the newer, fashionable Japanese nationalism was beginning to find its expression in Bushido, the modernized code of chivalry.

Li Hung-chang did not die, and he rose admirably to the occasion: impassive at the moment of danger, smiling after it, he assured his embarrassed hosts that so trifling an incident counted for nothing by comparison with his pleasure in being so honorably welcomed by the great Japanese nation. The empress dressed Li Hung-chang's wound with her own fair hands. The conference, which had opened in an icy atmosphere, turned into a competition in courtesy. The Jo-i assassin's bullet was expensive in square miles of territory and millions of taels. Still, the treaty was certainly not a bad one. China—but not Japan—recognized the "independence" of Korea, and ceded the Liaotung Peninsula, Formosa, and the Pescadores. She undertook to open four ports to Japanese trade, to pay an indemnity of two hundred million taels, and leave Weihaiwei in Japanese hands as a pledge for the payment of these reparations.

It was not all that had been hoped for; it was much more than Japan ever received. On April 26th, six days after the signatures of the treaty, Germany, France, and Russia approached Tokyo in concert, and "advised" the Japanese Government to renounce her claim to the Liaotung Peninsula, in consideration of a further thirty million taels' reparations. The Liaotung Peninsula was that part of southern Manchuria whose conquest had been so costly; its strategic value was enormous, for it dominated the gateway to Peking. Thirty million taels was no sort of compensation for its loss. But Japan could not—yet—afford to reject the "advice" of three great powers. She was obliged to give up southern Manchuria.

But there remained Formosa. That, at least, was now Japanese.

137

Admiral Kabayama was appointed governor of the island. When the question of installing him in office arose, it appeared very much as if that would not simply be a matter of presenting the islanders with a certified copy of the Treaty of Shimonoseki.

Which was why, on May 25th, Togo's light cruisers appeared once again off the coast of Formosa, in advance of a naval force escorting sixteen transports. Aboard the transports, in addition to certain line regiments, were the Imperial Guards, "shock" troops from whom the Imperial General Staff expected great things.

Li Yung-fu, the Black Flag leader, had decided to treat the Treaty of Shimonoseki as null and void, and had assumed the title of President of Formosa. His new emblem was a yellow tiger showing its teeth, on a blue ground. The Japanese ships were confronted with this flag as they came in sight of the forts of Tanshui. Tanshui was the port of Taipei, at that time the capital of Formosa. A fort on one of the hills fired a twenty-one-gun salute—a national salute—while a rattle of musketry fire broke out all along the shore, from cover. The Formosans were not using blanks: bullets were heard whistling overhead. Togo, in command of the vanguard, paid no attention to these piratical manners, but continued to steam offshore, looking for a landing place.

On the following day the landing force set foot on the island of Santiao Chao and marched on Keelung. On June 3rd the Imperial Guards attacked the place, while the fleet bombarded the forts on the high points above it. Everything went as planned, until a tropical downpour of rain, descending in sheets, so spoiled visibility that the fleet gunners could hardly see as far as the muzzles of their own guns. The Japanese were forced to cease fire. That, however, did not prevent the Guards from advancing, which they did, irresistibly, through deluge and mud. Keelung was taken. The Japanese infantry, still wearing the heavy cloth uniforms issued to them for the campaign in Manchuria, plunged into the steam bath of the jungle, cut their way through marshes and bush, flung the Black Flags out of Tanshui, and, hauling down the Yellow Tiger, ran up the Rising Sun in its stead. Prisoners, both bandits and

138

regulars, were crowded onto the beaches. They were herded into the transports, ferried across the strait, and put ashore on the Chinese mainland.

The campaign was going well, but in no way resembled a pleasure outing. Summer was on the way. The expeditionary force suffered from malaria and dysentery. Togo, half paralyzed by his atrocious rheumatism, remained on the bridge of his ship, issuing his orders from a chair. For it was he who really carried out the plan conceived in outline in Japan, but perfected on the spot: capture of the south-coast ports after the north had been mastered; destruction of the pirates' bases; then the punitive expedition. The hand of Japan was daily tightening its grip on Formosa. At the end of October, Admiral Arichi, the officer commanding the main fleet, was recalled to Japan, and Togo was left in supreme command of the naval forces in Formosan waters. Moving from point to point along the coast according to need, he transferred his flag from one ship to another. Every officer reported to him and came to him for orders. For a large part of the imperial fleet, Togo was now the commander in chief, the admiral.

On November 16th—by which time the conquest of Formosa was virtually complete—Togo was recalled to Japan. A few days later he crossed the threshold of his house, and his wife, Masuko, with her hands on her knees, greeted him with the three traditional bows. The news awaited him that by order of the mikado he had been awarded the Order of the Golden Falcon, fourth class, and the Order of the Rising Sun, fourth class. At the same time he learned that he was being relieved of his command at sea and appointed a member of the Council of Admirals and Chairman of the Naval Technical Board.

The next four years in Togo's life can be told in a few lines. There would, indeed, seem to be no point in recounting them at greater length. What is there to say of a man impassive by nature, silent by choice, when that man is a shore-based naval officer during a period when nothing happens? We have no reason to suppose that his inner life was violent or even disturbed. At least this is a change from the method of the modern novelist.

Togo wore a beard, which was black. His manner had changed a little; he had come to terms with himself, had an air of authority and ease. In present-day language, he was "relaxed." His phlegmatic temper had been modified by a touch of humor. He was affable in his attitude to junior officers.

May, 1896: Togo became head of the Advanced Naval College, better described as the school of naval warfare. He by no means considered the appointment as a retirement. He had hardly been appointed before he summoned his staff of instructors, and ordered numerous reforms in the curriculum—among which a thorough study of chess became obligatory. One of his staff officers was ordered to translate a famous work on strategy by the Russian Admiral Makarov.

Togo was promoted to vice admiral. He represented the navy at the funeral of the mikado's mother. He took a fortnight's leave to undergo the cure at the Kugahara medicinal waters, for his rheumatism. However, by and large, his health was good.

1899: Appointed commanding officer of the naval base at Sasebo. Another shore job. However, for the time being, the appointment was of more use to Togo than a command at sea. The last years of the century were years of rapid technical progress in all the world's navies. Moreover, this was the period when Japan finally abandoned her policy of alternately buying a ship abroad and building one at home. The Imperial General Staff had been forced to adopt an adequate naval program. The weapon which was being forged under Togo's eyes and with his agreement was a homogeneous fleet: four battleships, one of which was the *Mikasa*, six armored cruisers, torpedo boats and auxiliary vessels. English, German, and French, as well as Japanese shipyards, collaborated in this shipbuilding program.

As to the strategic importance of Sasebo, at the southwestern extremity of Japan, it is hardly necessary to emphasize it. Whenever

Togo could arrange it, he went to sea in one of the ships placed under his orders, and resumed his old trade of pilotage and hydrography. He learned by heart every pebble of the Korean Strait, its currents and prevailing winds. It was second nature to him to learn all he could about any place where he happened to be. Thus as commanding officer of the Sasebo base, he cruised the Strait of Tsushima, studying its coasts and waters, as if one day he might be required to navigate it blindfold.

Four and a half years passed, years during which Togo was deprived of the one thing that really rejoices the heart of a sailor: a sea command. All of his staff were struck with his thoroughness in the fulfillment of his duties; even in tasks more suited to a professional teacher or an industrialist than a naval officer, he never spared himself. These years, for all that they take but a few lines in the telling, counted for much in Togo's career. His invincible perseverance, his unrelaxing attention to duty, the care and thoroughness with which every task was performed, were all, so to speak, petals of that still folded bud which was to burgeon into the glorious flower of complete success.

The nineteenth century drew to a close, and the twentieth dawned. After four years of tranquillity, something was happening at sea. Togo was recalled to sea duty. On May 20, 1900, he was appointed Admiral of the Fleet. The Boxer Rising was already raging.

The story of the Boxers is as picturesque and captivating as any historian could wish. But to study it in detail and unravel its manifold tangled threads would be a work of several years. The trail one would have to follow through Chinese history might well turn out to have no ending. Which is no doubt why the true and complete history of the Boxers, bandits, spiritualists, and chauvinistic patriots, has yet to be written.

The Boxer Society (in Chinese *I Ho-chuan,* which may be roughly translated as The Fist of Concord and Justice) affiliated, like several other secret societies, to the Sect of the Big Knives and the Sect of the White Water Lily, was also associated with the freemasonry of the "Triad" which, half a century earlier, had given rise to the T'ai P'ing movement. It was an association of miracle-workers and sorcerers, heralding a new millennium, and convinced that they could render themselves invulnerable by means of certain drugs and exercises. These rather unsavory persons were unleashed like mastiffs against the foreign community in Peking by the Dowager Empress, Her Majesty the Sacred Mother Tzu Hsi, after she had shut up her nephew Kuang Hsu for life in the confines of a small temple because he had wanted to modernize China and come to terms with the foreigners.

Let us, however, be quite fair. China, the old China, had a great deal to put up with at foreign hands. From the time that the Japanese victories had revealed the Manchu dynasty's decrepitude, the policy of the Western powers toward China might be called "slicing the melon." Germany had seized Kiaochow to avenge the murder of two missionaries. Russia had obtained the cession of Port Arthur, as a pledge. Great Britain had occupied Weihaiwei, with a "right" to collect customs duties in the Yangtze basin. France had a lease of Kwangchow and a railway concession. To the Great Powers a slice of China, like a country house to a rich businessman, seemed to be a normal possession.

China reacted by unleashing the Boxers, and the European powers "protested." They sent warships to Taku, not far from Tientsin, terminus of both road and railway to Peking.

The first ship sent by the mikado's government to protect the Japanese in China was the cruiser *Kasagi*. Two smaller ships soon joined her. The situation, meanwhile, was deteriorating, the Boxers having cut the Peking-Tientsin railway. Vice Admiral Edward H. Seymour, commanding the British squadron, set out from Tientsin for Peking at the head of a small expeditionary force. On June 12th Sugiyama, councilor of the Japanese legation in Peking, was assassinated and his body mutilated. Togo, who was watching events from Sasebo, was given orders to sail. He hoisted

142

his flag in the *Tokiwa*, and was at Taku on June 22nd, where Rear Admiral Dewa, sent on before him, explained the situation and handed over the command.

On June 17th the Chinese garrisoning the northwest fort of Taku had opened fire on the railway station where the foreign landing parties were mustered. An attack on the fort had been launched at once: 350 Japanese had formed the rear guard, a rear guard that had turned into a vanguard when the momentum of the troops leading the assault had slackened. The first foreign flag to be run up above the fort had been a white handkerchief with a rough red circle in the center, that circle being, in fact, a bloodstain: nothing else had been available by way of a Japanese flag. Meanwhile, Tientsin was besieged by the Boxers, all communications with Peking were cut, and no one knew what had become of Admiral Seymour and his relief column.

Twenty-three warships lay at anchor off Taku: seven British, two Russian, four German, one American, four French, one Austrian, one Italian, and three Japanese. An odd spectacle. A conference of admirals met almost daily aboard the modern Russian armored cruiser *Rossya*. Togo attended on the first day, and thereafter sent Rear Admiral Dewa in his stead; he considered the time spent in chatter as time wasted. Nothing was being accomplished, and each nation's staff of officers seemed chiefly bent on impressing the others.

Togo inspected the military works ashore, steamed up the Taku River in a launch, took note of the want of any real cooperation between the allies. In addition he spent a good deal of his time in examining the foreign ships, particularly the Russian, through his binoculars. The Russians seemed ready to return the compliment. On June 29th Vice Admiral Alekseev, governor general of the province of Kwantung and commander in chief of the Russian Far Eastern Fleet, arrived aboard his flagship the *Petropavlovsk*. Alekseev had more seniority than Togo, to whom it occurred that he ought perhaps to pay the Russian a courtesy visit. But before he had made up his mind to do so, he saw the Russian admiral's

143

launch leave the side of the *Petropavlovsk* and, describing a wide curve, draw up to the *Tokiwa's* ladder. Alekseev, bearded, begilt, bestarred, and bemedaled, was all smiles. No one could have shown himself more amiable, obliging, and at ease, more ready to prolong the conversation. For the progress made by the Japanese Navy, he was all admiration, and he had, he said, no doubt that the tactical training of its officers was on a par with the splendid maintenance of its ships and the good order and discipline of its crews. Togo bowed his acknowledgments. Alekseev went further: it was the merest prudence on his part to want to know what a good Japanese like Togo thought of the leasing of Port Arthur by Russia. Togo, apparently, did not think of it at all, but continued to smile pleasantly and let Alekseev do the talking. In due course the Russian took his leave, without having learned anything whatsoever. Togo, for his part, drew his own conclusions from his patient observations.

"The Russian Navy is by no means so formidable as many think," he was to tell a naval officer friend a little later on. "Their discipline can hardly be called strict, and I have noticed gaps in the training of their ships' companies. The Russians are much too ready to use their warships as freighters for military supplies. Any ship used frequently as a cargo carrier soon loses her fighting quality."

Meanwhile it was becoming more and more urgent to go to the rescue of the foreign communities in Tientsin and Peking, now besieged by the red-turbaned Boxer bandits. The Japanese were soon fighting beside German, English, and French troops, and even, when necessary, Russian. The Japanese had received considerable reinforcements: between June 22nd and June 29th, nine transports had been convoyed across to Taku, one of their passengers being Major General Yasumasa Fukushima. Japan had no intention of playing second fiddle to any of her allies.

On June 25th Seymour and his column, safe and sound, were relieved. On the 29th, Fukushima attacked the force besieging Tientsin; and fighting developed in the streets of the city. On

144

July 13th the Tientsin fortress was assaulted. Once again, it was a Japanese detachment which, after fierce fighting, managed to place a mine under the fortress wall. The Japanese infantry went in through the breach.

In the month of August, Togo received orders to hand over his command to Admiral Dewa and return to Japan. The Imperial General Staff wanted to know whether the Boxer "war" was to be treated simply as a police operation by the Great Powers, or whether they had decided to liquidate China as a sovereign state. In that case, Japan must play her proper part and the whole fleet would be mobilized. The Admiral of the Fleet would be required to take his part in the mobilization, and in deciding on the plan of campaign. Togo's orders included a postscript: he was to return home by way of Korea. It might be as well to take a look at that officially independent but actually vassal country.

Once again, then, Togo made an entry into Seoul. He was received in audience by the king—who had promoted himself Emperor. And he returned the courtesy by giving a party aboard his ship, which lay at Chemulpo, at which two of the king's ministers represented the Korean Government. He saw nothing, during his visit, to make him think that Korea's political decline as a state had been arrested, much less reversed. Little by little, Japanese "protection" was taking the place of national institutions.

On August 20th, Togo's flagship dropped anchor in Kure. The Boxers besieging the Peking concessions had surrendered five days before. Once again Japanese troops had been an honor to their country, and not only by fighting heroically. Their discipline had not wavered during the orgies which followed the victory. Impassive, but doubtless entertaining certain interesting ideas, the little soldiers had watched their European allies sack and pillage the temples and the Winter Palace.

At the beginning of February, 1901, Togo received disturbing news of his mother's health and immediately asked for leave to go to her. Masuko—the once charming girl-wife, the youthful mother of the samurai, who had stood braiding her hair as she watched the black ships of the barbarians bombard Kagoshima—was now a shrunken old woman, her mouth sunken and her hair drawn tight to her scalp, a woman, living but almost mummified. Togo arrived in time to hear her dying sigh. She was eighty-seven years old; and eyewitnesses say that the admiral wept at her deathbed.

The Boxer Rising was important in its influence on the collective mind, the national consciousness, of Japan. Contact with European diplomacy and European soldiers greatly diminished Japanese respect for Europe. Japan had discovered that Occidentals were in no way superior to Asiatics as soldiers. She had also discovered that her European mentors, albeit worthy of admiration for their skill in the applied arts, were, morally, by no means their betters. Their glowing phrases and unctuous pronouncements, their wily circumlocutions, all too often cloaked nothing but vulgar greed. They were to suffer the consequences for this.

In conformity with the international agreement arrived at after the Boxer Rising had been crushed, the powers withdrew their forces from Manchuria. All, that is, except Russia. Questioned as to their intentions, the government at St. Petersburg replied: "Yes, we shall be withdrawing our troops. We shall carry out the operation in three movements." But not a Russian soldier budged.

Russia's ambitions and objectives were obvious. They were, most unfortunately, identical with Japan's. Japanese diplomacy began to feel its way, using certain discreetly worded proposals: it might be possible to envisage leaving Russia a free hand in Manchuria, on condition that Japan received a *quid pro quo* in Korea. But no: the Russian Bear was equally interested in Korea. This was really too much.

Too much, yes. But the mikado's advisers hesitated to face the prospect of war with Russia. Part of the trouble was the Franco-Russian Alliance. To affront two great European powers at once would be overbold. Brought up short by this obstacle, the Japanese military planners turned to their country's diplomats for help. No

146

stupider nor less obstinate than their military friends, they were not found wanting. They had their answer ready by January 30, 1902: it took the form of an Anglo-Japanese Alliance.

The text of the treaty was short, and, at first glance, in no way sensational. The high contracting parties recognized each other's interests in China; Japanese interests in Korea were recognized; both sides declared their freedom from aggressive intentions toward anyone whomsoever. The object of the treaty was described as being neither more nor less than the protection of these interests. But the real marrow of this apparently meatless bone was to be found in an addendum to the effect that should one of the high contracting parties be obliged in defense of its interests to go to war with a third nation, the second party would remain neutral "and make every effort to prevent other nations from going to war with its Ally." And if, nevertheless, other belligerents did take a hand, the other high contracting party would go to the help of its Ally—"would carry on the war in concert with him and would not sign a peace excepting by agreement with him." In plain English—Japan no longer need fear that any nation on earth would join Russia against her.

And what, meanwhile, was Togo doing? Togo, raised to the first class of the Order of Merit and presented with the Grand Cordon of the Rising Sun, Togo, whose manifold merits were now recognized by all the highest authorities in his country, had once again been brought ashore. He had been appointed commanding officer of a naval base which was being completed and armed in feverish haste and regardless of expense. The base was Maizuru, on the Sea of Japan, facing Vladivostok.

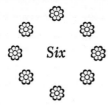

Six

I have before me as I write the illustrated supplement to the *Petit Journal* for February 21, 1904. Headlined on its garishly colored front page is the following: *8th February, 1904. Opening of hostilities between Russia and Japan. Sudden strike by Japanese torpedo boats against Russian fleet in Port Arthur.* Below this we are shown the Russian battleships sweeping a very rough sea with their searchlights, while the tiny Japanese torpedo boats bound toward them, pouring out clouds of black smoke: The side of one of the tsar's ships is being torn open by an explosion. This composition is probably a faithful image of the reality.

The news of the outbreak of Russo-Japanese hostilities on February 8th must have reached Europe by cable on the 9th, but the *Petit Journal* could not make use of it in its issue of February 14th because details did not arrive until later. Here is the article inside the weekly, which was so sensationally illustrated on its cover. It is worth quoting in full because it gives an idea of the European political climate at the time:

"Formerly, when two peoples went to war, they did not do so without an exchange of challenges. The knights of old sent a gauntlet to their enemy; monarchs dispatched a declaration of war to their adversary. 'Be on your guard; I am on mine.' This was good manners, and both sides knew what to expect.

"Of all the European nations, only England several times ignored this noble custom. Her ally, Japan, has now, for the second time, shown an astonished world that she has no more regard for such subtle refinements than perfidious Albion.

"As early as 1894, at the time of their difference with China, the Japanese sank an enemy transport seven days before warning the foreign legations of the declaration of war.

"They have just repeated this easy exploit, this time against the Russian fleet moored in the bay of Port Arthur.

"On the night of February 8/9, the Russian ships, having completed their trials, were lying at anchor, awaiting sailing orders. It must be admitted that this was signally imprudent, considering that the Japanese fleet was known to be in the vicinity. It was an imprudence which has cost them dear.

"Totally unsuspicious, they were not yet guarded by the powerful rays of their electric searchlights, and the lookout on board was no more than the usual watch kept in peacetime. This want of activity is, however, to some extent understandable. Officially, the state of peace between Russia and Japan had not yet been broken.

"Under cover of darkness the Japanese torpedo boats were able to approach the Russian fleet without having to cross a danger zone. Arrived within range, at about midnight they fired their torpedoes, and three of the heaviest ships in the Russian squadron were hit: The *Cesarevitch,* a battleship built in France in 1901;

the *Revizane*, a battleship built in America in 1900; and the *Pallada*, a first-class cruiser built in Russia in 1902. These three ships, notably the *Pallada*, suffered serious damage, although not so serious as the English newspapers were delighted, at first, to announce.

"Thus, war has begun by an act of violence, without previous declaration of war or notification of hostilities; and, suddenly and brutally, [Japanese] guns have set at naught all the efforts of diplomacy, and the hopes of peace-loving people."

The journalistic style reads as quaintly as will our own half a century hence. As to the substance, it should be remembered that a popular newspaper, then as now, is careful not to go against its readers' feelings: Japan, as an ally of "perfidious Albion," was unpopular in France.*

By the time the news of Japan's act of aggression reached Europe, the Japanese High Command had been looking on war as inevitable for at least four months. It was on October 17, 1903, that Togo, summoned to the Admiralty by Admiral Yamamoto, was told that "to all appearances, there is going to be war." Admiral Ito, chief of the imperial General Staff, was present at the interview· Yamamoto had explained the whole General Staff plan to Togo, as well as the plans of the Naval Staff. And he had added, "I have the pleasure of informing you that the High Authorities have decided to entrust supreme command of the fleet to you."

Togo's acknowledgment was a silent bow.

The work of putting the fleet on a war footing began at once. The ships that would do the fighting were grouped in three squadrons. The first two squadrons constituted the main line of battle, and were called the Combined Squadron. On December 28th, Togo officially took command of it, with supreme command over the entire fleet. His flagship was the battleship *Mikasa*.

* Which does not alter the fact that the account was a true one and that surely its greatest interest for us, in 1960, is the light it throws on subsequent events. The Port Arthur attack might almost be considered as a "dummy run" for the Pearl Harbor attack.—TRANS.

The minister for the navy, and the chief of the imperial General Staff asked him to give some thought to the question of which senior officers he wanted as his immediate subordinates. He replied that he had already done so, and handed them his list.

The names of the officers, written with a brush on Togo's list, will make their appearance in due course. But there is this to be said about them now: Togo's choice was so judicious that almost all these senior officers were to remain in their commands until the end of the war. It has been suggested by some historians that the real strength of the Japanese Navy in its struggle with the Russian Navy was that it possessed not merely one outstandingly able admiral, but a number of men who were capable of replacing Togo at a moment's notice. It may be so. But it was Togo who chose them: from the moment of assuming his new command, Togo the Silent, who might well have been supposed absorbed, exclusively, in the commands and tasks which had hitherto been given him, proved that he had at least one of the qualities indispensable in a high commander; he was a judge of men.

War had not yet broken out. The Admiral spent nearly all his time in his Spartan stateroom aboard the Mikasa. Its walls bore no ornaments; its steel bulkheads were not concealed under wooden paneling; and there was hardly any furniture. When action stations was piped aboard a Japanese warship, there was nothing to be dismantled, nothing to remove, nothing to stow away. What was Togo doing? Dictating orders and reading reports all day long. Concerning what? In plain terms, the problem of taking the Japanese fleet into battle with the Russian fleet in the best possible conditions and with the maximum chance of coming off victorious. This entailed, above all, gaining all possible information about the enemy. Hence Togo's absorption in the papers forwarded by the Intelligence Service.

Japanese agents were everywhere: in Port Arthur; in Vladivostok; all over Manchuria. They were even in St. Petersburg, and the Baltic and Black Sea ports. A number of these men were actually officers in the army or navy. Those operating in Port Arthur, working in the Russian naval dockyard, had begun by living and working for several years as coolies in Canton. They had grown pigtails and learned Chinese. At night they concealed themselves in clefts in the rocks ashore, whence they signaled their information, by means of lanterns, to apparently harmless Japanese fishing boats at sea.

From Europe, too, intelligence flowed in a steady stream. Information concerning the general political and military situation, for example: "Russian public opinion is still almost completely uninterested in the Far East; moreover, it does not approve of its government's active Far Eastern policy." Togo was informed of the ridiculously slow progress of work in Russian naval yards, and of the inadequate training of Russian gun crews. He was kept in almost daily touch with movements of the whole Russian fleet, whether the Baltic, Black Sea, or Pacific squadrons. A whole group of warships was undergoing refits in Kronstadt. At Port Arthur a heterogeneous flotilla lay at anchor—seven battleships belonging to four completely different classes; twelve cruisers, only two of which belonged to the same class; and twenty-five destroyers of seven different types.

Togo's intelligence reports informed him: "Ships built in Russian yards fail to reach the speeds contracted for. The armored cruiser *Rurik* cannot steam above 15 knots owing to the worn condition of her boilers. The battleship *Sevastopol* can do no better than 14 knots: a general overhaul of her engines is now being carried out, necessitated by the discovery of faulty construction; spare parts are expected from Russia. The battleship *Cesarevitch* is replacing the defective shell hoists of her 12-inch guns. We have confirmed that the range of operation of the 220-ton destroyers is less than 100 miles. . . . Work on the project of deepening the inlet and basin of the inner harbor at Port Arthur, with a view to rendering the squadron independent of tides, has still not begun. It still takes, as a rule, twenty-four hours to get the whole squadron to sea. The Chinese dock has been only slightly enlarged; it can barely hold cruisers of 6,000 tons. . . ."

152

Should all this make the Japanese resolutely optimistic? Optimism and pessimism were words which had no meaning for Togo. For the first time in her history at a nation, Japan was about to attack a European power. Handicapped as that nation might be by political incompetence in high places, by the mediocrity of her military and naval high commands, and by underground revolutionary sabotage, her fleet dated from Peter the Great, and was, in point of tonnage, the fourth largest in the world—after the British, the French, and German.* That was the fact Togo bore in mind as he made his plans.

Togo was about to attack this formidable fleet with a weapon which had cost the Japanese people, the people of a poor nation, a terrible price in self-sacrifice: in round figures, 213 million yen. Nothing was neglected. Togo's flag flew at the mainmast of the most advanced battleship of her day: 15,300 tons, a speed of nearly 19 knots, four 12-inch guns and fourteen 6-inch. Her firepower and armor were superior to those of the most up-to-date battleships in the British fleet. And there were two more of her class, as well as three only a little less powerful. Admiral Kamimura's heavy cruisers were among the best of their type. All the most recently built warships in the Japanese Navy were, in firepower—guns and torpedoes—engines, and wireless equipment, better than the ships of the Russian Navy. According to such information as can be gathered, the range of Japanese naval guns was, caliber for caliber, between 15 and 20 per cent greater. As for the ships' companies—we have learned to judge their quality. We have seen Japanese sailors in the ice of Chihli, in the snowstorm and tempest off Weihaiwei, and in the tropical humidity of Formosa. The enlistment of the volunteers who composed the best part of all crews was for eight years' active service.

* In point of number of ships, the Russian fleet was the third largest in the world; but in tonnage it was only fourth. Great Britain had 59 battleships and a total of 428 ships; France 30 battleships and a total of 421 ships; Russia had 19 battleships and 272 ships in all. The German fleet numbered only 209 ships, but of these 29 were battleships, giving her the advantage of Russia in tonnage.—TRANS.

January, 1904: More than one hundred warships lay at the naval base of Sasebo. Coal bunkers and ammunition magazines were full, and all war supplies were constantly maintained at maximum. The fleet was at one hour's readiness. From the *Mikasa*'s quarter-deck, where Togo took his few minutes' daily exercise, he could see and consider the formidable gathering of ships for which he was responsible. At this point it is important to understand the conditions under which he would have to make use of the mighty weapon his country had placed in his hands.

First, it was absolutely essential that the Japanese fleet strike such a blow at the Russian fleet, before it could be concentrated in Far Eastern waters, that it would be unable to prevent the Japanese from transporting their army to the mainland. Unless that could be accomplished, there could be no victory for Japan.

In the second place, this advantage must be gained with a minimum of loss. For the Russian Far Eastern fleet could be helped, reinforced, and even replaced from European waters. What use would it be to Japan to destroy the enemy's Pacific fleet, if her own were seriously weakened and therefore unable to fight again? The ships which Togo had under his eyes at Sasebo represented his country's lifeblood; their loss would be the end of her existence as a nation. If, whether in a first fleet action or in subsequent engagements, they were sunk, Japan would be as powerless as Korea, and as exposed to foreign domination. Such, then, was the value of the stake which the Japanese placed on the table when they played Togo as their trump card.

We already know the outcome of the gamble. We know that Togo did not disappoint his country. But it was not without difficulty that he fulfilled her hopes. Not without delays and hesitations, not without having to overthrow, avoid, or wear down numerous obstacles. And, probably, also not without difficulties of the spirit, inevitable because of the exceptional nature of his case: it had been his fate to be born into the Middle Ages, and to find himself playing a great part in the twentieth century. Our interest and sympathy for him are aroused at least as much by

154

his inner struggles and by his early lack of success, as by his masterpiece—Tsushima.

At the beginning of 1904, Togo was fifty-six. To the young officers who had been commissioned since the Sino-Japanese War, he was a far-famed warrior, already venerable. His career had begun before the establishment of the imperial navy; his exploits could be seen in historical perspective; his impassive reserve had made him a legend.

The entire fleet is under the orders of Vice Admiral Togo, a young commander was to note in his private diary, *and we must all rejoice that it is so. However, I am glad to be commanding a torpedo boat, which keeps me at some distance from him.*

A British war correspondent, H. C. Seppings Wright, who was also an artist, was granted permission by the Japanese Admiralty to spend a few days on the *Mikasa.* Togo received him affably and made him free of the whole ship. Wright observed everything, and above all the man on whom the eyes of all Japan were fixed. Tirelessly, he sketched and scribbled: "The admiral has a pleasant face, marked by lines of thought . . . the face might be that of any man of studious habits, yet there is something impressive in its expression. The eyes are very bright, black like those of all Japanese, with a slight fold at the corners, which hints at humor. The nose is fine and curving downwards, the mouth well-shaped, the lower lip somewhat prominent. The head is strong and shapely, the hair fine and cut very close. The face is framed by a sparse beard, turning grey at the chin. The moustache is thin and black." To this we may add a point overlooked by the Englishman but which, as we shall see, is not without importance. In January, 1904, Togo's hair was coal black.

February 6th, 1904: time two o'clock in the morning. In the darkness covering Sasebo harbor a white light began to wink from the *Mikasa's* mainmast yardarm: *Admiral to all ships . . . Admiral to all ships . . .* Aboard every ship the signalers of the watch stood ready to receive the admiral's signal. Commanding

155

officers of all ships in the Combined Squadron, the Third Squadron, and all flotilla commanders were to go aboard the flagship immediately. A few moments later dozens of small red and green lights were converging on the *Mikasa*.

Togo was in the reception room of his suite, standing behind a table on which lay a *sambo*, an unlacquered tray used exclusively for the most solemn ceremonies. On this tray was placed, not a tea service, but a single object, a drawn sword, short, pointed, its blade gleaming. The ultimate weapon—the one that a samurai turns against himself when even the longest of his swords has suffered defeat.

Togo looked at the silent and motionless assembly of officers, and spoke to them, softly:

"We sail this morning. Our enemy flies the Russian flag."

Then, after a brief silence, he added that he would begin by reading them the Imperial Order to the Army and the Navy, dated February 5th:

"In consideration of Our profound desire to maintain peace in the East, We caused Our government to initiate negotiations with Russia on the subject of the situation in Korea and in China. But We now find Ourselves obliged to conclude that the Russian Government is not genuinely desirous of maintaining peace. The territorial integrity of Korea and China has a direct bearing on the independence and defense of Our Empire. We have therefore instructed Our government to break off negotiations with Russia and We have decided that We are free to take action to safeguard Our independence. We count on your loyalty and courage to carry out Our decision, and to keep the honor of the Empire intact."

After another short silence, Togo read aloud a second document, which was his General Fleet Order Number One:

"The fleet will sail at nine this morning and will steer a course for the Yellow Sea to attack the enemy squadrons at Port Arthur and Chemulpo. Rear Admiral Uryu, commanding the Second Squadron, will take command of the Fourth Division, reinforced

156

by the armored cruiser *Asama* and by the Ninth and Fourteenth torpedo-boat flotillas. He will attack the enemy ships moored at Chemulpo and will cover the landing to be made at the same place. The First, Second, and Third divisions, and all other torpedo boats, will make directly for Port Arthur. The torpedo boats will go forward in advance and they will attack the enemy on the 8th under cover of darkness. The squadron will follow up the attack on the following day. The salvation of our country depends upon this war. We shall work together with all our strength to break the enemy, without losing heart, for the satisfaction of His Majesty."

The detailed orders completing this general order were distributed to the officers, who thereupon returned to their respective ships.

At nine in the morning the *Mikasa*'s anchor was raised and, with the whole imperial fleet at his command, Togo put to sea. The torpedo boats were first out, making their way between the big ships, each with its plume of smoke. The sun was shining, and a light breeze was driving a few rose-pink clouds across the sky. As the torpedo boats steamed past the *Mikasa*, the spectators crowded on the quayside and jetties, heard a faint clamorous cry, like the wailing of a child, whose noise just reached them across the water, indistinct but rhythmic. The sound was the voices in chorus of the flagship's ratings, transformed by wind and distance, calling a greeting, which was also a salute, to the crews of the torpedo boats. First, Second, Third, Fourth flotillas; and immediately behind them came Admiral Dewa's ships, steaming into their line-ahead formation—*Chitose, Takasago, Kasagi, Yoshino*, plus three armed freighters as auxiliary cruisers. Next, Kamimura's big armored cruisers, *Izuma, Azuma, Yakumo, Tokiwa, Iwate* and, in the middle of the squadron, like a redoubtable champion, the *Mikasa*. The crowds on the jetty picked out Togo's flag, the Rising Sun surmounted by a bar. After him came the battleships, *Asahi, Fuji, Yashima, Shikishima, Matsuse*. Astern of these came Admiral Uryu's cruisers, *Naniwa, Akashi, Takachiho*,

157

Nitaka, and the armored cruiser *Asama* which Togo had added to their strength. Last of all, three transports crammed with troops, their heads appearing above the bulwarks like thousands of black dots. No doubt they were staring back at the crowd that was watching them put to sea. Altogether, a magnificent and impressive spectacle.

On the following day, late in the afternoon, the squadron dropped anchor at Ronde Island, forty-four miles east of Port Arthur. Admiral Dewa's cruisers had scoured the Yellow Sea without once catching sight of the Russian flag. The troop transports, escorted by Admiral Uryu, were well on their way to Chemulpo, where the troops were to disembark. According to the most recent intelligence, two Russian warships lay at that Korean port. Admiral Uryu's orders were to destroy them.

A signal was run up on the *Mikasa,* ordering all torpedo-boat captains to come aboard the flagship. When they were all mustered, Post Captain Shinamura, Togo's chief of staff, showed them into the admiral's stateroom. With a wave of his hand, Togo invited them to sit down round the table, where he joined them. On one bulkhead was affixed a large chart of the Yellow Sea, and facing it a large-scale map of Port Arthur and the harbor roads. Copies of the latter were given to the officers commanding torpedo boats in the First, Second and Third torpedo-boat flotillas; those of the Fourth and Fifth flotillas were given a map of Dalny. Then Togo addressed them:

"Gentlemen, tonight you will have the chance, in Port Arthur and Dalny, to put the last several months' training to the test of reality."

The command of a torpedo boat, the largest of which displaced four hundred tons and the smallest one hundred tons, called for a robust physique, keen senses, and good reflexes. The officers gathered round Togo's table were, accordingly, all young men. Togo gave them their instructions in much the same manner as would be employed, nowadays, by the senior air officer of an

158

aircraft carrier briefing his pilots. In pointing out the positions of the Russian ships in the harbors, marked on the charts which had been given them, the admiral added that the information on which this marking was based could be regarded as perfectly reliable; it had just been received from a Japanese staff officer suitably disguised, who had got right into the heart of the fortress. No detail had been neglected.

Togo next reminded them of the need for caution in approaching their target area: all lights doused, extreme care in stoking to avoid flame or sparks from their funnels, and full speed ahead only when the moment came to launch their attack. Tactical details of the operation were left to the initiative of the flotilla commanders. Rendezvous after the operation—Chemulpo. Togo concluded his briefing as follows:

"Let me remind you that your attack must be delivered with the greatest possible vigor. For this is war, and only those who act without hesitation can hope for success. Our task, gentlemen, is quite simple, and all I ask of you is, be worthy of the trust I am putting in you, and for which I am responsible to His Majesty, the Emperor."

Togo rose, and all the company followed his example. They thought that the session was over. But at this moment the admiral's stewards appeared, carrying trays bearing glasses of champagne. Togo drank to the operation's success, and to the happy return of all taking part in it. He shook hands with the officers, and dismissed them, each to his own little ship.

The sky was clear; a light wind was blowing from the northwest. A signal was hoisted aboard the *Mikasa: Proceed to attack according to plan. I wish you success.* From the destroyer which carried the First Flotilla's commander, who was the senior officer, came a signal in response: *I answer for our success.* One after the other the flotillas vanished into the evening mist.

A little later the main body of the fleet also put to sea, proceeding at half-speed toward Port Arthur. At about one-thirty in the

159

morning Togo was informed by his chief of staff that flashes of light in the sky, cloud reflections of searchlight beams, had been observed far ahead. The torpedo boats had attacked.

Broadly speaking, the plan entailed three distinct operations: the landing of troops at Chemulpo; the attack by torpedo boats on Dalny and Port Arthur; the destruction, by the Japanese fleet's gunnery, of the Russian fleet in Port Arthur. This third operation we will follow by means of a chronological account:

February 9th, dawn: Order to the fleet's battleships and heavy cruisers to have their boilers at full pressure and prepare for action. Order to Rear Admiral Dewa to steam ahead with his light cruisers to try to bring the enemy ships to battle out of range of their land batteries.

9:45 in the morning: Dewa's cruisers in sight again and his report deciphered: the greater part of the enemy naval force lay in the roads outside the harbor. Dewa's cruisers had steamed within seven thousand yards without getting the Russians to open fire. Several Russian ships appeared to have suffered damage during the night torpedo attack. Dewa reported: "I consider the opportunity for an immediate attack to be favorable." Togo's order followed: *Formation line ahead First Division, Second Division, Third Division.* The five battleships led the way, followed by Kamimura's armored cruisers and Dewa's light cruisers.

11:20 in the morning: the Russian fleet in sight, maneuvering in the roads in the utmost confusion, in a hurried attempt to put to sea. The *Mikasa* signaled: *I am attacking the enemy's largest ships.* The battle flag was run up to her mainmast top.

11:26: Signal from the *Mikasa: Victory or defeat depends on this first battle. Let every man do his utmost.*

11:55: Change of course, the fleet turning west so as to steam past Port Arthur. Almost at once the *Mikasa* opened fire at eighty-five hundred yards. Hits were observed both on the Russian ships trying to take up station, and ashore. Russian ships and shore batteries returned the fire. The battle had begun. The Russians, six battleships and seven cruisers, achieved their line-ahead formation and steered a course due east. Broadsides were exchanged. The range fell to five thousand yards. The *Mikasa* was hit by three shells, one exploding near the mainmast: seven casualties, including a flag officer, but none of them fatal. Her masthead flag was carried away. It was replaced at once. The *Fuji, Shikishima,* and *Matsuse* were also hit.

12:20: The First (battleship) Division went about on a southerly course. The Second (heavy cruisers) Division exchanged shots with the enemy.

12:26: The Second Division turned south. The enemy, taking advantage of this maneuver, intensified his fire. The *Azuma, Yakumo,* and *Iwate* were hit. The Third Division (Dewa's light cruisers) exchanged shots with the enemy: all of the ships were hit.

12:37: Signal from Togo to Dewa: *Withdraw out of range.* The Japanese were breaking off the action.

This conclusion—or rather inconclusive ending—is a great disappointment. It leaves one at a loss, and under the impression that Togo had suddenly shown himself not up to the level of events. Some light can be thrown on the enigma of his behavior by giving his reason for what he did: the Japanese fleet broke off the battle because the Russians refused to put out to sea: their fleet remained well within the protecting barrage of the heavy shore batteries of the Port Arthur forts.

It cannot be denied that when we consider the concentration of the Japanese fleet, the torpedo attack, the final signal announcing that this first battle would decide the issue of the war—this simple explanation does not satisfy us. We remain under the impression that Togo had blundered.

Dozens of strategists have held post mortem examinations of the initial operation before Port Arthur. One reasonable conclusion emerges. Togo's plan of attack failed to take full advantage of the opportunity, because it was too slow. The situation as described in Dewa's report was extremely favorable, but it called for instant exploitation: a majority of the Russian ships had not even got up steam, and Togo could have opened fire on them before they were in a condition to move, and when they were still helpless to fire at all. True, there were the fort batteries. Even so, the Japanese would have had to withstand the fire of the shore batteries only, and not of the shore batteries and the guns of the Russian fleet.

But in point of fact, not even the shore batteries could have opened fire had Togo been quick enough, for at nine o'clock in the morning they were not ready! The guns were neither in place nor provided with ammunition. That, however, was not known until later. The Japanese agents who had given so much invaluable information had presumably not been able to get into the forts themselves. The total want of readiness on the Russian side on the morning of March 8th should have been Togo's highest trump card; but it was not only unknown to him, it was inconceivable. No commander in chief can be expected to base his plan of attack on the assumption that the enemy will be grossly negligent of his own safety. And Togo was peculiarly incapable of such an idea. For Togo, every Russian gun was ready for instant action and the roads of every Russian harbor were mined. It was always in his mind that Japan's naval strength had been placed in his charge; which, given the circumstances, meant the whole future of his country. It was his conviction that the treasure he guarded must be exposed only to the mimimum risk.

It is certain that had Togo brought his whole fleet up to Port Arthur, instead of sending only Dewa's light cruisers, he could not have failed of decisive victory. One can argue endlessly as to whether he was right or wrong not to take the risk of doing so, since he could not have known that there was, in fact, no risk at all.

At all events, by 11:20 in the morning the Russian shore batteries were ready to open fire and the Russian ships had steam up. It is surely no exaggeration to say that in these conditions Togo showed himself a sound leader in not trying to make up for the mistake of his initial slowness by a second and graver error;

162

as it would have been to persist in the face of definitely superior firepower. The temptation must have been great. It cannot have easy or pleasant to give the order to break off the engagement only seventy-one minutes after his *Victory or defeat* signal. But a commander in chief is no real war leader, no master of warfare, if he subordinates his tactical or strategic decisions to the preservation of his personal pride.

In perfect formation the fleet made for Chemulpo, its offensive and defensive strength virtually intact. Its casualties were four dead and about sixty wounded. While it was on the way, Togo received Admiral Uryu's report, by wireless, of the Fourth Division's action at Chemulpo. The two Russian ships found in the harbor, the gunboat *Koreetz* and the cruiser *Variag*, of 6,500 tons, had been destroyed, in conformity with orders, without the slightest damage to the Japanese. Details were not known until the fleet arrived at Chemulpo. Surprised by the arrival of an overwhelmingly superior naval force, the Russians, accepting battle with heroic determination, had steamed out to encounter the enemy. After an action lasting a little over an hour, during which the *Variag* was seriously damaged, the two ships had been forced to retire into the harbor, where they were scuttled by their crews. The landing of the Japanese troops had then proceeded without difficulty.

The five torpedo-boat flotillas which had carried out the attack on Port Arthur were punctual at the rendezvous. Several of the ships had suffered damage and casualties.

Shortly after this, the Japanese Intelligence Service was able to let Togo know the Russian losses. Two battleships, the *Cesarevitch* and the *Revizane,* and one cruiser, the *Pallada,* had been hit by torpedoes and had drifted aground. The *Cesarevitch* and the *Pallada* had been refloated, but not the *Revizane.* During the gunnery duel the *Novik, Askold, Bayane,* and *Diana* had been seriously damaged. The *Poltava* had been in collision with the *Savastopol* and had holed her, but not seriously, below the water line.

To sum up: although the plan to wipe out the Russian Far Eastern Fleet had not been an unqualified success, it had been so much weakened that it would not, for some time, be in any condition to dispute Japan's mastery of the Yellow Sea; and Chemulpo, the important base in Korea, had been occupied.

March 12th: Togo received a signal from the mikado: "We learn that in accomplishing its task of disembarking our land forces in Korea, liberating the west coast of Korea, attacking enemy warships in Port Arthur and destroying several of them, the Combined Squadron has demonstrated its great worth. We are highly satisfied and ask our officers and ratings to make even greater efforts." The final phrase expressed a certain reserve. Togo, in his acknowledgment, humbly implored the emperor to believe that the fortunate results obtained were due solely to His Majesty's greatness as Supreme Commander on land and sea. In the name of all his company he promised that great efforts would be made to win complete and sole mastery of the sea and thus execute the imperial will.

Before the introduction of aircraft and long-range submarines, there was a superlative, as it were artistic, form of naval victory, in which the enemy was decisively defeated in a great fleet battle. Most "classic" naval battles are of this kind, the simple and perfect form of sea fight in which everything is settled in a few hours. Such a battle is the naval strategist's dream. From such a battle, the victorious admiral emerges to return home in glory at the head of his fleet. And even though severely mauled in the battle, the winning fleet is more unquestionably victorious than any army can possibly be, not even having to prove its victory by occupying the field of battle.

After what had happened off Port Arthur on the morning of March 8th, Togo must have begun to realize that a victory of that kind—if he was to win a victory at all—was not what he could expect.

The Japanese Intelligence Service was still sending information.

164

The naval attack on Port Arthur had administered a kind of nervous shock to the Russians. The native Manchurian population was in flight from the coast. Russian officers and officials were sending their families back to Russia. The railway station had been besieged by refugees, and trains stormed by frightened crowds. The cutting of the telegraphic cable which linked Port Arthur with Chefoo—immediately opposite on the Chinese coast—had, by depriving Port Arthur of general news touching the situation in the Far East, produced a demoralizing effect almost equal to that of the bombardment itself. Detachments of the Russian Army guarding the coast, unfamiliar either with the outlines of their own or the enemy ships, were forever flashing back warnings of Japanese ships in sight, thereby increasing the general panic.

Meanwhile, the throwing up of earthwork defenses had been begun on the orders of the brigadier commanding the Seventh Brigade of East Siberian Infantry, General Kondratenko; the work was being pressed on with remarkable energy, day and night. And the approaches to the harbor were being mined, some mine fields being already in place.

The most valuable and least pleasant item of information, however, which reached Togo at this time, came from St. Petersburg by way of Tokyo: "It is increasingly probable that a large naval force will be concentrated in Russia and sent to reinforce the Russian fleet in Port Arthur."

A renewed attack by torpedo boats supported by Dewa's cruisers had been tried, but it had proved impossible to press it home owing to a snowstorm, and the result, this time, had been nil. It was clear that the Russians were determined to keep their ships under the protection of their shore batteries; as a consequence, time would soon be on their side.

Aboard the *Mikasa*, moored at a jury-rigged anchorage off Mokpo at the southernmost extreme of Korea, Togo spent several days conferring with Shimamura, his chief of staff. Shimamura had an idea: to seal off the entrance to Port Arthur. It could be done by sinking freighters laden with stone, cement, and inflammable material directly across the mouth of the inner anchorage.

If the operation succeeded, the Yellow Sea would be clear of enemy warships, the troop transports from Japan could cross unmolested, and the imperial fleet, freed from convoy duties, could try something else. Try what? That was Togo's secret. At all events, those concerned were given their orders on February 15th: "The operation will be carried out at 3:30 in the morning of the fourth day after the squadron puts to sea, and any enemy ship attempting to interfere with it is to be destroyed. A torpedo boat will be attached to each blockship, to pick up survivors." No one thought there would be many survivors from the blockship crews. The crews would, accordingly, have to be composed of volunteers.

When volunteers were called for on the *Shikishima*, with the order, "Volunteers, one pace forward, march!" the entire crew took one pace forward. The number of volunteers obtained from the whole fleet was twenty times the number required. Seventy-seven were chosen, five being executive officers and five engineer officers.

These picked men manned the block ships on February 19th. Togo invited the officers to dinner and solemnly drank their health. At four in the afternoon of February 22nd the fleet put to sea and at five in the afternoon of the 23rd dropped anchor twenty miles southwest of Ronde Island (forty-four miles east of Port Arthur). Shortly thereafter the blockships and their torpedo-boat escorts steamed away westward.

The sun was setting. The five heavily laden old tramp steamers moved slowly through the calm sea, and for once the honors were for them, not for the warships. As they steamed past the fleet, the ships' bands greeted them with music, and the ships' companies lining the bulwarks cheered them loudly, no doubt with the customary cry of *Banzai!* Against the flaming western sky the dark outline of the *Mikasa* stood out starkly, and it was on her that the eyes of the men manning the blockships were fixed.

At sea off Port Arthur on February 24th, Togo received a report of the operation from Dewa, who had again been sent forward as an observer. Only two of the blockships had been scuttled across the harbor mouth; two others had run aground on the rocks; the fifth was not to be found. The attempt to block the harbor had failed. Later it was learned that the blockship crews had behaved magnificently, heroically steering full steam ahead in line-abreast under a hail of shot and shell from Russian guns and machine guns, directly into the blinding glare of the Russian searchlights, which made it impossible for the Japanese pilots to see. The torpedo boats had carried out torpedo attacks and done their best to attract enemy attention to themselves. They had, moreover, cruised about the spot until eight in the morning, when it was broad daylight, making sure that no survivors from the blockships had been overlooked. Of the seventy-seven picked volunteers, only ten lost their lives. But the tactical outcome of the operation was exactly nil.

Proof was soon forthcoming, for the next morning, Dewa, cruising off Port Arthur, sighted three enemy ships at sea: two cruisers, *Askold* and *Novik*, and the heavy cruiser *Bayane*; they had clearly not been prevented from leaving the harbor. Dewa immediately informed Togo by wireless, and gave chase. Togo, too, joined in the hunt, barely missing a drifting Russian mine. They were too late. The Russians were again under cover of their land batteries.

The Japanese battleships and cruisers, setting their guns at maximum elevation, began a bombardment of the town, docks, and ships, firing over the Golden Hill. For five-and-twenty minutes Togo's guns thundered. But they could not bring the Russian fleet out of Port Arthur.

Shortly before the end of February, Togo received an interesting item of intelligence from inside Port Arthur: "There is much

167

talk in military and naval circles here about the imminent arrival of Admiral Makarov. His arrival is awaited with high hopes and much excitement."

Now Togo was the man who, as principal of the Naval College, had had Makarov's *Reflections on Tactics* translated into Japanese. And he had, to some extent, made Makarov his model.

The two sailors were about the same age, but the Russian had begun his career in a navy already ripe in tradition and experience. As a lieutenant he had invented a mat for sealing off leaks in a ship's hull, which was adopted in all navies. During the Russo-Turkish War of 1877–1878, he had distinguished himself by forcing an entrance to the harbor of Batum at night, and there torpedoing and sinking several enemy ships. At the time, the self-propelling torpedoes which he had used were as new and sensational as they were capricious. Makarov had also invented a type of caisson by which ships could be repaired without being put into dry dock. He had been responsible for the nose cap which gives a shell more power of penetration, and for the idea of ice-breakers for arctic waters. In addition to all this, he had published books on oceanography, crew training, gunnery, shipbuilding and on naval tactics.

Makarov, the son of a petty officer, because of his plebeian origin, had had the greatest difficulty in making his way into the exclusive caste of the tsar's naval officers. He was, without any question and by a very long margin, the most intelligent, able and—as he was shortly to prove—courageous of the Russian admirals. He was worshiped by his ratings, to some extent because of his modest parentage, but also because he was accustomed to speak to them without either insulting or striking them. On the lower deck he was known as The Beard, a nickname which was not a pejorative but was due to his magnificent beard which, parted in the middle, flowed luxuriantly over his chest.

Since the beginning of the war, while the fight for Port Arthur was going on, the fleet in Port Arthur had been commanded by the incompetent Admiral Stark, while Makarov was kept at

168

Kronstadt. At last some glimmering of sense had filtered through the amorphous Russian bureaucracy. Makarov was now on his way and soon to arrive at Port Arthur.

The news was made official by the Russians at Port Arthur, who could hardly contain their joy. British and American newsmen began making the wires hum with the conjoined names of Makarov and Togo. European and American newspapers published articles under headlines of this order: *Sensational Duel. The White Admiral Versus the Yellow Admiral.*

Togo kept his own council. Thoughtful before his big chart of the Yellow Sea, he sent Kamimura with a squadron of heavy cruisers to take action against the Russian cruisers which, from their base in Vladivostok, had begun raiding attacks in the Strait of Korea. And he established a cruiser patrol across the Narrows, between his provisional base in the Hall Islands and the Shantung Peninsula.

Makarov arrived in Port Arthur on March 8th. Stark had flown his flag on the battleship *Petropavlovsk.* Makarov preferred to make the cruiser *Askold* his flagship. True, she was only of five thousand tons, but she was the greyhound of the fleet, with a speed of twenty-three knots. That choice seemed significant. Western war correspondents began sending home stories which read like contributions to the sports page. There was speculation as to which of the duelists would strike the first blow. It did not last long. On March 9th Togo launched his fourth attack on Port Arthur.

As usual, the Japanese torpedo boats went in first. But this time they met with opposition before reaching the outworks of the harbor: Makarov had patrols at sea. The little ships engaged in a furious cannonade at three hundred, then two hundred yards, down to almost point-blank range. There was no decisive result, and the Russian big ships did not emerge from harbor.

There was a feeling that things would be different, however, on the next day, March 10th. A Russian torpedo boat, the *Steregoustchy,* was caught and cut off by the Japanese Third Squadron.

She fought gallantly, at point-blank range, until she could fight no more, her engines smashed and her crew lying dead at their posts. The Japanese took her in tow, sure of their prize. But, unknown to them, two Russian survivors had shut themselves in the engine room; rather than see their ship captured, they opened the stopcocks and scuttled her at the sacrifice of their own lives.

This tragic little battle had been anxiously watched from Port Arthur. Presently, a cruiser put out, to help or avenge the little *Steregoustchy*. She was the *Novik*, and she was soon followed by the *Askold*. But the blue cross of St. Andrew, Makarov's flag, no longer flew from the *Askold*'s mainmast but from the *Novik*. Makarov had transferred to the first ship ready to put out, so as to take charge of the fight in person as quickly as possible.

However, there was no battle. The *Novik* and the *Askold*, steaming in pursuit of the Japanese torpedo boats, came within range of the main body of Togo's fleet. Unless he was prepared to sacrifice two cruisers, there was only one thing to be done, and Makarov did it; he put about and returned to harbor.

Nevertheless, this sortie had made an impression, and not only among the Russians. The Japanese considered that here was one Russian, at least, who behaved like a samurai.

Makarov had hardly made fast his ship, and the cheers which greeted him were still sounding bravely through the port, when they were drowned by the din of exploding shells: 208 of them —12-inch shells—came screaming over the Laotieh Shan. The tide was low, the Russian fleet caught as in a net, unable to move; and the shore batteries, masked by the mountain or their range too short, could not return Togo's fire.

Togo had foreseen this, had thought it all out in detail. Day by day he was perfecting and organizing this kind of battle of attrition, which circumstances forced on him. The bombardment over, Togo returned to his base in the Hall Islands. He had work to do—regrouping the squadrons, studying reports of damage and casualties, sending one or more ships home for a refit, checking stores and provisions—in short, he had to carry on with the administration of the fleet as if he were an accountant, so precious was it; and so impatient for battle that not the least of his contributions to maintaining its morale at a peak was that of husbanding its strength. For the Japanese imperial fleet had no need of a Makarov to restore its confidence and energy; what it needed was a man who would keep it in a state of immediate readiness twenty-four hours a day; and who, the moment Makarov tried to get his fleet out of the trap of Port Arthur—and try it he would, that was obvious—would be prepared to bring the Russian instantly to battle. Such a man was Admiral Togo.

Almost always alone in his stateroom aboard the *Mikasa*, almost constantly smoking his pipe, drinking his cup of sake after each meal, Togo seemed, while his fleet lay at anchor, to be husbanding his own strength much as he husbanded his fleet's. Those who had dealings with him at the time received the impression that they were talking with a naval-base commander relaxing in all the tranquillity of peacetime. Togo received visitors seated on a swivel chair at his desk, and would indicate that they were to be seated by a gesture toward the couch. There would be maps and charts spread out on the table. The bulkheads were decorated with a few drawings, mostly representing his first battles off Port Arthur; they were the work of the admiral's chief steward, and by no means masterpieces of art, but Togo was attached to his devoted servant. If a visitor happened to refer to the drawings, the admiral made no answer, but glanced at them; and his dark eyes would gleam suddenly with a feeling that was part malice, part kindness.

Ashore, the winter campaign was proceeding. Along the wretched, muddy roads of Korea, the Japanese soldiers made their way, advancing relentlessly, marching twenty miles a day, each man with a sixty-pound pack on his back. Distance, cold, fatigue, and privation were their most dangerous enemies.

Not that the Russian infantryman was a bad soldier. In defense, he was outstandingly good. But though the Russian troops were

171

perfectly capable of holding and throwing back a direct attack by the enemy, they seemed incompetent to maneuver in the field, and the Japanese had only to make a swift and energetic flank or enveloping movement to force the Russians into a hasty retreat. The Russian want of flexibility was, for the most part, a product of the Russian staff officers' immoderate attachment to railway lines. It was not strategy they had in mind, but personal comfort. The example was set in the highest ranks.

At the beginning of the war, Admiral Alekseev, governor general of all Russia's Far Eastern territories, and supreme commander on land and sea, had a special train at his disposal: it included drawing-room cars, a restaurant car, and sleeping cars. The train was long, since the admiral's staff was composed of a crowd of gorgeously uniformed officers. When this train was on the move, it was preceded by a sort of pilot train, or shield train, in case of mines, attacks, or attempts at assassination. As Admiral Alekseev loathed traveling at night, and was accustomed to rising very late, his train spent the night and the best part of the morning in some station, or shunted onto a siding. Moreover, the admiral could not bear to have his sleep disturbed by locomotive whistles, consequently, all railway traffic in the neighborhood was stopped as soon as he went to bed.

When Admiral Alekseev was relieved of his post and replaced by General Kuropatkin, the general insisted that he, too, must have his special train. His chief of staff thereupon demanded a like privilege, an example that was promptly followed by all army corps commanders. The thing became a matter of prestige, almost a point of honor. And since each general was anxious to leave his comfortable home on wheels as rarely as possible, it followed that all military operations must, as often as possible, be confined to the near neighborhood of railway lines. Whence arose a certain tactical and strategic rigidity in the conduct of the Russian defense of Manchuria.

At sea, Togo lay on watch over the Russian fleet, and tirelessly kept up his high-elevation bombardment of Port Arthur. A cruiser,

172

posted at the harbor mouth, acted as observer for the gunners. But Makarov had realized what was happening, and by placing an observation post on a hilltop, he enabled his own battleships to return the Japanese long-distance fire.

On March 22nd the *Petropavlosk*, the *Sevastopol*, the *Pobeda*, and the *Peresvet* put out from harbor. Togo immediately sent Dewa and his light cruisers to draw them into the open sea, but in vain. The four ships persisted in hugging the coast, keeping within the protection of their land batteries. However, on the following day, Togo learned that Makarov had taken advantage of this brief cruise to give the ships' companies some training in close-formation maneuvers. The Japanese spies were also able to let Togo know that the battleships' gun mountings had been modified and the range tables lengthened. This last item was important, for it meant that Makarov intended to come out and fight a gunnery battle. Impossible, however, to discover when. Togo decided not to wait and be satisfied with his long-range bombardment of Port Arthur; he gave orders to make another attempt to block the harbor mouth.

This time the blockships were armed with small guns, not so much as a means of fighting back when the Russians shelled them, as for their psychological effect on the crews.

Volunteers were as numerous as on the first occasion, and included all the survivors of the original attempt. However, only the officers, whose experience would be valuable, were accepted, Togo refusing to let the same men take the same appalling risks a second time.

This attack was the sixth that Togo had directed against Port Arthur, and, like the others, it failed. Despite the unbelievable bravery of blockship and torpedo-boat crews, the way into Port Arthur remained open.

On the following day Togo wrote, with his own hand, a funeral oration for one of his officers, Hirose Takeo, killed during this action. He then sent off a long signal to General Staff Headquarters. Those who had not seen this signal thought that Togo

173

was making his report, and probably adding that he was now giving up all idea of blocking the entrance to Port Arthur. But his chief of staff and his cipher officer knew better: Togo had made his report, certainly; but, for the rest, he had asked that a greater number of blockships be placed at his disposal. And there was something more: "While waiting to make a fresh attempt, I request that Captain Oda be placed at my disposal forthwith." Captain Oda was the leading Japanese expert on naval mines.

As soon as this officer arrived on board the *Mikasa*, he was closeted with Togo and Shimamura in the admiral's office. The chief of staff spread a chart on the table.

"Here," said Togo, "is a fairly accurate plan of the Russian-swept channels outside Port Arthur. We were able to fix them by the courses steered when their ships put out. Your problem is to mine them. If you can do so, we shall launch an attack designed to lure the enemy out of harbor. Do you see any difficulty?"

To which Oda replied, "None, Admiral."

The mine laying began late at night on April 12th. The night was dark, and the darkness was intensified by fog, rain, and snow. The *Koriu Maru*, with Captain Oda on the bridge, did her work escorted by torpedo boats. The poor visibility both helped and hindered the mine layer: helped her by making her invisible to the lookouts and sentries in Port Arthur, and hindered her by making it difficult for her navigating officer to determine his position. Fortunately, the Russians caught a glimpse of what looked to them like Japanese torpedo boats, and switched on their searchlights. Their beams could not penetrate the fog, but their luminous disks gave the *Koriu Maru* a bearing. At six twenty-five in the morning of April 13th, Togo received the signal he was waiting for from Oda: *Operation completed.*

April 13, six-thirty: Five minutes after receiving Oda's signal, Togo had given the order to sail—the fleet lay twenty-five miles west of Ronde Island. One of the fleet's officers noted in his private diary: "I do not know exactly why, but this time I have a feeling that something is going to happen."

The fleet had recently been reinforced by two new battleships lately delivered by European yards and christened with the names of two former Japanese warships: *Nichine* and *Kassuga.* It was aboard the original *Kassuga* that Togo had returned in triumph from the civil war of Hakodate. That was thirty-five years ago. A long time: and no time at all. Then he had fought as a medieval samurai, a petty feudal vassal; now he was about to try conclusions with one of the best admirals of the modern world.

Eight forty-five: signal from Dewa—*The greater part of the enemy force has put to sea and is engaging our ships.* At last! But no: confronted by an obviously superior force of Japanese warships—six battleships, four heavy cruisers, and four light cruisers, Makarov, with only two battleships and four cruisers, withdrew under cover of his land batteries. Togo did not give chase.

He had in mind the previous night's operation in the mine fields. With his binoculars to his eyes, he watched the Russian squadron's maneuvers. Makarov was flying his flag in the *Petropavlovsk,* leading the other ships in line-ahead. He was apparently making for the harbor. But again—no: the Russian changed course, bearing east, the other ships following suit. His attempt to bring Dewa's cruisers to battle alone having failed, he was taking advantage of being at sea to exercise the ships' companies in close-formation maneuvers again. And right under the enemy's nose! Well, why not? Makarov knew that if he could hold out until help came from Europe, which sooner or later it must, he was saved.

But what was that column of black smoke, rising so suddenly from the *Petropavlovsk?* Time, nine forty-three. Togo stood on his bridge, glasses at his eyes, watching one of the most sensational events of the war. As he watched, the black smoke thickened, changed color, became yellow, and then seemed to glow like a great cloud of fire. Followed the dull boom of the first explosion, then a second. The stern of the Russian battleship seemed suddenly enveloped in a whirling storm of flame. Then more smoke. Then nothing. Literally. Within two minutes the great battleship had vanished, sunk like a stone.

Aboard the Japanese there was a long moment of silence, then exclamations, scattered and amazed. Togo, on his admiral's bridge above the *Mikasa*'s navigation bridge, said not a word. But he could not prevent himself from walking to the covered end of the bridge in order to read what the staff officer of the watch had written in his log: *Nine forty-three. The* Petropavlovsk *blew up and sank.*

A few days later it became known that the greatest of the Russian admirals had been killed when his flagship blew up. The Makarov-Togo duel was over.

A number of Togo's flag officers came to him with the idea of making a signal to the enemy fleet expressing their condolences: this was in the new Bushido tradition, which was all the fashion at that time. Togo uttered a curt "No," and that, of course, was that. The admiral was obviously right: How genuine could the feeling behind such a signal have been? The mine which killed Makarov had been laid by the Japanese, with every intention of killing him if possible. A mine is not the most chivalrous of weapons, but it is a weapon, not a natural hazard. No doubt Togo would have preferred to defeat and kill his enemy in a gunnery battle on the broad ocean. The chances of war, however, had made it necessary to use a mine. Besides, it was not a question of what Togo might or might not think. He spoke for Japan. The personal feelings which had not been out of place in the old, feudal wars could no longer be allowed to count.

The Japanese mines had not claimed only that single victim. Half an hour after the *Petropavlovsk* blew up and sank, the battleship *Pobeda* struck a mine and was seriously damaged. The Russian squadron beat a hasty and disorderly retreat into Port Arthur, and it seemed probable that it would no longer dare emerge from harbor, even for exercises in the outer anchorage.

It was at about the same time that Togo received information from Headquarters of the General Staff about the forthcoming operations ashore. The First Army was about to force a crossing of the Yalu and invade Manchuria, where it was to be met and reinforced by the Second Army. To this end, the Second Army was to be landed—the landing operation to begin on May 1st— at Bitsevo (or Bi-Tsi-U), on the east coast of the Liaotung Peninsula. The admiral was requested to ensure the success of the landing operation by such naval action as he judged opportune. This was not a question, simply, of Port Arthur, nor merely of tactics, but of strategy.

The first possibility to be considered was that the Russian cruisers based on Vladivostok might take action against the Japanese sea communications. Without enthusiasm, but also without hesitation, Togo prepared to detach a force capable of preventing any surprise action in that quarter. One squadron of heavy cruisers, one of light cruisers, two torpedo-boat flotillas, and some auxiliary cruisers were placed under Kamimura's orders. The rest of the fleet would be responsible for keeping the Yellow Sea clear of enemy warships.

The second decision: the Elliot Islands must be prepared as a naval base for the main body of the fleet. This involved dredging operations, mine laying, and the building of piers and breakwaters. Togo knew all there was to know about such work, including the name of the man most capable of getting it done quickly and thoroughly. "I request that the fitting up of the Elliot Islands as a base be placed in charge of Rear Admiral Mioura Ko." Headquarters had every confidence in Togo's judgment, and back came a signal: *Request granted.*

"I request the immediate allocation and preparation of blockships for a new attempt to seal off Port Arthur."

Granted, without argument.

Such is the outcome of power of command. The swiftness with

which the General Staff gave him what he wanted was the measure of Togo's standing at home—and also of his share of responsibility. His countrymen were staking their lives on him.

On April 30th came news which might have been generally expected, and which, in any case, Togo had been expecting, and which, now that it had come, transformed a threat into a certainty, giving the future a new and less rosy look: the Russian Baltic Fleet had a new title: it had become the Second Pacific Squadron.

On May 2nd the third attempt to bottle up Port Arthur was made. It was at once the most considerable and the most determined of the three. Twelve cargo ships were used as blockships. They were all lost. A sudden gale of wind from the south, lashing the sea into enormous waves, turned a planned operation into a desperate venture. The lifeboats turned turtle; to those killed by enemy gunfire was added the toll of men drowned; the wounded, cast ashore by a raging sea, where the Russians were waiting for them, fought like demons to avoid capture. Almost all who had vounteered for the undertaking lost their lives.

However, on the following day Togo was able to make this report. *It seems that the harbor is now completely blocked for cruisers and large ships.* And, in fact, the blockships had steamed very close in to the harbor, and not a single Russian ship had since put out. Obstinacy and courage carried to the extreme of self-sacrifice had at last brought its reward.

Or so it appeared: and so, in a manner, it was, but in no way in the manner supposed by Togo and the Japanese. In point of fact none of the blockships had been scuttled in a better position than the more determined or more fortunate of those taking part in the earlier attempts. The entrance to Port Arthur was not blockaded. On the other hand, something else, something of which the Japanese knew nothing, had happened.

Alekseev had delegated provisional command of the squadron to his senior flag officer, Rear-Admiral Vitheft, at the same time ordering him, "by reason of the serious weakening of the Russian naval forces, to undertake no offensive action." Togo had believed and reported that the Russian squadron in Port Arthur was imprisoned at last; and so, indeed, it was, but for other reasons. The heroic fighting spirit of the Japanese volunteers and of all the sailors in the fleet had not been in vain. In war, no action long persisted in ever fails of a result.

There are men who seem to make their way through life preceded by unseen guardian angels, so easily does the road to success open before them. There are others who are obliged to rely solely upon their own determination and their faith in themselves to reach their goal. Such a man was Togo, and the gods of Japan, whoever they be, seemed to think—at least at the beginning of May, 1904—that he was worthy of the honor of meeting with the maximum of difficulties.

On May 12th torpedo boat Forty-eight blew up in the course of a mine-laying operation. Her captain and five men were killed, and all the other members of her crew wounded. On the 13th the steam launch *Miako*, moored at Cape Robinson on guard duty with the dredgers, suffered the same fate.

On the 14th, Dewa's division was steaming through thick mist, on its way from Port Arthur waters to the new base in the Elliot Islands, when the *Kassuga* collided with the *Yoshino*. The *Yoshino*, taking in water through a large hole in the hull, turned turtle and sank. Only one lifeboat got clear: it contained twelve ratings and a portrait of the mikado, which they had been anxious to save. Thirty-two officers and two hundred and eighty-seven ratings lost their lives. The *Kassuga* herself was so badly damaged that she required a month's refit in a Japanese dockyard.

On the morning of May 15th Admiral Nasshiba was on his way from Port Arthur with three battleships—*Hatzudze, Yashima,* and *Shikishima,* one cruiser, the *Kassagui,* and the gunboat *Tatzuta.* At ten-thirty the *Hatzudze* struck a mine, and a few minutes later the *Yashima* struck a second mine. Both ships went down, the *Hatzudze* at twelve thirty-three after striking another mine, the *Yashima* at six o'clock in the evening while she was being towed.

179

Four hundred and ninety-two men lost their lives. Admiral Nasshiba, a survivor of the *Hatzudze*, had transferred to the *Tatzuta*. The same evening, proceeding in thick fog, she ran aground on an island. On the following day the *Oshima*, a gunboat, run down by a sister ship at nightfall, sank. And at ten twenty-two the same evening the destroyer *Akutsuki* struck a mine and blew up before Port Arthur.

Eight ships had been lost in six days. On one of these days, and without even a brush with the enemy, Japan had lost one third of her battleships.

The British war correspondents on the *Mikasa* watched Togo with intense professional curiosity and secret compassion: Japan had put so much of her strength into his hands, and staked her hopes on him: and now he was bound to report these disasters. Togo was equal to the occasion. He remained easy and affable, making no allusion to the fleet's losses except in the orders designed to palliate them as soon as possible. It was, doubtless, during the dark days which followed that unlucky week that he finally won over the admiration of his whole entourage. Thousands of messages of sympathy, forwarded by the Admiralty, poured in from his countrymen, both friends and strangers. It may be doubted whether he had leisure to read them.

There was at least one, however, which was brought to his attention; it was a postcard, obviously written by a schoolgirl, and signed only with her given name: *Mister Togo, please take great care of yourself.* Togo looked thoughtfully at that awkward, childish writing. All that we know about him—and it is not much, for he revealed so little—must lead us to think that adulation made no impression on him and did not interest him, yet that card may well have made him ponder. A lesser man might have shrunk from what it revealed: that the men who ruled Japan had done nothing to prevent an unprecedented concentration of national responsibility upon his person; they had even encouraged it.

On June 6th Vice Admiral Togo received the signal promoting

him to Admiral's rank, the highest in the Imperial Navy. His new flag, a red sun with rays on a white ground, innocent of border, was run up to the *Mikasa's* mainmast head.

On the same day General Nogi landed at the head of the Third Japanese Army in the Bay of Talien Wan, on the east of the Kwantung Peninsula. The Third Army's objective was Port Arthur. The place was a fortress, and so well provided with natural defenses that it could not be taken from the sea alone; there had never been any question of that. All that had been hoped for was that the Russian fleet could be lured out of harbor, brought to battle, and destroyed. That had not proved possible. Admiral Togo and General Nogi had now to meet and coordinate their plans to combine forces and crush Port Arthur between the Japanese land and sea forces. The two leaders met and agreed on the actions to be taken.

On June 23rd, at four-thirty in the morning, the Japanese torpedo boat on watch at the entrance to Port Arthur made a signal to Dewa, who was patrolling the offshore waters with his cruisers: *Enemy ships in harbor getting under way.* Dewa made a signal to Togo at once, and at eight-thirty a second: *The enemy squadron is putting to sea.* It was a fact: the Russians were preparing to sail. Togo knew, by then, exactly how long it would take them and, consequently, how much time he had at his disposal. His wireless operators had already signaled orders to the fleet and fixed a general rendezvous.

At about eleven Vitheft's ships appeared in the harbor mouth, proceeding with incredibly slow caution behind a screen of mine-sweepers, feeling their way through the channel, and sweeping it for good measure as they went. At three in the afternoon the first sound of gunfire gave Togo a hint as to where he should seek the enemy. Two flotillas of Japanese destroyers had attacked the Russian minesweepers, and the Russians had counterattacked. Three hours later Togo had the enemy's line of battle clear in his binoculars.

The *Cesarevitch*, Admiral Vitheft's flagship, was leading the line. After her came the battleships *Revizane, Pobeda, Peresvet, Sevastopol,* and *Poltava,* the heavy cruiser *Bayane,* the light cruisers *Diana, Pallada,* and *Askold.* Starboard of the line steamed the *Novik,* leading seven destroyers. At a glance, therefore, Togo was forced to realize, first, that the harbor mouth had never been blocked at all and, second, that the Russian ships most seriously damaged by Japanese attacks had been repaired. They were all there, excepting only the *Petropavlovsk.* All the exhausting work of the past winter, the endless, watchful cruising in storms and snow, the night raids by torpedo boats, and the sacrifice of freighters as blockships, the careful and costly long-range bombardments, not to mention all the men and ships swallowed up by the Yellow Sea—for all this there was nothing to show but the absence of the *Petropavlovsk.* The price was very high.

There could be no question, however, of wasting precious time in crying over spilled milk. Under the golden light and blue sky of late afternoon, the Russian fleet was steaming slowly south. Ahead, the *Cesarevitch* was visible to starboard, and the distance was steadily diminishing. It must have appeared to Togo that Vitheft intended to make his way out of the Gulf of Korea, keeping close under the north coast of Shantung.

The Japanese fleet was smaller than it had been, reduced by the losses suffered in May and by the ships detached under Kamimura. Togo could muster only four battleships against the Russian six; moreover, these were all that Japan had. Only three of Japan's eight heavy cruisers were available—*Asama, Nichine,* and *Kasuga.* There were eight light cruisers, a veteran sloop *Yayeyama,* six flotillas of destroyers, and some torpedo boats. Finally, there was the old Chinese *Chen Yuen,* taken over by the Japanese after the fall of Weihaiwei. It was late in the afternoon, but, being June 23rd, the day would be a long one. Moreover, there would be a full moon. There would be virtually no darkness. And the Russian fleet was at last beyond the protection of its shore batteries and minefields.

Togo could, by this time, be certain that he would one day have to fight the Baltic Fleet, now the Second Pacific Squadron. Ought he to risk the Japanese fleet, deprived as it was of Kamimura's cruisers? Togo had no hesitation: his orders were already given.

As the Russians steamed ahead on a southwesterly course, Togo changed his own course to starboard, aiming to "cross the T" and so bring the enemy to battle in conditions advantageous to his fleet. His guns were at maximum elevation. In the total silence which reigned on the *Mikasa's* decks, the voices of the range finders could be heard calling the ranges from the gun-turrets: "15,000 yards—14,500—14,000 . . ." Togo gave orders to increase speed. In a few minutes, the battle would begin.

"The *Cesarevitch* is turning to starboard."

There followed some seconds of baffled doubt on the *Mikasa's* bridge. What did this change of course imply? The doubt did not last long. Following their flagship, all the Russian ships were going about to starboard, and on a northerly course. They were making for Port Arthur. Vitheft was avoiding battle, and once more Togo was frustrated by Russian caution.

Meanwhile, General Nogi's troops had attacked Port Arthur's land defenses. The Russians showed their usual mettle when on the defensive. Even so, they were driven back from the outer bastion, and their commanding officer, General Stoessel, ordered them to fall back on the second line of defense.

On August 10th, at six thirty-five in the morning, Shimamura entered Togo's office with a signal in his hand. The admiral was already at work. The chief of staff passed the signal to his commanding officer and said, "Same again, sir."

The signal emanated from the cruiser *Fuso,* which had received it from the torpedo boats on watch outside Port Arthur: *The enemy squadron is preparing to put to sea.*

Togo did not pause to wonder whether Vitheft was putting out in order to fight the Japanese or once again to maneuver within the protection of his shore batteries and minefields. When the Russians raised anchor, the Japanese fleet moved in: it was a rule, almost a reflex. Shimamura knew exactly what orders to distribute: a glance from Togo was enough to set the wheels turning.

Neither Togo nor Shimamura could know, of course, that three days earlier Admiral Vitheft had received a categorical order from Alekseev: by order of the tsar: the fleet in Port Arthur was to force its way through to Vladivostok, avoiding battle if possible.

While Togo was sailing from Ronde Island with the First Division, all the ships that were at Dalny and the Elliot Islands received orders to join their commander in chief immediately, and were informed of his course and speed.

It was about noon when, yet once again, Togo picked up Vitheft's ships with his glasses. Six battleships and three cruisers in line-ahead, with the fast cruiser *Novik* steaming abeam of the line. The sky was clear and there was a fair, brisk wind. Togo hoisted his battle flag and ordered action stations sounded.

The Russian squadron was steaming southwest at a moderate speed. The situation was strikingly similar to that obtaining on June 23rd. As on that day, and for the same reason, Kamimura was absent and battle would have to be joined without his ships. Togo's line of battle included, in addition to the *Mikasa*, the three battleships *Asahi*, *Fuji*, and *Shikishima*, and the new heavy cruisers *Kassuga* and *Nichine*. South of this group, and making up to them at full speed, Dewa's three cruisers were in sight, led by a third heavy cruiser, *Yakumo*. On their way to join Togo from the north were several other, older cruisers, including the former Chinese *Chen Yuen*.

We can transport ourselves without difficulty aboard the *Mikasa*: the battleship was 462 feet from stem to stern, and both funnels and masts were taller than later ships of her class. Looking forward and to starboard, we can see the Russian line of battle, and beyond it the heights of Port Arthur.

Togo's first care was to give the enemy elbow room, not to crowd in on him, but to let him come out, in case the battle ended

184

before it was started, as had happened on June 23rd. This was the reason for Togo's "Ninety degrees to port all together" order. The resultant line-abreast thereafter resumed line-ahead formation, steering east-northeast, the *Mikasa* astern. At one-fifteen the *Mikasa* opened fire, the rest of the fleet following suit. The enemy replied. The sea began to be dotted with the water spouts of shells. Togo changed his line's course to northeast.

The enemy were still maneuvering, and their next move was a starboard turn which seemed designed to bring them astern of and round the Japanese line. Almost at once the *Mikasa* signaled: *Turn to starboard 180 degrees all together.* Now the Japanese formation passed through line-abreast to line-ahead again, but with the *Mikasa* leading. Speed was increased to seventeen knots. This complicated maneuvering had, of course, a definite object: Togo was determined to keep his line at right angles to the enemy—to "cross the T" and frustrate Vitheft's attempts to give him the slip. Every move made until this moment had been orthodox textbook tactics. It was now three-thirty. A 12-inch shell struck the *Mikasa's* mainmast, killing twelve men. The battle continued.

Vitheft made the next move, changing course to port. His object was apparent: he was trying to get out of his unfavorable position, to avoid being the upright of the "T" which his opponent was bent on crossng. Above all, he wanted to pass astern of the enemy line. It was Togo's business to prevent him.

But he had to consider that if he signaled another "all together" turn, so as to achieve his object without increasing the distance between the fleets, the *Mikasa* would again become the rear ship of his line. In those days, when sea fights, at least fleet actions, consisted of gunnery duels between battleships, no admiral liked what we may call a "line-astern" formation, that is, line-ahead reversed, because by that maneuver the flagship, carrying the commanding officer, was not first but last to reach the best position for observation, decision, and action. To prevent this, instead of ordering a change of course by an "all together" turning movement, Togo ordered a change of course "in succession." This means that the leading ship alters course in the required direction, and the rest of the squadron follow, each in her leader's wake. Thus, like a great water snake, the Japanese line of battle turned west, then north, then east again. This maneuver took a long time. When it was complete, the two lines of battle were again steaming parallel on an easterly course. But Togo saw at a glance what this turn "in succession" had cost him. Vitheft had gained a dangerous lead, and with nothing to bar his way was steering for the open sea of the Gulf of Korea. By then it was about three-thirty in the afternoon.

If Vitheft escaped, if he succeeded in passing the Strait of Korea, it meant the end of Kamimura's division. His armored cruisers might engage one or even two Russian battleships with good hope of success, but certainly not six. And if Kamimura's cruisers were lost, there would be no hope of facing the former Baltic Fleet—now the Second Pacific Squadron—on anything like equal terms.

Moreover, with Vitheft in haven at Vladivostok, there would have to be a new siege undertaken, far from Japanese bases and from the arms and equipment already landed. It would leave Vitheft free to bring his ships out to support the new fleet from Europe. In short, it would probably mean the loss of the war for Japan.

Such must have been Togo's reflections as, to all appearances as impassive as ever, he stood on his bridge with his binoculars glued to his eyes and his face turned toward the enemy. It is hardly too much to say that at this juncture the fate of the Japanese Empire was in Togo's hands. His last signal still fluttered from the *Mikasa's* halyards: *Admiral to all ships: Make all possible speed.* The empire's fate was in the hands of the little lean yellow stokers aboard every ship who were now shoveling coal into their devouring furnaces for dear life. Stoking in warships at that period was a purgatory even at moderate speeds. Today not even the most hard-bitten Polish miner would work under such conditions. And what Togo had asked for was not moderate speed, but all possible speed.

Fortunately for the Japanese Empire, the Russian stokers had to keep under way ships whose real speed had never approximated at all closely their designed speed. At fourteen knots they were "all out." The Japanese fleet could make seventeen. Little by little the Japanese were recovering their lost distance. But their turbines were not the only things which were revolving: so was the earth. If Vitheft could hold a fraction of his lead until nightfall, he was saved. Togo's vital race was being run not only against the Russian admiral, but against the sun.

Every smokestack in the fleet was vomiting dense clouds of black smoke. The Russan cruisers had taken shelter behind their battleship line. Togo signaled his own to do likewise. There was no point in attempting secondary engagements. The important point was not to lose a second.

Togo was gaining on the Russians: little by little, but gaining. And it must have been slowly born in on Vitheft that he was not going to escape without a fight. His one hope, therefore, now lay in delaying his enemy by inflicting damage on him. So, at five-thirty, he gave orders to open fire. The first ship in readiness fired: she was the *Poltava*.

Naval historians have made a careful study of the Battle of the Yellow Sea. In the first place, the situation was dramatic for both sides: the issue of the battle would be decisive. Second, and far more important, this new contact between the two fleets was to be the fastest running gunnery duel ever fought out at sea. Witnesses reported that the vibration of the engines was perceptible even on the armored decks; it was even noticeable during the almost incessant discharge of the twelve-inch salvos. The *Mikasa's* mainmast, already damaged by the shell which had killed twelve of her company, was quivering like an oak in a hurricane.

Six o'clock: The battle was still raging. Togo gave his orders under a hail of shells such as no officer of his rank has since experienced. He was covered with blood—officers and ratings had been killed within a yard of him—but still calm and easy in his manner. Implored by all to continue his direction of the fleet from the shelter of the armored blockhouse on the bridge, he refused, explaining simply (like Beatty after him) that he could see the battle better from where he was.

The enemy line was not only sustaining the Japanese bombardment but giving as good as it got. All down its length, the Russian guns flamed and thundered, and the heavy smoke of each salvo drifted down on to the sea. From a distance it did not look as if any Russian ship had suffered damage.

In the Japanese line of battle a series of incidents and accidents had occurred to remind those apt to forget it that battle at maximum speed and maximum rate of fire is an appalling strain on even the best of equipment. Five out of sixteen 12-inch guns were out of action, either owing to enemy hits or to accidental breakdown. Fortunately, Japanese flesh and blood was even tougher than Japanese steel. The stokers kept steam up at maximum pressure without flagging; and the gunners kept every available gun firing at the maximum rate.

Six-twenty in the evening: A hit was observed on the Russian flagship: but it appeared to have made no impression. True, from Vitheft's bridge Togo's line, including the *Mikasa*, which had suffered serious damage, must have looked as fresh as the Russian line from Togo's.

It was now six-thirty, and, considering the situation objectively, there was no reason to believe that Vitheft's dash for the strait could be stopped before nightfall. Togo, in fact, had every reason, at this juncture, to feel that he had made a major blunder when he ordered the Japanese fleet to go about in succession rather than all together. A mere question of maneuvering was enough to lose him the battle.

Six thirty-seven: the *Cesarevitch*, hit by another shell, suddenly began to list, and swerved away sharply to port. The *Revizane* and *Pobeda* followed her, hesitated, nearly ran foul of each other, swung back to their original course, and steamed in a circle.

188

The *Peresvet* hove to. The Russian fleet abandoned any formal formation. The battle was won.

Two well placed shells were all that was required to change the course of the battle which, if not the most decisive, was certainly the most significant in its consequences, of the whole Russo-Japanese War. Nothing could be easier than to call it a stroke of luck. But we have been able to see for ourselves that luck was not always on Togo's side. Indeed, luck on occasion was definitely against him. But given Togo's perseverance combined with the law of probabilities it was to be expected that sooner or later one of his purposes would be accomplished. Of the two shells which hit the *Cesarevitch,* one at least was unquestionably aimed at her. What was a stroke of luck for Togo was the fact that the first shell actually landed on Admiral Vitheft in person. All that was left of him after the explosion was a blood-stained leg. His chief of staff and other officers on the bridge were wounded. The flag captain, Post Captain Juanon, kept his ship on her course and the line in the right direction for a little while longer. But at six thirty-seven, the second shell exploded in the blockhouse on the bridge, and everyone inside it was either killed, wounded, or choked by the fumes. The steering gear and all the apparatus controlling the gun sights were put out of action. With the *Cesarevitch* steaming helplessly in a circle, the whole Russian fleet behaved for some decisive minutes as wretchedly as a decapitated duck. Aboard the flagship herself, her second in command, at his action-station under the armored deck, did not immediately realize what had happened. He then ordered the signal: *The admiral hands over command to Rear Admiral Prince Oukhtomsky.* Oukhtomsky attempted to make the signal *Follow me,* but both his masts had been shot away and his signal was flown from the forebridge staff, where it was invisible to the fleet. Eventually Oukhtomsky succeeded in conveying the news of Vitheft's death to the fleet, and as the Japanese battleships narrowed the range, their line forming a vast curve which cut across his eastward

189

course, and as the intensity of their fire continued undiminished, he ordered the scattered squadron to retreat to Port Arthur.

Twilight was at hand. Togo, making use of his cruisers as well as his battleships, surrounded the enemy exactly as Ito had surrounded the Chinese years before, as night fell, off the mouth of the Yalu. And as on that occasion a beaten but not entirely helpless enemy contrived to regain his base under cover of darkness.

"Admiral Togo," writes one historian of this battle, "disdaining to put out his hand and take the prey which was his for the taking, gave the Russian ships time to break off the battle." Such considerations are of interest only in so far as they throw light on what was in Togo's mind. Togo himself never explained or commented on his battles, never spoke or wrote a word about them apart from his official reports. He died without once answering such questions as "Why did you do or not do this, that, or the other?"—except with a polite smile. Thus it is only in Togo's comportment, in a thorough examination of his orders and directives, that we may be able to discern the probable motives of his actions. To all appearance, Togo could have pounced on the demoralized and leaderless Russian fleet and finished it off. For a few hours, at least, he had overwhelming superiority, and the risk in closing in on the enemy would have been slight. Why, then, did he not take the risk?

Possibly Togo had been impressed by the immensity of the historic circumstances in which he found himself. Commentators are apt to judge the decisions he made on the evening of August 10, 1904, by the criteria established by famous Western admirals. To do so is to overlook the fact that only forty years before a European fleet had appeared to punish Japan as if she were a tribe of savages. Less than forty years before August 10, 1904, Togo himself had been fighting in medieval armor. The imperial fleet he commanded was less than thirty years in being. Togo carried on his shoulders an enormous responsibility for his country's fate, and he was fighting against the fourth—or perhaps third—most powerful navy in the world. The fleet now making for Port Arthur

190

was not the whole Russian navy. There were the ships in Vladivostok to be held in check, and the Baltic Fleet, to deal with which it was essential to conserve ships, guns, provisions, and crews. Togo could take no risk whatever, however slight, *without the justification of an essential victory.*

So on the evening of August 10th, Togo could and should have given the Russian fleet out of Port Arthur the *coup de grâce.* But his patient, slowly maturing professional skill and confidence had not yet developed to the point where he was capable of making such use of the enormous striking power at his disposal—the power of a modern line of battle. Togo was not yet ripe for the kill; he had not yet sufficient knowledge of his own strength. Instead he hung about his retreating enemy, bombarding the Russian ships from a reasonable distance and, as darkness fell over the Yellow Sea, once more unleashed his torpedo boat pack.

Vitheft was dead; the *Cesarevitch* dragged her broken carcass as far as Kiaochow on the Shantung coast where the Germans interned her. The *Askold* and one torpedo boat put in to Shanghai where they, likewise, were interned; the *Diana* suffered the same humiliation at Saigon. The *Novik*, after a swift coaling at Tsingtao and a remarkable raiding cruise to the east of Japan, went down with all hands fighting heroically to the last, off the coast of Sakhalin.

"Although the greater part of the enemy fleet was able to regain its harbor," Togo dispatched to the mikado in reply to the imperial signal of congratulation to his fleet, "we have other plans and are ready to throw ourselves completely into the task of bringing the war to a victorious conclusion." It was the war, not a single battle, that mattered. Whatever reservations we feel obliged to make concerning Togo's ability, whatever regrets that his talent was wanting in dash and fire, we must respect his lack of vanity. It is not so very common in either generals or admirals. He has been reproached for his failure to see that fame was within his grasp, that evening of August 10th, but how many irredeemable follies have been committed in pursuit of such fame?

191

Kamimura, after four months of ups and downs in his unequal struggle with the Russian cruisers based on Vladivostok, had finally obtained the upper hand at the battle of Cape Urusan on August 14th. As a result, his squadron was again free to rejoin the fleet in operations against Port Arthur.

At Port Arthur, Japanese Army artillery had begun bombarding the Russian ships, which were obliged to huddle together in the West Basin to escape the falling shells, as one takes shelter from the rain by keeping close against a wall. From time to time Russian torpedo boats made a dash out of harbor and tried to bombard Japanese positions ashore. On August 16th General Nogi sent an officer under a flag of truce to the fortress, offering General Stoessel "honorable terms" if he would surrender. The proposal was signed jointly by Nogi and Togo: "Our army has almost completed its arrangements for a general assault which will begin very soon. Once this attack is launched, the fate of Port Arthur will be settled. . . ." For the purpose of avoiding a "useless" effusion of blood, Nogi and Togo proposed the evacuation of noncombatants, and a surrender which would otherwise be imposed by force. These proposals were not accepted, and the general assault was launched on August 19th.

In the course of the next few days General Nogi and Admiral Togo were forced to recognize that their suggestion of honorable surrender had contained at least one incautious phrase—"Once this attack is launched the fate of Port Arthur will be settled."

For four days Nogi's assault had been maintained with massive forces and ferocious energy. By the evening of the fourth day the Japanese had managed to capture three of the outer strong points but nothing else. Once again the Russian troops had demonstrated their outstanding quality on the defensive. During the four days they suffered four thousand casualties; the Japanese casualties were fifteen thousand. Nogi realized to the full what he was up against, and on August 24th he wrote to Togo: "We have been made to realize that even courage without equal cannot, of its own accord, defeat an enemy engaged in defending a well armed fortress to the last man. We shall hold the

192

forts we have captured and, using them as bases, we shall take
the others one by one."

One by one. Togo found nothing to reassure him in that particular choice of words. His ships, damaged in the battle of August
10th, needed a thorough refit, not in jury-rigged bases, but in
home dockyards before they would be ready to meet the Second
Pacific Squadron. Nogi knew this. He would have liked nothing
better than to take Port Arthur at one blow, and so relieve Togo
of anxiety. But Port Arthur was turning out to be a very tough
nut to crack. After the first general assault, General Staff Headquarters sent an officer named Tokuya Izumi to Nogi, to bring
back an eyewitness account of what was happening. This messenger told the general that he also had orders to see Admiral
Togo, and asked if there was any message he could take from
the general to the admiral.

"Tell him that I am deeply distressed at the failure of our
attack," Nogi replied. "Our casualties have been heavy. I am
determined to renew and sustain the attack for as long as necessary." For some moments he reflected, and then added, "It may
seem out of place for a soldier to offer an opinion in matters
naval, but ask the admiral if it would not be possible for one
or two ships to be sent at a time to Japan, very secretly, so
that our fleet can be built up again to its full strength before
the enemy's naval reinforcements arrive."

Tokuya Izumi promised to convey this suggestion.

"How long do you think you will need to take Port Arthur?" he
inquired.

Nogi shook his head. "Certainly not less than three weeks. The
truth is, I cannot possibly make a reliable estimate."

The man from G.H.Q. would have liked to be able to give Togo
a definite date. Given a definite date, plans could be made, decisions
taken. But Nogi could not, in honesty, give him a date.

"What do you think about it all?" the messenger asked Togo
when, in due course, he paid his visit to the admiral. Charac-
teristically, Togo replied,

"Think about it? Nothing. We shall see."

193

It was at about this time that unwelcome news arrived from Europe. The Second Pacific Squadron was about to sail from the Baltic. More than forty warships would be putting out from Libau. The preparations were well advanced.

More than forty ships. Faced with the reports on the state of his fleet and his supplies, and of the refitting which was necessary, that figure was bound to make Togo thoughtful. As for sending his ships back to Japan for refitting one at a time, the notion did not appeal to him. He wanted to take his fleet home himself, and supervise the work to be done on it. But he could not do so while a single ship remained in Port Arthur; and Port Arthur still held out.

One of Nogi's officers came to see Togo at this juncture and told him that the general had decided to undertake the assault of a hill called, locally, High Mountain without further delay. Nogi was no fool, and he was ready to try anything and everything to help the admiral. Togo had sent on to him the account of the Second Pacific Squadron's readiness to sail, without comment; this, then, was Nogi's answer.

The so-called High Mountain was actually a hill about 670 feet high. But it overlooks the West Basin of Port Arthur, and part of the East Basin. After a three-day artillery preparation, the new attack was launched. Like its predecessor, it was only partially successful. High Mountain Hill remained in Russian hands, the Japanese capturing another of the heights, Long Mountain Hill, from which a part of the inner harbor was visible. Togo tightened his blockade, while first guns and then 15-inch mortars, were hastily installed on the newly conquered hill. Hastily—yes, for haste was now all-important. Mortar shells rained down on the Russian ships, causing them serious damage; on the other hand, the Second Pacific Squadron had set sail from the Baltic. It was no longer a hypothesis, a project, a vague threat, but a reality. The stems of forty ships were plowing the waves, and their destination was Japan; not one of Togo's ships had yet been in for refit, and Port Arthur was still holding out. It was October 3rd. Togo wrote to Nogi that it was absolutely essential to destroy the Russian squadron in Port Arthur as soon as possible. Togo, the admiral, had to write this to Nogi, the general. Rarely in the whole course of history has a sailor been obliged to address so humiliating a request to a soldier. Very dearly indeed was Togo paying for his want of boldness on the evening of August 10th. But Togo was quite free from vanity, and he counted on Nogi's friendship.

Nogi's answer came on October 13th. The work preparatory to a new attack on High Mountain Hill was not complete. That position would not, therefore, be one of the objectives in the forthcoming attack. Togo sent one of his staff officers to protest: it was absolutely necessary to attack High Mountain Hill before anything else.

"Very well," Nogi agreed, "but we shall attack on November 26th."

Six weeks to wait. It was long, very long. But Togo realized that Nogi could not attack any sooner. Meanwhile, he sent all his big ships to sea for tactical exercises.

On November 26th a mine exploded beneath one of the principal Russian forts—Number Two—and the Japanese infantry charged into the breach. Once again, they were hurled back; five thousand men fell in this attack, which was purely diversionary.

The attack on High Mountain Hill began on the 27th. In numerous documents describing this battle—even in Japanese accounts—the same phrase occurs: "After five days of furious fighting . . ." How else could those five days and nights of savage hand-to-hand fighting be described? It would seem, by all accounts, that the Japanese attacked more ferociously even than—for example—the American infantry at Tarawa in World War Two. And the Russians defended their position as ferociously as the Japanese must have defended Tarawa.

At all events, as a result of this fighting, High Mountain Hill was won.

One hour later the Japanese artillery was in position. Two hours later, these new Japanese land batteries opened fire on the Russian fleet. The first shell fell on the *Poltava;* her men had to scuttle her to prevent her from exploding, and she sank to the bottom. On December 6th the *Revizane* and the *Peresvet* were both sunk by shellfire; and on the 7th the *Pobeda* and the *Pallada.* The *Sevastopol,* towed into the outer harbor on December 9th, and there attacked for five nights by Japanese torpedo boats, in a continuous whirlwind snowstorm, was holed like a sieve, ran her stern aground on the sand, and there stuck, a useless hulk. The Russian squadron was wiped out—at last.

But this destruction had not been achieved only at the army's expense. On October 10th the cruiser *Akashi,* on blockade duty, had struck a mine and blown up. On December 13th another cruiser, the *Takassago,* had suffered the same disaster, going down with 279 hands. Nogi sent his condolences to Togo, concluding, "I hope that, now the Russian squadron is almost completely wiped out, you will be able to return to Japan."

Togo landed at Dalny on the 19th and went first of all to a point on the shore whence the *Sevastopol* could be seen, aground, without guns or crew, lying over on one side, the very image of courage at long last defeated. Having looked for a long time at this last of his adversaries, Togo went to confer with Nogi. It was his turn to tender condolences: in the course of his attacks on Port Arthur, Nogi had lost two sons.

On the 23rd Togo received orders from the Admiralty to leave enough ships cruising off Port Arthur and in the Strait of Korea to intercept the surviving Russian vessels, and to bring the remainder of his fleet back to Japan for the necessary refit. The Battle of Port Arthur—which was to end in Russian surrender on January 2nd—was virtually over.

On December 30, 1904, Togo, with Admiral Kamimura at his side, stepped out of a train in Tokyo. He was met on the platform by an officer of the imperial household who informed him that the mikado wished to see him at once.

"Very well," Togo replied, and the party of officers crossed

196

the concourse of the Shimbashi railway station and came to the top of the steps which led down and out into the city streets. And there, despite his habit of absolute self-control, Togo stopped short. For, restless before and below him was such a sea as he had never dreamed of, an ocean of heads and faces, from which rose a great sound, as of a storm. There were thousands upon thousands, wave upon wave of heads, and above them a foam of waving hands, flags, and hats. The cheers from this vast crowd were unceasing. The people of Tokyo seemed to have been raised to a state of exaltation by the sight of one man's face—the face of the man who stood disconcerted at the top of the steps, between gorgeously bedecked staff officers. The face they gazed at was not the one they knew: day after day of sea and sun, wind and rain, fog and cold, mist and heat had given their hero a mask of bronze.

Surprised—never before had any man seen Togo at a loss—he took off his cap in a motion of acknowledgment to the crowd. At that there was a moment of total silence, of stricken calm in the midst of the storm of acclamation. In that instant the people had realized what the war had meant to their admiral: his hair had turned as white as snow.

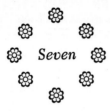

Seven

Immediately upon leaving the palace after his audience with the emperor, Togo had himself driven to his own house. He crossed the threshold of his small but leafy garden and saw his wife and sons lined up before the house to receive him, bowing with their hands on their knees. Until very late that night, he sat and talked with them; as usual, he did most of the listening.

On the following day he received the official messages of congratulations from the emperor and empress, and answered them according to protocol, using words prescribed by a rigid etiquette, and which must not be departed from. His first visit was to his mother's grave; his second to General Nogi's wife. She, when he expressed his sympathy for her great loss, answered him thus:

198

"My two sons showed themselves worthy of their vocation as soldiers. For me, that is consolation enough."

Togo's leave lasted three days. He then resumed his duties, going every morning and evening to conferences at the Admiralty. Present at these meetings were the minister for the navy, the heads of several other government departments, and a number of high officials. Their business was to prepare a suitable reception for the Second Pacific Squadron, the Russian fleet that was on its way from Europe.

First things first: the High Command. Togo had ready the list of officers composing the various staffs, as he wanted them. He read it aloud. The ministers looked at one another, then nodded. The business was settled. We need not here burden our memories with fifty names, all difficult to bear in mind: it will be sufficient to recall that Dewa and Uryu, both promoted to vice admiral, kept their cruiser flotillas, that Shimamura, hitherto Togo's chief of staff, was made a rear admiral and given command of a division in the Second Squadron, under Kamimura. Togo's new chief of staff was the newly promoted Rear Admiral Kato.

Needless to say, several conferences had to be devoted to the battle plans elaborated by Togo. At the time, of course, these projects were secret. Subsequently, the Japanese archivists and official historians revealed them, but only in part.

Meanwhile, "now throve the armorers," for, from dawn till dusk, and from dusk till dawn by the light of arc lamps, work was proceeding on the fleet in the nation's dockyards. Engines, turrets, guns, navigation and range-finding gear—all were dismantled, repaired, checked, adjusted, and refitted, with new parts wherever necessary. The fleet's charts of all the seas about Japan were overprinted with a grid of coded squares to facilitate the signaling of the positions of Japanese or enemy ships. Signaling stations were set up on islands and capes, and several new wireless stations constructed.

The *Mikasa*'s refit had been given priority. Togo went aboard on February 6th and on the 21st put to sea for the new operational

199

base he had chosen. Dewa was detached with a force of cruisers to reconnoiter along the South China coast; other ships of the fleet were leaving the dockyards every day and putting to sea immediately for exercises and gunnery training.

For Togo, the decisive battle had already begun; in fact, it would be fair to say that it had begun as early as February, as soon as he had chosen his operational base, since that choice, the outcome of his strategic thinking, fixed the geographical position of the Japanese fleet—the position in which the admiral had chosen to receive the Second Pacific Squadron. What had been his line of thought? First, he must have put himself in his adversary's place; second, he must have verified and checked as precisely as possible all the information he possessed; and, third, where there were gaps in his information he must have done his best to fill them with hypotheses based upon a balance of probabilities.

What, meanwhile, was the line of thought occupying the mind of his opponent, Admiral Rojestvensky, admiral of the fleet which was on its way to Japan? Obviously, he had realized that the surrender of Port Arthur left him with only one harborage for such a fleet as his: the only suitable port remaining in Russian hands was Vladivostok. The self-evident solution to his problem was to get to Vladivostok and, from that base, operate against the Japanese fleet.

There was a second possibility: he might begin by occupying some other port, in Chinese waters for example, as his base. But which? The Anglo-Japanese Alliance meant that all British bases were denied him. Would France lend him a base, or allow him to occupy one? Russian diplomats answered that one: No; France would remain strictly neutral, and Russia could not contemplate trying to force her hand for fear of provoking trouble with England.

China, despite the nibbling at her territory by colonialist powers, still possessed excellent potential bases at some points of her coast line. But it was known in Tokyo that in the event of Rojestvensky trying to make use of a Chinese base, the Anglo-Japanese Alliance, again, would come into play, a fact that was

200

equally well known to the Russian admiral. There remained Japan's own southern bases in Formosa and the Pescadores. Togo knew them well enough to believe that his opponent would hardly find them convenient: the anchorage was quite inadequate for a large fleet, and the climate and pilotage were both unsatisfactory. Besides, the whole world knew and had long known that these two places, quite apart from their natural disadvantages, were one mass of Japanese mine fields. All things considered, Rojestvensky was almost certain to choose Vladivostok.

From which direction would he approach it? The charts showed three possible courses. Rojestvensky could steam round Japan to the east and try to get through La Pérouse Strait, between Hokkaido and Sakhalin. The strait was narrow and easy to mine, infested by mist during the early months of the year, and could only be reached after running the gantlet of the Kurile Islands reefs. No admiral was likely to choose that way. The Russian might try to take his fleet through the Tsugaru Narrows between Hokkaido and Honshu; but this strait was also very narrow, was swept by violent tidal currents, was flanked by Japanese bases, and, like the La Pérouse Strait, was mined. Togo rejected this second hypothesis, and concluded that Rojestvensky would make his way through the Strait of Korea.

Thereafter he based all his decisions on this conclusion. He placed the main body of his fleet at Masan on the southeast coast of Korea. It was there that Russia some years before had tried to get a base for her ships. The basin, which is extensive and well sheltered, is protected by the island of Kose. The base chosen for the cruisers was Osaki, in the island of Tsushima, in the middle of the strait.

On April 9, 1905, Togo received an item of information that had been transmitted to him with quite exceptional speed and exactitude. On the day before—April 8th—the Second Pacific Squadron, passing through the Strait of Malacca, had steamed past Singapore. After a cruise of sixteen thousand miles without a base of any kind, Rojestvensky's fleet was entering the China Sea.

201

There is no want of sources to refer to when we come to reconstructing the Russian squadron's extraordinary journey; yet it is by no means easy to form an idea as to what really happened in the course of that strange adventure. Happened, that is, from the point of view of the thousands of men engaged in it, and of how they behaved to one another.

The evidence most commonly relied on by naval historians is that of Commander Semënov. Semënov had served with the fleet at Port Arthur and had been aboard the cruiser which was disarmed and interned by the Germans at Kiaochow after the battle of August 10, 1904. He returned to Europe, was attached to the Baltic Squadron, on the staff, and returned to Japan as an officer in the flagship. His account of the long cruise, and of the Battle of Tsushima, is called *Rasplata,* that is, Chastisement. Semënov was a man of keen sensibility and some talent as a writer. His talent is apparent in his book, equally remarkable for its thoroughness and its fiery momentum. But although Semënov had evidently made it his business to represent the Russian defeat as the ineluctable consequence—the punishment—of Russian decadence, he could not prevent himself—and who shall blame him?—from being what he was, a naval officer. There can be no doubt that, from time to time, he conceals certain mistakes, acts of stupidity and incompetence, and that he skims lightly over certain actions which did his profession little credit.

In addition to Semënov there are Rojestvensky's official reports and his depositions in the course of his subsequent trial. The defeated admiral made a truly noble—and quite systematic—attempt to cover his subordinates: that in itself makes it difficult to use his own evidence. And, naturally enough, there were certain facts which he himself played down or of which he gave a partial and personal rendering. The evidence of Nebogatov, another defeated Russian admiral, brought to trial in November, 1906, provides us with supplementary revelations concerning the "unforgivable defects" of the Russian fleet: he would have been wiser to hold his tongue—the court condemned him to death, a sentence later commuted to ten years in a fortress-prison.

Yet another famous source of information is Alexei Novikoff-Priboy's *Tsushima*. Three hundred thousand copies of this book were sold in Russia in 1933, and as many in the following year, plus half a million copies of an abridged paperback edition. This work provides us, in my opinion, with the most vivid and spectacular evidence, but which can only be accepted with a certain reserve.

Alexei Silitch Novikoff-Priboy was an assistant steward in the battleship *Orel*. His account was written from a diary of notes kept from day to-day, then burned when his ship was surrendered, reconstructed in a Japanese prisoner-of-war camp with the help of a dozen or more other Russian ratings, burned again during a riot in the camp, and again rewritten. Taken back to Russia after the war, the papers were buried during the Revolution, lost, found again twenty-two years later—in 1928—completed and the gaps filled in with the help of the U.S.S.R State archives. Meanwhile Novikoff, a self-educated man and a great reader of proletarian writers, had made a name for himself in Soviet literature.

Like Semënov, he has a good natural style, easy, popular, and vigorous. His judgments of naval actions are often stupid, and his opinion of the behavior of the tzar's naval officers full of Bolshevik prejudice, like his "choice" of documents drawn from the national archives for reference. But, all said and done, his evidence cannot be rejected. Too many passages ring true. I have myself, as a cadet-officer of the navy serving on the lower deck, lived with naval ratings. I have heard articulate members of a ship's company describing—and dramatizing in the plebeian manner—events of which I had been an eyewitness. Reading Novikoff, I sometimes get the feeling that I can sense the reality beneath all his exaggerations and special pleading. Still his account is chiefly valuable for what journalists call "color."

When, in St. Petersburg, the question of sending a fleet to the relief of Port Arthur arose, socially brilliant young officers in ward-rooms, naval officers' clubs, and society drawing rooms, joyously toasted the prospect. But the responsible authorities were not so sanguine. It would have been ridiculous to send only old and ill armed ships. On the other hand it could not be denied that the most powerful units of the Russian fleet had never yet made even a maiden voyage. The ships in question were five battleships, the building—or at least fitting—of which was still being completed in the naval dockyards at Kronstadt and on the Neva. Two of them had been launched in 1901, two more in 1902, and the fifth in 1903. And the work of finishing these warships had been carried on very slackly.

The experts consulted said that it would take at least a year to finish them. And, if they *were* ready, it must be realized that they could not possibly make the journey, since modern battleships consumed far too much coal. No battleship was built to steam from European Russia to Japan.

A great many things were going far from well in the tzarist Russia of 1904, but here and there were still to be found men who were interested in their work, especially technicians. A gust of brisker, fresher air blew through the administration offices; the dockyards began to work at a faster tempo. It began to look as if the new squadron might be ready by mid-September. And Admiral Rojestvensky was appointed to command it.

At fifty-six years of age and in full-dress uniform, the gigantic Rojestvensky was a splendid spectacle. His mighty shoulders glittered with gilded epaulettes decorated with monograms and black eagles. His vast chest displayed rows of medals. A stripe of silver braid ran down the sides of his trousers. His torso was crossed by the scarlet satin ribbon of the Order of St. Anne, and a tangle of silver aiguillettes hung from his right shoulder. Above this powerful and gorgeously caparisoned body was poised a face by nature severe, framed in a closely clipped pepper-and-salt beard. The black eyes gave expression to a will of iron.

Rojestvensky had never led a fleet, or even a flotilla into battle.

That was not his fault; it was history's. His command of the Russian Far Eastern Squadron during the Sino-Japanese War had consisted of conferences, receptions, and a few maneuvers. Rojestvensky had also served in London as naval attaché; and as chief of the General Staff in St. Petersburg. However, as a young man he had shown courage during the Russo-Turkish War: as captain of a small torpedo boat he had shown great audacity in attacking enemy warships.

He might, perhaps, have been less violent, not so quick to anger, had circumstances provided him with more opportunity to work off his natural aggressiveness. In default of that opportunity, he terrorized his own circle. At the 1902 maneuvers, when the Tzar Nicholas II and his guest, Kaiser Wilhelm II, were standing within six feet of him on his bridge, Rojestvensky, seeing a Russian ship make a mistake, stamped furiously on the deck and flung his telescope into the sea. His chief of staff went in fear of his life.

In naval and military circles, however, this kind of behavior was not particularly out of the way, and surprised no one; manners and the whole style of living were still, among many Russian officers, almost those of the old boyars. It was of no more consequence to insult a naval rating than to insult a house servant. Certain other officers, men who had read Tolstoi and even Gorki, took the contrary, the "humanitarian" line, lending their men books and encouraging them to exchange confidences. This inconsistency of relationship between officers and men was, obviously, totally different from the consistent policy followed in the Japanese fleet.

On August 14th Rojestvensky hoisted his flag in the *Suvorov*, which lay at Kronstadt. On August 25th the squadron put to sea for a short training cruise. On September 11th it sailed for Libau on the Baltic coast. The battleship *Orel* ran aground in the channel, as the fleet was steaming out; two days were required to refloat her. At the beginning of October, the fleet reached Reval, at the mouth of the Gulf of Finland.

There were still some details of fitting and training to be completed. Rojestvensky ordered more exercises at sea and was, if one may judge by his order of the day Number 51, not particularly pleased with the result. "Today, at 0200 hours, I ordered the *Suvorov's* officer of the watch to give the alarm for an attack by enemy torpedo boats. Eight minutes later, nothing whatever had yet been done. Ships' companies, including officers, were all asleep, excepting the watches, and they were half awake, and had no idea what to do with themselves. Not one searchlight was ready. No one took any action about deck lighting, although such lighting is indispensable to gun crews in action." On October 10th the tzar arrived to inspect the fleet. He made an appearance on the bridge of every ship and delivered a short speech to each ship's company. He called upon his sailors to avenge Russia on the insolent enemy who had disturbed her peace. Obliged, as he was, to repeat the same harangue, over and over again, he spoke without any spirit. The crews responded with the regulation three cheers. On October 11th the squadron put to sea, dropped anchor once again in Libau, where it remained until the 15th and then, at last, set off for Japan.

The problem of coaling had been solved, at least in theory. The squadron was taking colliers with it; and the Russian Government had signed a contract with a German firm which had undertaken to send large freighters laden with coal to various predetermined rendezvous on the squadron's course to the east. The Russians were also counting on the benevolent neutrality of France, whose government had agreed—in theory—to allow the warships to make use of their colonial harbors.

The Russian ships, painted dark gray with yellow funnels, made a fine appearance at sea. The dark gray of their hulls was visible from a great distance; and the yellow funnels were, in due course, to facilitate the work of Japanese range finders, but these two defects were not yet apparent. The main body of the fleet consisted of its seven battleships, five of which were new. The theoretical performance of these ships was excellent, especially in the matter of speed. Unfortunately, this speed had proved un-

206

attainable in practice; something always went wrong before the maximum was reached.

The range-finding gear was the last word, the same as that used by the Japanese. There was this difference, however: it had only just been installed in the Russian ships, whereas the Japanese gunners had had many months of thorough training with it. Russian wireless ratings and officers were excellent and intensely interested in their work: this made them all the more furious when, in a sudden concern for economy as inexplicable as it was petty, the dockyard authorities decided not to install the latest Marconi sets, as used by the Japanese, and substituted Slaby Arco apparatus, inferior in both range and quality.

Despite some inferiorities and the inexperience of technical-branch officers and ratings with gear which, in any case, was not completely fitted and tested, the Russian squadron still represented a redoubtable line of battle. But it was setting out on its immensely long cruise in very adverse conditions, and all hands were well aware of the fact. As a result these men, officers and ratings who were to show the highest courage under the devastating fire of the Japanese fleet, began by making themselves look ridiculous before the watching eyes of the whole world.

On the night of October 21/22, the fleet then being in the North Sea off the Dogger Bank, the depot ship *Kamchatka*, which was steaming behind the fleet, made a wireless signal announcing that she was being attacked by Japanese torpedo boats. There followed a wireless dialogue between *Kamchatka* and the flagship *Suvorov*:

We are being pursued by torpedo boats.
How many? What is their bearing?
They are attacking from all sides.
How many torpedo boats? Give details.
About eight torpedo boats.
At what distance from you?
One cable length.
Have they fired?

We do not know.

Give your course. Are the torpedo boats pursuing you? In any case change your course. Once out of danger give us your position.

At eleven o'clock, *Suvorov* called *Kamchatka:*

The admiral asks if you can still see torpedo boats.

We can no longer see them.

Meanwhile, the whole squadron had received the order *Prepare to repel torpedo-boat attack.* Action stations was piped in all ships, and guns loaded. The lookouts peered into the surrounding darkness. A little after midnight, rockets went up from the surface of the sea. The *Suvorov* switched on her searchlights and opened fire. The entire fleet followed suit, shooting more or less at random. Formation was lost. The "battle" lasted about twelve minutes. By a miracle, no Russian ship was hit by Russian shells.

As for Japanese shells, torpedoes, or torpedo boats, they did not exist. The rockets had been fired by fishing trawlers out of Hull, England. One trawler was sunk, and numerous fishermen killed and wounded. The Russian squadron went on its way, without bothering about its victims. The whole business made the worst possible impression. Great Britain mobilized a part of her fleet. Russia was forced to agree to pay a large sum in reparations.*

The Russian Government should have made an example— perhaps they did—of certain officers of the *Okhrana* who were entirely to blame. Before the fleet sailed they had sent in alarming reports, which were passed on to the admiral, according to which the Japanese had been buying small vessels in Europe with a view to making a torpedo attack on the Russian fleet in the North Sea. But even so, the fleet's reaction had been excessively jumpy, officers had lost their heads, and total chaos had reigned. This incident naturally had a very bad influence on

* There was a question of refusing to allow the Russians to pass the English Channel. And Rojestvensky's fleet was shadowed by British warships for many days thereafter.—TRANS.

morale, on the state of mind of both forecastle hands and the afterguard.

At Tangiers, Rojestvensky divided his squadron in two, himself leading the main body down the west coast of Africa and round the Cape of Good Hope; the smaller division, going through the Mediterranean and the Suez Canal, had orders to rejoin the admiral off Madagascar. Reinforcements, consisting of two cruisers, were to follow shortly afterward.

Coaling an old-fashioned battleship was not a pleasant pastime. The Russian sailors had to shovel the coal into sacks, their difficulties aggravated by the fact that half the fuel was dust. Their strength was sapped by the West African climate. The French Government, which had become much less helpful since the latest Russian reverses in the Far East, refused to allow coaling to be done in their harbors, so that it had to be done in the open roads, while the ships rolled in the Atlantic swell.

Cattle on the hoof was being carried aboard the ships to feed the crews. Once these animals had been slaughtered and eaten, the Russian ratings had to fall back on salt meat. It stank. No ship's company which is badly fed is ever anything but dissatisfied with its condition. Relations between officers and men became strained. The weather was fine, but the fleet was often forced to heave to or at best go dead slow ahead, while damage to one of the ships was repaired. On one point at least the dockyard experts had been right: the warships of 1904 were not round-the-world cruisers.

Nevertheless, the long cruise had to be completed. Rojestvensky's division of the fleet rounded the Cape of Good Hope on December 19th, set a course for Madagascar, and dropped anchor in St. Mary's Bay, near Tamatave, on January 1, 1905. On the same day General Stoessel was sending an officer to General Nogi, with orders to negotiate the surrender of Port Arthur. Rojestvensky's sailors heard the news a few days later: it was like being hit on the head with a club.

The squadron which had sailed through Suez arrived safely at the rendezvous, followed in February by the reserve ships from Libau. Counting store ships and colliers, the fleet now totaled forty ships. Not one of them but was infected by pessimism, and suffered occasional outbreaks of violence. Newspapers sent to the officers from Russia, once read and discussed in the wardrooms, were apt to find their way to the forecastles. The articles which were favorite reading were those contributed by a naval officer named Klado to the newspaper *Novoie Vremia*. Lieutenant Klado consistently predicted every kind of disaster, and the melancholy side of the Russian temperament took pleasure in absorbing this poison.

There was a sublieutenant named Virubov, on the *Suvorov*, who wrote a certain letter to his father—probably unaware that it would be opened by the secret police, and copied. The copy went to swell the files of the imperial archives—files which, in due course, were to provide the Soviet authorities with an inexhaustible source of propaganda:

"This Klado of ours is first-rate. Somebody ought to have attacked the Ministry of the Navy, as he is doing, long ago. And even he has not told a hundredth part of all the dirty and idiotic things which that splendid institution has done and is still doing to bring our wretched fleet to ruination. If, God willing, I ever see you again, I shall have things to tell you which not even the most heated imagination could conceive."

It would have been surprising if, in such circumstances, discipline improved. There was a stirring of embryonic mutinies, notably on the *Orel*, the ostensibly chief grievance being, once again, the quality of the food. Rojestvensky visited the ship in person. The reproaches that he heaped on the crew took the form of shouted insults. He asked that the ringleaders be pointed out to him, and the officers selected a few men, more or less at random. Eight ratings were shoved to the middle of the deck.

"Look at them!" the admiral shouted. "Traitors to holy Russia! Not one human face among them! Jailbirds' faces, the lot of them!

210

What did they pay you to sell out your country? Come on, I'm asking you what the Japanese paid you to sell us out!"

Shortly after this incident, foreign newspapers carrying long accounts of the events in St. Petersburg on January 22nd were passed round the fleet. An immense procession of workingmen, with their wives and children, estimated to number three hundred thousand souls, and let by a priest, Father Gapon, had gone to the tzar's palace "to ask for reforms." The demonstrators carried holy icons and portraits of their tzar, the Little White Father of his people. The troops guarding the palace had opened fire, and the cavalry had charged. Some of the papers confined their estimate of casualties to the generalization that there had been "a large number of victims." Others gave figures: two thousand dead.

This news would have been less pernicious in its effect on morale if the fleet could have put to sea and done some fighting. But Russian public opinion was now demanding stronger reinforcement before the fleet went into battle. As a result, Rojestvensky was waiting for a fourth squadron, under the orders of Admiral Nebogatov. This reinforcement comprised a number of old warships previously withdrawn from service.

Some historians have written that Rojestvensky was in no hurry to press on toward Japan. Novikoff-Priboy, who certainly does not usually spare the admiral, says that, on the contrary, Rojestvensky was so furious at the delay that he smashed up the furniture of his stateroom; and also that he "decided to drive his men so hard that they would have no time to think of their condition or of what was happening in Russia." The recipe is an old and well tried one. Maneuvers, coaling fatigues, dummy night attacks, landing and embarkation exercises—careening the ships' hulls—he kept them uninterruptedly hard at work. In fact, Rojestvensky rather overdid it; moreover—and it is here, surely, that he really was undeniably at fault—his reprimands were invariably wounding and delivered in public. This was hardly calculated to restore harmony.

As a last straw, there were foreign merchant ships lying in the anchorage at Nossi-Bé, and traders ashore. And the stuff most

211

readily sold, at a high price, to demoralized men, has always been alcohol—at least when the men in question are Occidentals. The officers' stewards carried tales of wardroom extravagances to the lower deck, where imaginations heated by liquor transformed them into wild orgies. Things were going from bad to worse.

It was, therefore, fortunate for the Russians that the Japanese Government continued to protest loudly in Paris against the Russian use of Madagascar as a naval base. Paris informed St. Petersburg that it would have to stop, and Rojestvensky received orders to put to sea. He left Nossi-Bé on March 25th, and, as we have already noted, passed through the Strait of Malacca on April 8th. His circumnavigation of Africa had been followed with keen attention and lively interest in all the world's chancelleries, and when the cables began humming with the news of his arrival off Singapore the whole European press was loud in its praise of the Russian exploit, including even the British newspapers. Thus, for example, the St. James Gazette went on record with: "We had underestimated Rojestvensky. We salute him with all the respect due to courage and energy." There can be no doubt that the Russian admiral had accomplished a remarkable feat in moving a large naval force so far from its bases. Nothing of the kind had ever been done before.

Togo had been kept well informed by Japanese Intelligence of the difficulties encountered by the Russian admiral in the course of his voyage. Those agents who watched the fleet through glasses as it steamed slowly past Singapore had some interesting points to make in their ciphered cables to Tokyo: the Russian ships were not good at keeping station; the battleships were so heavily loaded that their armored decks were often awash; and they did not fail to notice the striking, almost black, paint of the hulls, and the glaring yellow of the funnels.

On April 14th the admiral of the Japanese fleet learned that the Russian squadron had dropped anchor in the bay of Kam Renh, on the coast of Annam, and had carried out a fleet exercise. On the 26th, he learned that it was at Wanfrong, forty miles

212

farther north. On May 13th news reached Togo that Rojestvensky had been joined by Nebogatov at the head of the fourth squadron. Whatever might be the value of this reinforcement, it had turned up and it would count for something in the coming battle. On May 18th a Japanese agent forwarded the information that "a large fleet of fifty ships flying a flag with a blue cross had left the bay of Wanfrong on a northerly course." That, as far as we know, was the last information of his enemy's movements that Togo received. No mention is made in Japanese histories of a fact which is not, however, without importance: as the Russians steamed past Shanghai, all service ships—auxiliary steamers, colliers, store ships, and transports—were detached and sent up the river Woosung, which opens into the delta of the Yangtze, while the warships, accompanied only by the hospital ships and depot ships, continued on their northerly course. Numerous observers concluded that this could have only one meaning: Rojestvensky intended to accept battle in Japanese waters.

Togo could bring only four battleships into battle, against Rojestvensky's eight; but only five of the Russian battleships were completely modern. Togo had eight heavy cruisers—two of them very powerful, to oppose to Rojestvensky's three. He had absolute superiority in light cruisers and torpedo boats. Comparing fire-power, the Russians had almost twice as many large-caliber guns. But the number and rate of fire of medium-sized guns on the other side meant that the Japanese could hit three times as hard as the Russians in weight of shells per minute. The Japanese ships were faster. As for the difference not, indeed, in courage, but in the fighting value of the ships' companies on each side, we have already said all that needs to be said.

As is customary before the issue of final operational orders, Togo received all his ship and flotilla captains on board the flagship, and addressed them, beginning, "The keen desire of the Combined Squadron to encounter our powerful enemy is at last about to be realized."

The Admiral's calm and low-pitched voice made all the greater impression on his officers for being so rarely heard. In the barely furnished stateroom where those slight short yellow-skinned officers stood, stiff and rather crowded, their leader's voice was clear against a background of total silence. For this was Togo the Silent speaking. He told them, first, that nothing had been neglected in preparing the fleet for battle: there are sometimes occasions, at the height of an action, when a fighting man is brought bitterly to regret his neglect of some apparently trivial preparatory detail. The fighting men of the Imperial Fleet could safely clear their minds of any such anxiety: they could forget everything else, and concentrate their whole strength of mind and body on the actual fighting.

Let us continue to listen: the words Togo uttered were not conceived for that special occasion; they were not the ordinary exhortations of the ordinary commander fulfilling the tradition of delivering a vigorous speech before battle. Instead he was giving expression to his experience as a warrior and as a sailor, and his words were informed by a common sense which amounted to something more: he said a great deal that was of the essence in a few very simple words, and what he said was designed to be of immediate service to the officers who heard him:

"Those who have not often taken part in a modern naval battle are constantly apt, in the heat of an action, to overestimate the enemy's strength and situation, in the first place because they cannot perceive the damage wrought by our own fire in the enemy's ships, whereas the damage sustained by our own ships is tangible and visible. There are some who, seeing an enemy ship trying to escape by making its way through our line, believe her to be attacking us boldly; others, drawing near to a ship out of control and firing at random, receive the impression that her firepower has enormously increased. Such examples are not rare. And often, in the midst of an engagement, we think that we are losing, whereas it is the enemy who has already lost. When we give our enemy seven chances of winning, against our own three, the

214

chances, in reality, are even. In a naval battle there is never any occasion to think defensively, for a determined attack is always the best form of defense."

One is struck, when considering the preliminaries and opening moves of the Battle of Tsushima—which the Japanese call the Battle of the Sea of Japan—by the schematic, one might almost say harmonious, pattern of the succession of events. Hitherto, Togo had made but slow and halting progress toward victory, obstinate and laborious, frequently suffering checks and setbacks, feeling his way, failing, going wrong, beginning afresh. But now it began to seem as if events fell neatly into the places he had designed for them, disposing themselves with the elegant symmetry and unparalleled swiftness that distinguishes the perfect fatality of classical tragedy.

But—and let us make no mistake about it—this is far more apparent than real. It is my belief that one can have but a partial and even false view of Tsushima if one considers it otherwise than as the culmination of Togo's whole career. Tsushima is nothing less than the result and totality of all Togo's acts of will. The battle was his masterpiece. At the moment when he was preparing to advance and encounter his adversary, he held in his hands a weapon forged by himself, thoroughly tested and tried in battle. But above all—and this is the accomplishment which, as students of humanity, must interest us most—the Japanese admiral's decisions were no longer particular applications of general rules that he had learned. They were the reflexes of a complete and self-confident commander. Hence the swiftness, the assurance, the *elegance* of the battle; hence, too, the apparent docility of events. They seem suddenly to be bowing and bending to one man's will; but what we are, in fact, witnessing, is the effect of the accumulated weight of past efforts, making itself felt at a decisive moment.

On the evening of May 26th, Togo lay at anchor in the base he had chosen for the main body of his fleet; Masan, on the Korean coast of the Strait of Tsushima. With him was the First Division,

composed of four battleships and two new and powerful heavy
cruisers, Admiral Kamimura's cruisers, Admiral Uryu's cruisers,
and most of the torpedo boats. At the base on the bay of Osaki in
the island of Tsushima lay Admiral Kataoka's cruisers. About
seventy miles to the south, more cruisers and auxiliary cruisers were
at sea, patrolling and sealing off the strait. Behind them, as a second
patrol line, were Dewa's fast cruisers.

It must be confessed that few of us ever have occasion to look
at a large-scale map of Japan, and the word *strait* naturally con-
jures up a vision of a piece of water which is, in fact, *strait*, that is,
narrow. But the width of the Strait of Korea between Korea and
Japan is about one hundred nautical miles.*

The Strait of Tsushima is the neck of sea between the Korean
coast and Tsushima Island, which lies in the middle of the Strait
of Korea.

The night of May 26/27, 1905 was cloudless, but misty. The
moon, in its last quarter, was about to rise. It was at this moment
—about two forty-five, that the officer commanding the auxiliary
cruiser *Shinano Maru,* one of the advance patrol ships, Commander
Narigawa, sighted, at some distance ahead, a vessel that did not
look like a warship, carrying lights differing from those carried by
merchantmen. Visibility failing to improve, Narigawa, keeping
a close watch on the suspect through his night glasses, altered
course toward her. She was carrying three lights one above the
other, blue, white, and red.

Presently the moon rose over the eastern horizon, and the
ship's outline could be made out more clearly: two funnels, three
masts and, to all appearances, no guns. Narigawa approached
her and steamed round her stern. Above the three colored lights
a signal lamp began winking. Narigawa realized that the *Shinano
Maru* had been sighted, and was being questioned or signaled;
and, at the same moment, that this encounter was an exciting one:
the steamer was a hospital ship. A few moments later a rift
in the mist revealed the impressive battle line of the former Baltic

* A nautical mile is 2,000 yards.—Trans.

216

Fleet, the funnels of its ships pouring out long plumes of black smoke as the hulls plunged through the foaming sea. It was four forty-five when Narigawa sent off the most important wireless signal of his lifetime: *Enemy fleet sighted in square 203 appears to be steering for the Western passage past Tsushima.*

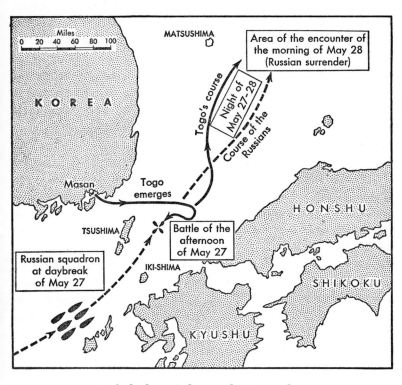

Unified plan of the Battle of Tsushima

The signal was picked up and retransmitted by Kataoka, and the Admiral received it at five minutes past five. When his flag lieutenant rushed into his stateroom, the signal in his hand, even the impassive Togo could not forbear a sigh of relief as he read it. Rojestvensky was behaving according to plan: Togo's plan. He would be punctual at the rendezvous fixed for him.

The admiral dictated a signal to Tokyo. *Have just heard of the sighting of the enemy fleet. My fleet will move out to attack and destroy the enemy. Weather fine and clear. Sea very rough.* And with reassuring automatism, the Japanese naval machine began to operate.

Less than an hour after receipt of the *Shinano Maru*'s signal, the *Mikasa* put to sea, leaving the shelter of Masan at the head of Togo's line of battle: *Mikasa, Shikishima, Fuji, Asahi, Kassuga, Nichine,* four battleships and two heavy cruisers. It was six in the morning, and there were no people on the docksides to see the fleet sail. The bay was deserted, and green seas were running high.

At six-thirty-five, the *Shinano Maru* signaled that the cruisers were relieving her in keeping touch with the enemy.

Rojestvensky's fleet, having reached a point nearly twenty thousand miles from its home port, plowed steadily on toward the Sea of Japan as if it were making for some promised ocean, some sea of dreams. Each ship rose and fell with a kind of tragic solemnity, in stately progress through the long ocean swell. The shadowing Japanese cruisers, some ahead of it and some hugging its wake, kept their distance, watchful, their guns mute. Not so their wireless sets; these were talkative: *The enemy force, accompanied by transports, is formed in two parallel lines-ahead. The easterly line comprises the most powerful ships. Speed twelve knots. Course northeast.* On receipt of this information, Togo decided to meet the Russians at about two o'clock near the island of Oki-no-shima with his main strength, and attack the western line.

At eleven in the morning came the news that the Russian battleships had opened fire on Dewa's cruisers; and, a little later, that they had ceased fire. The cruisers had not fired back and had withdrawn out of range.

That first salvo was, in fact, the result of an accident. One of the *Orel*'s guns had gone off accidentally, and the whole fleet, under the impression that the admiral must have given the order, opened fire. Rojestvensky at once signaled *Do not waste your ammunition,* and the ships ceased fire. Aboard the Russian ships, officers and men went to lunch in messes and wardrooms, watch by watch, swallowing their food hastily. The accidental firing had had a considerable effect in raising their morale. Many of the sailors believed that a battle had been fought and the enemy forced to withdraw. Rojestvensky made a new signal: *Alter course north 23 east destination Vladivostok*. It was the anniversary of the tzar's coronation, and in every wardroom the officers rose to drink His Majesty's health in champagne, also toasting the tzarina and drinking to a Russian victory.

While they were doing so—the time was noon—the *Mikasa* was ten miles north of Oki-no-shima. In the Japanese ships all hands were at action stations and not a word was spoken. Dispersing mist still hung and drifted in masses above the surface of the sea. Togo ordered a change of course, steering west toward the enemy.

The original plan conceived by Togo for receiving the Russians comprised seven successive actions, spaced in time over four days, and in area over the whole Sea of Japan from south to north. The first of these actions was to be a torpedo-boat attack before Rojestvensky got into the Strait of Korea; the last, a major assault off Vladivostok. Owing to poor visibility and the very rough sea, Togo had been forced to order his torpedo boats to take refuge in the bay of Miura, in the island of Tsushima; this meant that the action must begin with the third item in the program: the big ships to engage the enemy in a gunnery duel in Tsushima Strait.

The two fleets were now drawing near to each other. Togo was kept constantly informed of his enemy's position, whereas Rojestvensky, having called in his cruisers, knew no more than that the Japanese line of battle lay somewhere to the north.

At one-fifteen the *Mikasa* sighted Dewa's cruisers. They were in contact with the enemy by keeping course east of Rojestvensky's line. A little later the Fifth and Sixth Japanese divisions, which were steaming ahead of the enemy, were sighted to the west. And at last came the moment when Togo glimpsed through a rift in the mist the sight he had envisaged for many months. In the midst of that green expanse, striped and tossed with white crests of foam, he saw the slowly moving dark hulls, the yellow funnels, the thick columns of smoke flattened and dispersed by the wind. It was one-thirty-nine.

Minutes, even seconds, would count now. Leading the Japanese battle line, the *Mikasa* smashed proudly through the waves, like some colossal tank, spray breaking over her prow, water washing over the deck as far back as the stern 12-inch turret. Across the front of the mainmast, and above the wide navigation bridge, was a narrower bridge for the staff. Togo was there, surrounded by his officers. All were wearing active-service uniform, black, buttoned up to the chin, the silk-braid stripes of rank barely distinguishable. That part of the mast which touched the bridge, and the periphery of the bridge itself, were padded with stout fenders, to reduce the danger from shell splinters. A staff officer asked Togo to exercise his command of the ship from the armored blockhouse. It was traditional, by then, to make this request, and it was known in advance that the admiral would refuse. He did so, with a smile that was faintly mocking.

"I shall soon be sixty," he said. "I have had my time. But you, who are young, must take care of yourselves. Into the blockhouse with you."

Needless to say, no one obeyed the order. Togo spoke quietly to his chief of staff. An order was passed forward, and presently a signal was run up to the *Mikasa's* mainmast signal halyards. The high wind made the flags crack like whips. *The country's fate depends upon this battle. Let every man do his duty with all his might.* It was a paraphrase, a century later, of Nelson's famous signal at Trafalgar: *England expects that every man this day will do his duty.**

The time was one fifty-five. Togo watched the Russian formation through his glasses. The Russians were steaming in two lines ahead, but not exactly in the manner indicated by the morning's reports.

---

* It is perhaps worth remark that Togo's signal was that of a man more modest than Nelson. Nelson's signal, as originally worded by himself, read, "Nelson confides that . . ." It was Hardy who suggested the modification "England expects . . ."—TRANS.

The starboard line, composed of the biggest ships—*Suvorov, Alexander III, Borodino, Orel*—was steaming ahead of the port line, which was led by the *Oslabia*. This heterodox formation was the outcome of Rojestvensky's unsuccessful attempt to get his fleet into single line-abreast, a detail which could not be known until later, and what he was now doing was trying to re-form line-ahead, with *Suvorov* leading. This evolution was still incomplete as Togo's line drew near. Watchful, Togo realized that Rojestvensky's course was veering north: it was north 23 east. The Russian was evidently making for Vladivostok. Togo's object must therefore be to bar the way and attack with his full strength. His first plan was consequently changed, as regards its purpose (to attack the leading ships of the port line), but not as regards the execution of the movement. It would still be necessary to attack from the west. Togo gave himself more room: course, north 38 east.

At two minutes past two, the fleets were about 14,000 yards apart, the enemy being to port forward. Togo's purpose, once positioned, was to steam full ahead at the Russian fleet. All this is simple and easily visualized. Both fleets were steaming full ahead toward each other, the Russian course being north 23 east, the Japanese south 23 west. If nothing had been changed, they would have steamed past each other exchanging broadsides. In short, a classic naval battle. But since the two fleets were moving in exactly opposite directions, there was a risk of their first engagement being brief and indecisive. After this the Russians would only have to hold on their northerly course toward Vladivostok. This Togo could not tolerate. At all costs he must avoid a second version of the running battle in the Yellow Sea: Rojestvensky must not escape to fight again. The moment had come to bar the way, cross the Russian's course, and fight him. In short, to go about at once.

It will be recalled that if this maneuver is carried out "all together," it is relatively swift but leaves the flagship, not at the head of the line, but in the rear. We can remember that Togo's most cherished theory was that an admiral should lead his battle

221

line. Togo and no one else must be in the lead, so that at the height of an engagement his captains would simply have to follow him. As long as the flagship is at the head of the line, and under way, however badly hit, the battle is not lost. Moreover, in the present case, a turning movement carried out "all together" would expose his weakest ships, the Japanese cruisers, to the Russian battleships' fire. Togo therefore rejected that course of action.

On the other hand, to go about "in succession" would give Rojestvensky a momentary but considerable advantage. In such a case, the ships of the line follow exactly in the admiral's wake. That is, each goes about when she arrives at the same point of sea, as if turning round an invisible marker buoy. While the maneuver is in progress, the enemy has to concentrate his fire only on that point; he is bound to do a good deal of damage. Moreover in such a movement the line assumes the form of a hairpin; during all the time the ships are in the leg of the hairpin farthest from the enemy, they are masked by those in the other leg, and therefore unable to fire.

Togo, of course, knew all this. He also knew that the line of battle he had created and trained would carry out the movement without hesitation or mistake, however violent the enemy fire. He knew that his sailors had cool heads and he had in mind the difference between the efficiency of his own gunnery, and the Russians'. He weighed the risk precisely and, having done so, promptly took it: *Alter course 180 degrees to port in succession.* The signal was acknowledged by the whole line. The *Mikasa* began to change direction. Time, five minutes past two.

Russian astonishment at Togo's maneuver was complete. Commander Semënov, describing his reaction, wrote as follows: "With my eyes glued to my glasses, I stared at them, and I could not believe what I saw. The Japanese were turning to port and in succession. . . . This maneuver meant each ship turning successively about the same point as the one ahead of her. Once there, she remained relatively motionless, greatly facilitating our task. Moreover, although the Japanese fleet was steaming at about fifteen knots, this turn would take at least a quarter of an hour, during which time the battleships which were on the new course would come between us and the guns of their other ships. 'What madness!' Reydkin exclaimed, who was so excited he could not keep still. 'In another minute we shall be hammering their flagship!' "

It was eight minutes past two. Rojestvensky had just given the order to open fire. Down came the hail of Russian shells, as expected by Togo. The sea round the *Mikasa* was churned into boiling violence; the flagship was surrounded by huge waterspouts; the air quivered with the bark and growl of the big guns. The Japanese line continued its maneuver, faultlessly, and without firing a shot. From eight minutes past two until eleven minutes past two the Imperial Fleet simply presented itself as a target to the Russian gunners. Post Captain Ayatsushiro, commanding the cruiser *Asama*, stood playing the flute upon his forebridge, encouraging his officers to keep cool during this terrible ordeal.

At last, the *Mikasa* having completed its turn, opened fire, and, following its example, each ship as she came round onto the new course followed suit. Their fire was concentrated on the *Suvorov* and the *Oslabia*.

At twenty past two a 12-inch shell exploded on the *Mikasa*, behind the bridge, wounding fifteen officers, and smashing the compass beside which Togo was standing. Togo, smiling, did not move. A few minutes later, one of the flagship's guns was hit and put out of action by a shell which pierced the gun turret. But in thirteen minutes the Japanese maneuver was complete, and no serious damage had been done. Rojestvensky had had his moment. Togo now had the advantage; his guns could speak and give of their best in the best possible tactical position.

The Japanese were using a new type of armor-piercing shell loaded with Shimose powder mixed with a new explosive still unknown to the Russians. These shells tore through armor plate as if it were paper. When they exploded they shot out great gusts of flame, and with the flame a toxic gas which choked any man who breathed it. As soon as the Japanese gunnery officers had found

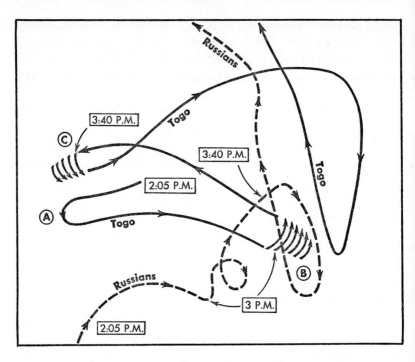

*Decisive engagement of the Battle of Tsushima, afternoon of
August 27*

A. From 2:05 P.M. to 2:20 Togo carries out his change of course in
succession. It was in the parallel fight between 2:20 and 3 o'clock
that the battle was virtually won.

B. At about 3 P.M. Togo carries out a change of course "all together,"
steering northwest to cross the Russians' course and bar their way.

C. About 3:40 P.M. Togo's second change of course "all together."

the right elevation, conditions aboard the leading Russian ships
became nothing short of hellish.

In the *Suvorov*, Semënov was in a position to compare the
Japanese shooting with their shooting during the Battle of the
Yellow Sea. Listen to what he has to say: "It seemed impossible
to count the shells which hit us. Not only had I never seen such

224

a barrage, I could not even have imagined anything like it. Shells seemed to rain down on us without pause. Steel plates and parts of our superstructure were blown to pieces, and flying splinters did a lot of damage. Iron companion ladders were twisted into circles and guns literally torn out of their mountings. Such disasters could never have been caused simply by a shell striking, and certainly not by splinters. They could be caused only by the force of the explosion. The high temperature of that explosion spread a kind of liquid fire which smothered everything, further enhancing the terrifying effects of the shells. I saw a steel plate catch fire as it was struck; true, the metal itself did not burn, it was the paint which went up in flames. Objects as little inflammable as hammocks soaked in water caught fire like torches. There were times when it was impossible to see anything through binoculars, for the quivering of the overheated air confused everything."

It goes without saying that, since then, we have done even "better" in explosive force and power of destruction. But the unheard-of effectiveness of the Japanese gunnery and ammunition caused much the same impression on the Russians as an atomic weapon would do nowadays.

Togo could not of course estimate the damage done by each Japanese shell from the bridge of his flagship. But he was able to see that his shooting was three times as fast as the enemy's. Less than half an hour after the start of the engagement, he also realized that the Russian shooting was becoming sporadic and ineffectual. It would have been surprising had it been otherwise. Aboard the Russian ships, ravaged as they were by fire, range finders and all the other gunnery apparatus had been put hopelessly out of action. What was surprising was the fact that the Russian gunners were able to continue aiming and firing their guns at all.

In the years which followed the battle several Russian officers and ratings were to have occasion to give their personal impressions of Tsushima. Allowing them to have dramatized a little it is quite clear, if only from the recurrence of the same details which could hardly have been independently invented, that the situation

225

aboard the Russian ships became appalling after half-past two in the afternoon. In the *Suvorov* two gunnery officers in succession were wounded inside the armored blockhouse, smashed open by Japanese shell splinters. The second of these officers was killed as he made for the last serviceable range finder. On the navigation bridge it was an officer who stood at the wheel, covered with the blood of the quartermaster who lay dead at his side. A shell hit one of the casualty dressing stations, blowing a number of wounded men to pieces. The admiral, hit by a splinter, remained in the blockhouse. But he could do little to lead the fleet now: all halyards and yardarms were down, the signal-flag lockers were blazing; and finally, the mainmast, cut in two by a shell, went overboard.

In the *Oslabia*'s sick bay, the surgeon-captain and his lieutenant were operating, without chloroform, on the endless stream of wounded and badly burned men being carried in on stretchers. The deck was awash with blood and amputated limbs. Every shell which hit the battleship "produced an appalling din and made the whole ship quiver as if someone had dropped a hundred iron rails on the deck from a great height." When she began to list, the wounded, screaming with terror, fought each other viciously to be first up the companion ladders.

Often, during the course of the battle, cries of "Every man for himself!" and "Jump into the sea!" were raised aboard the Russian ships. On the other hand, here and there, and in greater number than was to have been expected in such conditions, men behaved with courage and even with heroism, remaining at their posts under a hail of steel splinters and in the clouds of asphyxiating gas liberated by the explosions, sometimes with a kind of bitter and despairing fatalism. All aspects of the intensely emotional Russian nature, capable of the best as of the worst, were in evidence.

The Japanese line kept faultless station; Rojestvensky's line bent before the violence of the Japanese bombardment like a tree before the fury of a storm. Its scarce moments of respite were due to the patches of mist which still drifted across the surface of the sea.

As if he could sense that the Russian ships could not stand up to such terrible punishment for long, Togo increased the pressure, altering course so as to begin the pitiless envelopment of the enemy's leading ships.

At two-forty-seven his course was east southeast and the range 4,500 yards. At two-fifty the *Oslabia*, "surrounded by an unbroken wall of enormous waterspouts, flames and black smoke," withdrew from the line of battle. Ten minutes later the *Suvorov*, afire from stem to stern, also quitted the line, falling away to starboard. The *Alexander III*, left at the head of the Russian line, suddenly altered course to due north, evidently headed for Vladivostok, her purpose being to slip out of the Japanese embracing movement by passing behind their line. But Togo was watchful. He felt victory within his grasp. Eight points to port all together, again, eight points to port all together and Togo's line was now on a northwesterly course. Now his ship was at the rear of the line but this was no longer important; the important thing was that it barred the way to Vladivostok.

At three-ten the *Oslabia* turned turtle and sank. Clusters of white-clad Russian sailors could be seen clinging, like a strange swarm of insects, to the steeply sloping deck; then, as the slope became sheer, sliding down into the sea. The Japanese sailors watched the tragic spectacle intently; this was something they had never seen—a mighty warship, sunk by their gunfire, going to the bottom.

Kamimura held to his southwesterly course, covering the First Division's change of course and concentrating the fire of all his cruisers on the *Alexander III*. She, in her turn, left the head of the line, giving way to the *Borodino*, which was already in flames. Togo, by another "all together" movement, led his line back on a northeasterly course and, with the *Mikasa* once again in the lead, threw all the weight of his firepower into hammering the sorely tried Russian fleet.

The *Suvorov*, apparently out of control, was at the very heart of this murderous onslaught, bombarded by Togo's ships from one side and by Kamimura from the other, and at the same time attacked by torpedo boats. An observer might have supposed her to be a target ship, moored there for gunnery-training purposes. Some of her guns were still firing, although it was hard to imagine how any living creature could still find a foothold on that mass of twisted, fire-blasted iron.

Russian shells were scoring hits more and more infrequently. Then their line collapsed entirely: battleships and cruisers, falling together into a shapeless huddle, moved aimlessly about in a circle formed by the Japanese line. From time to time they were hidden by mist. Their dispersion and very want of orderly formation gave Togo a new anxiety. It was still his principal aim to bar the way to Vladivostok to any Russian ship, even though it might be doubted whether any ships which had taken such punishment would be able to reach the port. Togo and Kamimura, sweeping the embattled sea at full speed, caught sight of the *Suvorov* near to the depot ship *Kamchatka*, which was drifting, immobilized. The *Suvorov* had been exposed to the fire of the whole Japanese fleet for five hours: she had driven off two torpedo-boat attacks. She was still afloat. A single 3-inch gun was still firing. "Commander Fujimoto's torpedo-boat flotilla received orders to attack the *Suvorov*," says the official Japanese history. "Although almost reduced to a still-burning cinder, and although she had undergone so many attacks and been a target for our whole fleet; although, finally, she could now fire only one small gun, this proud vessel continued firing, to prove her firm resolution to resist to the very end. And she did, indeed, continue firing while she could still float. In the end, at about seven-twenty, and after having been twice more attacked by our torpedo boats, she began to settle, and, majestically, sank out of sight."

As the *Suvorov* went down, there was a violent explosion aboard the *Borodino*, which was still trying to lead the remnants of the Russian fleet toward Vladivostok. The *Borodino* vanished beneath the surface of the darkening sea. Twenty minutes earlier the

Alexander III had gone down with all hands—not a single survivor was saved. The depot ships *Kamchatka, Ural,* and *Russ* had been sunk by gunfire. Two hospital ships had been captured. The third part of Togo's original plan was accomplished.

Night was falling. The sea was still rough, but the wind was declining to a breeze. It looked as if the elements were going to set the scene favorably for Togo's Act Four: a night attack by torpedo boats. Like hunting dogs they gathered, coming from every quarter of the horizon to form their pack. Togo gave orders to cease fire, gave his big ships their course for the night—due north; and fixed a rendezvous for the following morning off the island of Matsushima.

Night, aboard the Japanese battleships and cruisers, was spent cleaning up and washing down decks, bridges, and gun turrets; in bringing the wounded, and those whose duty had kept them all day long in the hot engine rooms and 'tween decks of the ships, up into the fresh air; and in lowering the dead into their coffins. Of these there were more than one hundred, and of wounded, five hundred and thirty. These casualties, considering the violence of the battle, were small. The *Mikasa* had been the enemy's main target, and had the largest casualty list. She had been hit forty-eight times. Of her entire armament, only five 6-inch guns could be called intact. The *Nichine,* rear ship of the line, had also suffered severely: admiral Misu whose flag she carried had been wounded. As for the *Asama,* her captain, after having played the flute on his bridge during those three terrible minutes at the start of the battle, had not, thereafter, been idle. Hit, at two twenty-seven, by a shell from the *Oslabia,* and forced to pull out of the line, hard pressed by the enemy while her steering gear was out of action, the *Asama's* stern was now eight feet under water. Nevertheless, at three-fifteen she had resumed her station in the line. The *Kassagin,* with a big hole shot in her hull, made for the nearby bay of Aburadani, escorted by the *Chitoze* to which cruiser Dewa had transferred his flag. Other ships had been damaged, but none seriously. And

Togo knew that he had sunk three of the four Russian battleships of the *Suvorov* class, which were considered in St. Petersburg to be unsinkable.

Night had fallen, and after sunset the Russians had set about attending to their terrible wounds. Doing honor to their incredible and traditional faculty for recuperation, they got the many fires in their ships under control, and stopped their numerous leaks. Makarov—alas for his country that he had not been there!— was still doing posthumous service, for the Russian sailors used the mats he had invented for stopping leaks in the hulls. The wounded—those who had survived but had had to be neglected in the heat of battle—were attended to. Because the dead could not be coffined—the few coffins carried had gone up in flames—they were thrown overboard. A hideous duty. And yet, aboard all the Russian ships for more than an hour, despair gave way to hope. The Japanese guns had fallen silent, and the lights of the Japanese ships had vanished into the darkness. Perhaps, after all, it might be possible to reach Vladivostok, to find a refuge, a haven, safety at least for a little while, and the company of fellow countrymen, the welcoming feel of Russian soil underfoot. It was only a dream. The truce lasted only an hour. Suddenly, the night was full of throbbing all about them: the mutter of engines at sea and the thrash of screws as the swell lifted them clear. Despair once more invaded Russian hearts.

The officers commanding the Japanese torpedo boats, aware of the day's results and provided with orders for their night's work, were afire to do deeds of prowess in their turn. They hurled their ships upon their wounded pry, launching their torpedoes, returning time after time to the attack and charging straight into the beams of the Russian searchlights. The battleship *Navarin*, hit by two torpedoes, sank with nearly all hands. The battleship *Sissoy Veliky*, and the cruiser *Admiral Nakimov*, also hit, managed to crawl as far as the shore of Tsushima Island, where they scuttled themselves to avoid capture. But not all the Russian ships tamely submitted to the attack. Gunners with

230

bandaged heads and burned hands contrived to work the breeches of their guns and open fire on the enemy hunting packs. Two Japanese torpedo boats were sunk by Russian gunfire, and six others put out of action, damaged by enemy shells or by collision in the darkness and confusion. The Japanese flotillas withdrew as dawn began to lighten the sky in the east.

The day promised to be fine and clear, which was exactly what the Japanese needed. The curtain was about to rise on Act Five.

Deployed as a wide fan of flotillas and single ships, the Imperial Fleet swept the sea in the general direction of Matsushima. At five-twenty Togo received a signal from Kataoka that the Fifth Division, steaming sixty miles south of the Admiral, had sighted several columns of black smoke on the horizon, bearing east. A few minutes later came more details: *Four enemy battleships and two cruisers in sight, course northwest.* The surviving Russians were making another attempt to reach Vladivostok. Once again, Togo steamed to cross their course.

This time he had everything in his favor, both strength and speed. The First and Second divisions received orders to intercept the enemy: the Fourth, Fifth, and Sixth to harry him from the south. A little after ten o'clock, the enemy came in sight. The old *Nicholas I,* flying an admiral's flag, was leading the line, followed by the *Orel,* and by two armored coast-guard ships, *Apraxine* and *Seniavine.* The cruiser *Izumrud* was steaming abeam of the line and a little ahead of the flagship.

At ten thirty-four the *Kassuga,* followed at once by all the other Japanese battleships, opened fire. The *Izumrud,* immediately increasing to full-steam ahead, left the line of Russian ships, steering due east. She was making her escape. Togo saw that she was doing so, and that the *Chitoze,* in prompt pursuit of her, was being outdistanced. It did not matter. One or two smaller fry were bound to get away: what mattered was the main body of the enemy, the remnant of his battle line. What remained of that could not escape; it was there, in front of him, encircled and again suffering a devastating bombardment.

231

This had lasted exactly nine minutes when one of the officers of Togo's staff said something about the *Nicholas I.* He had noticed something happening aboard the Russian flagship. He had seen the battle flag at her mainmast top jerking up and down in a peculiar manner. Next, it was seen to be running down to half-mast. At the same time, an international code signal was run up: X G H. The signals officer of the watch immediately translated: *We ask to negotiate.*

Togo made no move. He seemed turned to stone. The officers surrounding him were equally motionless, equally silent. They looked at the admiral and they looked at the Russian ships, still under heavy Japanese fire. But more than one mouth was opened in amazement or to utter an exclamation at what came next.

The other Russian ships, acting almost together, were striking their colors. And when the Russian flags had disappeared below their bridges, another flag was run up on every ship: the Rising Sun, national emblem of Japan. The Russians had struck their colors and run up their enemy's flag to make it quite clear that they were surrendering. It was a heartbreaking spectacle. Even on Togo's bridge there were officers whose hearts were thumping uncomfortably, officers with lumps in their throats and tears in their eyes.

Togo's eyes were dry. He still said nothing. He stared at the Japanese flags fluttering from the Russian mastheads. Russian guns were no longer firing, but Japanese shells were still exploding on the Russian ships.

"Admiral, they are surrendering," said one of the officers. "Should we cease fire?"

Togo made no move, said no word. Was he going to sink an enemy disarmed? Or could he not believe his own eyes? Every second that passed seemed unbearable to his expectant staff officers.

"Admiral, they are surrendering," said his chief of staff in a voice that was unsteady, almost shrill. "Does not the spirit of Bushido require us to cease fire?"

Togo took one more look at the signal flying from the mast

232

of the *Nicholas I* and at the Japanese flags on the other ships. "Cease fire," he said.

And he ordered all the ships to form a circle round the enemy. This scene was played out on May 28, 1905, at a quarter to eleven in the morning in waters situated approximately eighteen miles southwest of the Liancourt rocks.

No one, as far as I know, thought of timing the delay that occurred between the moment when the *Nicholas I* first struck her flag and Togo's order to cease fire. Judging from the accounts available, the delay may have lasted about one minute: perhaps less. It need hardly be said that Togo has been criticized and reproached for letting it occur.

I should like to be able to offer an explanation. I should like to be able to put myself in Togo's place during that minute and experience his train of thought just as he, before the battle, had made himself think as if he were Rojestvensky. But it is not easy. One can hardly get much farther than that this Japanese admiral, so long bowed beneath the burden of a crushing responsibility, may have had some difficulty in believing in his own victory. It may be, too, that he had a more or less subconscious wish to see the enemy fleet whose defeat had become perhaps his only reason for existence disappear beneath the surface of the sea, wiped out and for ever abolished. It is possible that during this minute or less Togo may have been tempted by the ideas advocated by partisans of total war, the war of extermination. That kind of war had existed long before his time, if only among tribal savages. And those Western journalists and historians who criticized Togo for that minute of silence, could not, of course, know that their reproaches were being addressed to the future preceptor of the mikado who was to visit the ruins of Hiroshima and Nagasaki.

After he had given the order to cease fire, Togo again fell silent, erect and motionless, his chin sunk upon his breast. Then he ordered an officer named Akiyama to go aboard the *Nicholas I*, taking with him Lieutenant Yamamoto, who spoke French; he was to bring the Russian admiral back with him. The torpedo boat *Kisi* came alongside the *Mikasa* to ferry them across.

They boarded the *Nicholas I* and were taken to the admiral's quarters. The admiral who received them was not Rojestvensky. Rojestvensky, inert and only half-conscious, was aboard the torpedo boat *Byedovi*. Gravely wounded, he had been taken off the *Suvorov* to the torpedo boat *Buiny*, but had been transferred when she was damaged. The man who received Togo's officers was Rear Admiral Nebogatov, who had brought the famous "Fourth Squadron" from Russia—the "self-sinkables," as these lame old ships were called in the Russian Navy. He it was who had taken the responsibility for the surrender. Wearily he contemplated the two small black-uniformed Japanese, one of whom spoke in a swift, musical gibberish, which the other promptly translated into French.*

"I am instructed by Admiral Togo to present his compliments. The admiral is glad that the battle has been brought to a swift conclusion. He has been deeply impressed by the bravery of your officers and ratings, and it is his wish to treat your fleet as a fleet which has surrendered with honor. Your officers may keep their swords. Your ships and their armament and your weapons must, of course, be left as they are, and you will have the goodness to notify your ships of this at once. Further, Admiral Togo wishes to meet you personally and I am to ask you to return with me aboard the *Mikasa*."

Nebogatov replied forthwith that he agreed to all the proposals and asked for a few minutes to issue the necessary orders.

He then went to his stateroom, to reappear presently in full-dress uniform and wearing all his decorations. His face was gray, however, a speaking image of affliction and despair. The whole ship's company were piped to lay aft on the upper deck. Turning toward them, in a voice sadly muted, strangely dulled, to which all listened in deathly silence, he began to speak. He said that they had all

---

* Readers will remember that all upper-class Russians commonly used this language among themselves, often in preference to their own, until 1914, although Russian was beginning to come into favor before that.—TRANS.

fought faithfully and with the utmost valor. But the battle was lost. He took full responsibility for the surrender. To carry on the fight would have been deliberately and hopelessly to choose the absolute certainty of being wiped out.

"Men," he concluded, "I have a long life behind me. I am not afraid of death. But I could not bear to lead you to your deaths, you who are still young. On my head be all the shame of what I have done. Let them summon me before a court-martial; I am ready to accept sentence of death. I shall soon have to put off this uniform. Whereas you can continue, in the future, to wear yours with honor. Farewell!"

The ship's company cheered him. Having saluted them, Admiral Nebogatov went down the gang ladder escorted by the two Japanese and followed by several of his staff officers.

Togo received him with the customary honors, and even with marks of personal respect. Their business, now, was simply to get the terms of capitulation down in black and white. A Japanese officer, this time a qualified Russian interpreter, read over the conditions:

The Russian ships which had surrendered were to be handed over exactly as they were to the Japanese fleet.

Their crews were to become prisoners of war.

Their officers could keep their swords.

Nebogatov asked if his officers might not be set at liberty on giving their parole never again to bear arms against Japan, and repatriated. The interpreter translated, and Togo bowed his head affirmatively. Nebogatov asked if the ratings, like their officers, could keep their side arms. Togo said No. To a question from Nebogatov about the kind of treatment the prisoners could expect, Togo replied curtly that the Japanese were not barbarians.

The Japanese admiral then drank a glass of champagne with his defeated enemy, to celebrate the end of the war. And he uttered a few courteous words paying homage to "the skill and courage which had been required to bring the Russian fleet without accident

235

a distance of seventeen thousand miles from its bases." But a little later Togo was to make a curious confession to his friend Ogasawaka.

"Whilst we were talking and sipping our wine, I was observing Admiral Nebogatov and his officers to see if they showed any sign of resentment. As they raised their glasses quite calmly, I felt assured that there would be no danger in sending only a few of our men aboard the prizes, to bring them back to Japan with their own crews."

Clearly, Togo had not lowered his guard. With his own eyes he had seen the enemy's most powerful ships sink beneath the sea; their remaining ships had struck their colors. But perhaps the Japanese was wondering if there was not some final ruse, some last maneuver which he must be on the watch for. This distrust seems to us incredible. But it is also revealing, throwing a little light on that minute of inaction after the Russian signal of surrender. It does indeed seem as if Togo had taken a minute to fully realize his own immense victory.

Four thousand eight hundred and thirty Russians had been killed, and one hundred and seventeen Japanese. Thousands of Russians had been wounded; one thousand Japanese. But, even more striking, whereas the Russian fleet no longer existed, Togo had lost only three torpedo boats. Even the cruiser *Izumrud* escaped from the last engagement only to run aground and scuttle herself on the coast of Russian Siberia, north of Korea. Three other cruisers were interned in Manila, and a torpedo boat in Shanghai. Of the whole armada, the only ships which reached Vladivostok were two destroyers, the *Brawy* and the *Grosny* and a small, fast cruiser, the *Almaz*. Encircling its prizes, the Japanese fleet set a course for Sasebo.

As soon as the fleet was in harbor, Togo sent Yamamoto across to the *Byedovi* to inquire after Rojestvensky. Post Captain Clapier de Colongue, the Russian admiral's chief of staff, told Yamamoto that the admiral was exhausted by his wound and that a visit might make him worse. But Admiral Rojestvensky would be informed at once of Admiral Togo's kind inquiry. At the last moment, as Yamamoto was preparing to go over the side into his boat, Clapier de Colongue recalled him: the admiral wished to see him. Rojestvensky had insisted on thanking Togo's messenger in person. He said that he was touched by Admiral Togo's concern for him, and sent his compliments.

On June 3rd Togo paid Rojestvensky a visit in person, at the Sasebo naval hospital. Japanese popular imagination made much of this visit of the victorious admiral to his brave but defeated enemy, and the scene was depicted in the popular colored prints. Rojestvensky is shown seated on his brass bedstead, his head bandaged. Togo, wearing a white tunic, and bareheaded like the officers of his suite, is shaking the wounded Russian's hand.

"Defeat," said Togo, on the occasion thus illustrated, "is an accident common to the lot of all fighting men, and there is no occasion to be cast down by it if we have done our duty. I can only express my admiration for the courage with which your sailors fought during the recent battle, and my personal admiration for yourself, who carried out your heavy task until you were seriously wounded. I am anxious to convey to you my feelings of sincere respect and deep regret. I hope that you will soon recover your health."

Rojestvensky kept Togo's hand in his own for some moments and then in a low voice replied:

"I thank you for coming to see me. Your sympathy comforts me. I feel no shame at having been beaten by such an opponent as yourself."

Rojestvensky and Nebogatov were both to return to Russia and face trial. Rojestvensky covered all his subordinates, and took the entire blame on himself. The Russian authorities were grateful to him for not trying to fix the responsibility for the disaster on his superiors, the rulers of Russia. The public prosecutor turned his indictment into what was virtually a speech for the defense, and the admiral was acquitted. He died two and a half years later. Nebogatov, condemned, in the first instance, to death, had his sentence commuted to ten years' close confinement in a fortress. His crime was a serious one—he had tried to place responsibility where it really belonged. Moreover, the Russian Government needed a scapegoat.

Some weeks after the Battle of Tsushima, a Japanese naval force escorting the Thirteenth Army Division transports, sailed from Sasebo for Sakhalin. This operation was to be the last of the war. Three new names were noted among the ships of the naval escort force: *Iki, Oki-no-shima,* and *Mishima.* These names were freshly painted on the bows, above the coat of paint which had obliterated the Russian names of Nebogatov's former ships.

For the defense of Harbin and Vladivostok, the Russians were obliged to send their troops by that interminable umbilical cord, the Trans-Siberian Railway. The Russian fleet having been eliminated, there was nothing to interfere with Japanese troop transports, and the Japanese Army leaders could quickly move as many soldiers as they needed into Manchuria. Thanks to the naval victory of Tsushima, the war was virtually won on land, as well as on sea. And no one could say how far inland from the Pacific coast of Asia Japan's expansionist ambitions might now take her.

Great Britain, Japan's ally, while officially rejoicing at her success, began to be worried. British politicians and diplomats, keeping a watchful eye on the Far Eastern situation, began to wonder whether it would not be advisable to set a limit to the victorious march of this new Great Power. The more so in that Japan had scored her triumph *as a naval power.* Had Togo's victory not, perhaps, been too complete?

Other nations were worried by Japan's success, notably the United States. On June 9th the American Government offered to mediate, and both belligerents accepted the offer: things in Russia were going from bad to worse, while Japan's finances were seriously strained by the war. President Theodore Roosevelt received the Russian and Japanese plenipotentiaries, and a peace treaty was signed, at Portsmouth, New Hampshire, on September 5, 1905.

238

Japan, unquestionably the victor, received Korea, which she considered hers in any case; Port Arthur, which she had had to take from the Russians after first taking it from the Chinese; and the southern half of the island of Sakhalin, plus some railway concessions and fishery rights.

After her victory over China, it will be remembered, Japan had felt that the Western Great Powers had combined against her, one of the Small Powers, to steal her victory. The disappointment following the Treaty of Portsmouth was even greater. Japanese mobs, despite their veneration for their great emperor, Meiji, rose in revolt in Tokyo, Yokohama, and Nagasaki. A little later, quieted by the mikado's calm and sensible message, and enlightened as to the financial situation—an empty treasury and a national debt of two thousand million yen—the Japanese people went patiently back to work. But, for the moment, nothing could restrain their fury.

On the night of September 10/11, the *Mikasa* blew up in harbor. The official report gave the cause as "spontaneous explosion in a powder magazine." This explanation is by no means unlikely. Something of the kind happened in the French Navy when the battleship *Liberté* blew up in Toulon roads in 1911, as a result of the powder in a magazine decomposing with an accompanying rise in temperature. Nevertheless, there has always been some doubt about the real cause of the *Mikasa* catastrophe. There were nearly six hundred dead and wounded.

At the time of the explosion Togo was in a train on his way to Tokyo. Had he set off an hour or two later, the man who personified the nation's victory might have fallen a victim to what was perhaps a demonstration of popular indignation with the treaty.

If that had happened Togo's career would end here. Should we, perhaps, decide that his story ends here in any case? Never again were his guns to give tongue, except in salute. Even so, there is a little more to be said. The man whose whole outward activity had driven toward the masterly victory he had just won is not fully revealed by his final achievement. It seems to me that his character should continue to interest us, even out of the context of war. Moreover, there is charm in some of the scenes from his life which have still to be accounted for here.

Victory was celebrated in grandiose style. The celebrations, indeed, were on an especially splendid and brilliant scale because it was necessary to make the people forget their disappointment with the Treaty of Portsmouth. However, the first of these public rejoicings was discreet and, as was proper, religious. It consisted of a thanksgiving prayer offered up by the admirals of the fleet in the garden of the imperial shrine at Ise. Togo stood in full-dress uniform before an altar to the ancestors. A Shinto priest robed in white kneeled at his side. There was not a breath of wind, and the trees were motionless. The other admirals moved to the altar, each in his turn to offer his prayers of thanks.

From Yokohama, Togo went directly to Tokyo, to make his official report on the operations of the war to the mikado. Through the windowpanes of his railway carriage he watched the people come running. The whole way between the two cities, on both sides of the track, was lined by the faces of his countrymen and the flags they waved to greet him. At Tokyo, as he stepped out of the train, he beheld an array of gorgeous uniforms, and, in front of them, a group of men in traditional costume: these were poets. They had been busy on their victory odes for weeks, and now read them aloud to the victorious hero. Thereafter, and not until that was over, the military bands struck up their martial music.

The procession of open carriages provided to carry the admiral and attendant notabilities to the palace had to make its way between cheering crowds. This tide of humanity washed up to the very gates of the imperial palace. Beyond them lay silence again, and solemnity, with every least word and motion governed by the strict etiquette of official ceremonial.

Togo and the three admirals who had commanded squadrons of the fleet, Kataoka, Kamimura, and Dewa, were ushered into a vast gilded hall—the gold-covered ceiling, walls, and floor. At the far end stood the mikado, surrounded by his great officers of state, the cabinet ministers. Like Togo, he wore an admiral's uniform. Togo held a document in his hand. He bowed deeply, and the other three admirals did likewise. Then Togo took a pace forward and began to read his report:

"During one year and a half, since the Combined Squadron put out to wage war on imperial orders, there has not been a single battle on land or sea in which our imperial forces have not been victorious. And now peace has been restored to us. And we, your Majesty's servants, can return in triumph to Imperial General Staff Headquarters. This triumph is entirely due to your Majesty's eminent dignity and incomparable worth."

At this point Togo marked a pause of several seconds. No one moved. It was as if all those magnificently clad personages standing stiffly in that golden hall had been turned into statues. Then Togo resumed his reading. In his low-pitched voice he read an abridged account of the whole campaign. It concluded thus:

"Having thus rendered an account of the course of our naval operations, I have the honor to submit that the execution of the Imperial Command has been carried to a successful conclusion."

Togo bowed; and it was the emperor's turn.

"It is well known, both in Our fatherland and in foreign countries, that the Combined Squadron has, under your command, rendered unprecedented services. Having heard this report on the war, We are highly satisfied with your loyalty, as We are with the courage displayed by your officers and your men."

The mikado fell silent. He had nothing more to say. The words which he had just uttered were those of the *Final Rescript*. Nothing could come after that: everything had been said.

The emperor withdrew. Togo, the other three admirals and their staff officers were ushered into the east antechamber, where a collation was served. This was followed by a reception at the Ministry of the Navy (Admiralty), then another at the minister's official residence. This was a luncheon, including toasts, official congratulations, salutes, felicitations, and group photographs in the gardens. The most remarkable aspect of all these ceremonies, from

241

our Western point of view, is, perhaps, the following: Togo had been ushered into the palace at eleven in the morning; at ten minutes to two in the afternoon his train left Tokyo for Yokohama. The swift timing of all these arrangements had been strictly adhered to.

The great naval review took place at Yokohama on the following day. The imperial yacht *Asama* steamed past an array of one hundred and sixty-five ships: eight battleships, twelve heavy cruisers and light cruisers, twenty-eight destroyers, seventy-seven torpedo boats, and—already—five submarines. Guns thundered in salutes and, as the imperial yacht passed, the officers and ratings on each ship's company prostrated themselves on the deck. Togo, standing beside the mikado—an unprecedented honor—said a few words about each ship as they drew level with it. But Togo was unable to present the most glorious ship in the fleet to his imperial master on that day of triumph: the *Mikasa* was not there. No human triumph is ever perfect.

It was natural that the government of a country where ancestor worship was the basis of the national religion should have given some thought to those who had lost their lives in the war. The gunners killed at their guns, the sailors who had been blown up with their ships, the drowned, the blockship volunteers, the soldiers who had paid with their lives for the taking of High Mountain Hill and the advance into Manchuria—all the dead must be honored; and the more so in that their families might well feel that they had died, to some extent, in vain. A very solemn religious service was held at the Aoyama cemetery, in Tokyo. The royal princes with their families attended, in the front rank of a vast crowd assembled before an altar decorated with foliage and laden with offerings. A pale sun shone on the scene. Togo spoke. He said that their victory, due to "the emperor's infinite greatness," had been obtained, "also," thanks to the self-sacrifice of the dead they were there to honor. His speech was, in fact—and inevitably—a sermon composed of ritual phrases; but those present would have been shocked to hear anything else. The intervals of silence between his long sentences were filled with bird song.

Finally—last image of war—as Togo moved through the silent crowd toward the gates of the cemetery, he was surrounded and accompanied by a company of touching little figures, all with jet-black hair and all clad in white, their eyes raised to him as if he were a god. These children in mourning were the orphans of the nation's heroes.

On December 20, 1905, Togo was appointed Chief of the Imperial General Staff. He gave a farewell party to his ships' captains on board the *Asahi*, his flagship. For Togo was not leaving the navy. He would still be in its service and, as supreme commander of his country's armed forces, the navy's future was, to some extent, in his hands. But he knew that he was giving up, and this time for ever, the most magnificent of all vocations and a service of superlative satisfaction, such as not even a ruling sovereign can expect—command at sea. The *Asahi* was his last ship. His words of farewell to the officers of his fleet were in some measure his testament. One of the ideas which he expressed was, consciously or otherwise, auto-biographical, for it referred to his own unwearying perseverance: *"The gods award the crown to those who, by their training in peace-time, are victorious even before they go into battle."* But another of his phrases was a warning: *"The gods soon take the crown away from those who relax in the pleasures of peace. The Ancients said, 'After a victory, tighten the straps of your helmet.'"*

Togo, as Chief of the Imperial General Staff from December, 1905, to December, 1909, strictly observed that rule. Throughout those years no war broke out between Japan and any other power, and yet the need to tighten helmet straps was self-evident. Japan, the newest great power, found herself engaged in competition with richer countries, and countries which did not have a recent war to pay for. It was Togo's job to get the utmost value out of the share of the Treasury's revenue obtained by the civil head of the Admiralty. Togo, studying the naval programs of the maritime powers, gave thought to the problem of exploiting the newest weapon, the submarine, which some believed certain to upset all the rules of naval tactics. And there was yet another new weapon which required attention, for far away in Europe a Frenchman named Blériot had just flown an "aeroplane" across a strait nearly as wide as Tsushima.

Nor were technical problems the Chief of the General Staff's only preoccupation. The United States was beginning to feel that Japan, despite the whittling down of her victory by the Treaty of Portsmouth, was becoming too powerful; that her expansion was counterbalancing Anglo-American influence in the Pacific Zone—an influence whose righteousness went without saying, of course. Hawaii, a strategic point for American power, had a population that included 79,000 Japanese as against only 12,000 Americans. Japanese emigrants were establishing themselves all over the Pacific area, including California, where they worked for practically nothing, thus displacing white labor. Mutual hostility became intense, and there were outbreaks between Americans and Japanese in San Francisco and Ogden, Utah. The two governments exchanged ill-tempered notes. On December 16, 1907, a formidable United States naval force of sixteen battleships was moved from Hampton Roads to San Francisco. In the end, a settlement was arranged. In November, 1908, Tokyo and Washington exchanged friendly notes, both undertaking to maintain the *status quo* in the Pacific and to respect China's territorial integrity. But for a time, although there was no open war, the task of the Chief of the Imperial General Staff was no sinecure, and certainly bore no resemblance to a peaceful retirement.

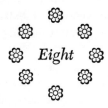

Eight

In the forenoon of May 29, 1911, the Japanese liner *Kamo Maru*, having recently emerged from the Strait of Gibraltar, was steaming parallel with the Spanish coast, three miles offshore and on a north-westerly course. The captain was on his bridge, and with him were his most illustrious passengers. He had invited them to see Cape Trafalgar as they passed it. They were the Prince and Princess Higashi-Fushimi, on their way to represent the mikado at the coronation of King George V, in London. Their Imperial Highnesses were accompanied by General Nogi, and by Admiral Count Togo, Knight Grand Cordon of the Chrysanthemum, Order (First Class) of the Golden Falcon, Member of the High Council of War. It was within two days of forty years since Togo had sighted Cape Tra-

245

falgar for the first time. More than half a lifetime and all one man's achievement lay between those two occasions. It was no ordinary achievement, no commonplace lifetime. The samurai of Satsuma, making his second journey to Europe, was the greatest fighting seaman since Nelson.

London was still the greatest city in the world. The front pages of the voluminous British newspapers were filled with biographies and photographs of Togo and Nogi. The two were photographed together perhaps a thousand times in the course of the coronation festivities and ceremonies. But when it came to what, for every true Briton of the epoch, was the grandest of all the shows, the culminating splendor—and incidentally the most sensational display of the times and one which no country in the world but Great Britain could have accomplished—the naval review at Spithead, Togo alone was invited aboard the Admiralty yacht *Enchantress*. "No other foreigner," the newspapers reported, "was on board." One million four hundred thousand tons of warships steamed past; eighteen nations were represented. Side by side off Spithead, among the other guest warships, lay the battle cruiser *Kurama*, her great Rising Sun at the mainmast head, and the Russian *Rossia*. Later, during a garden party, made gay by two thousand sunshades, King George V talked with both Nogi and Togo. The newspapers printed his parting words to the two distinguished guests as if they were a text to be remembered: "I hope that you will have pleasant memories of your stay in England."

Togo visited his old training ship, the *Worcester*. Once there had been difficulties about his boarding her at all; now he was received aboard with extraordinary honors, he who had once been "Johnny Chinaman." He made a speech to the assembled cadets. And at a gala dinner given by the Worcester Association the principal toast was "Admiral Togo—an example to every boy-seaman in the navy!"

The festivities over and the Imperial Highnesses on their way back to Japan, Nogi set off to visit the Continent. Togo preferred seeing Scotland. He traveled incognito in theory, although recognized, of course, wherever he went. One night he was ushered into what was needless to say the best bedroom in the hotel. As soon as he was alone, Togo called his aide-de-camp Tanigochi; he was disturbed at the spectacle of *two* beds in his room. Did not this mean that the hospitality with which he was being received was to include the services of a Scottish geisha? Tanigochi, whose room had only one bed, immediately changed quarters with his admiral, and was able to assure him, the following day, that no Scottish geisha had appeared.

In agreement with his government, Togo had accepted an invitation to visit William Howard Taft, President of the United States since 1909. He arrived in New York on August 3, 1911, having crossed the Atlantic in the brand-new *Lusitania*. Journalists and photographers stormed aboard the liner and began looking everywhere for a Japanese admiral; they were a good deal disappointed to be confronted with a man who was hardly Japanese at all and who wore a lounge suit and a felt hat.

Nevertheless, Togo was a success in America because of his simple manners and pleasant smile. His journey became a triumphal progress from banquet to banquet, each more gigantic and luxurious than the last, each host organization trying to outdo the others. The secretary of state, Philander C. Knox, who as the government's representative felt impelled to top everyone else, gave the admiral a gargantuan dinner which cost a hundred dollars a head. The table was decorated with a model of the *Mikasa* made of flowers; the dinner service was gold plate worth fifty thousand dollars; and nine kinds of wine were served. Caricaturists depicted the admiral defeated at last—by champagne—and crying, "I surrender!"

But Togo did not lose his head: he was imperturbable, unshakable. In the course of a visit which he paid to former President Theodore Roosevelt, his host showed him two swords which the mikado had sent him as a present some time ago. Togo and Roosevelt examined the beautifully worked handles and guards, priceless jewels of craftsmanship. Togo unsheathed one of the swords; and immediately his brow darkened and he frowned; there were stains of rust on the blade.

247

"I shall clean them at once," he said.

"I'll have them cleaned," Roosevelt assured him.

"It cannot possibly wait."

The admiral was given the nearest obtainable substitute for the traditional sand and cloth which should have been used, and he began to rub away at the rust. He cleaned first one blade, then the other. And as he did so, he explained that these swords were not simply objects, but in some sort materializations of the soul of the samurai who had made use of them.

Togo returned to Japan in mid-September. Exactly a year later Meiji, the mikado, the great emperor who had reigned for forty-five years and was venerated to the point of deity, died. It was Meiji who had inaugurated the modernization of Japan and had been her first progressive monarch. In spite of this, the funeral cart which Togo followed on foot was drawn by five oxen. The wheels, as they turned, emitted "the seven sounds of grief," for this cart was the work of "a family of Kyoto carpenters who specialized in this craft and whose ancestors had made more than one coffin for the imperial family."

On the day of the funeral, General Nogi and his wife, discreetly and according to the strictest ritual, put an end to their own lives, by dealing themselves *seppuku*, in their residence. Having buried his emperor, Togo had to bury his brother-in-arms.

Togo was sixty-five years old, and had been forty-three years in the service of the Imperial Navy. Emperor Yoshihito, Meiji's successor (he continued to be known by the name of Taisho), had just appointed him Admiral of the Fleet. His chest brilliant with a whole constellation of stars and orders and crossed by the ribbon of the Grand Cordon of the Chrysanthemum, his arms straight at his sides in sleeves golden with braid to the elbow, Togo, impassive as ever, posed for the photographers. His snow-white beard was clipped very short. His eyes were as piercing as ever. But there was, in his face, a barely perceptible tension, the shadow of a rictus due to pain. Since his return from the United States, his health had been poor. It was not rheumatism, his old enemy, which troubled him this time, but stone in the bladder. In November, 1913, he underwent an operation which gave him relief. And in the following spring he was back at work, still Admiral of the Fleet and a member of the highest councils of state, and, in addition, assuming new duties. He had been appointed to preside over the Office of Studies set up for the Prince Imperial's education.

The education of his divine pupil was no sinecure. Seventeen teachers were appointed to instruct the boy in ethics, history, geography, Chinese and Japanese literature, natural history, physics, chemistry, the French language—he already knew English—writing, law and legislation, and the history of the fine arts. Moreover, accounts of military and naval affairs were frequently read to him. Military education, which naturally had an important place in the school curriculum of a future monarch, included all those exercises to develop the body and the character, without which the finest ornaments of the mind are but vanity. Togo was on duty every morning at seven-forty.

In 1914, when Japan entered the war, Togo, Admiral of the Fleet, was not in command of the fleet. But every important command was in the hands of one of his pupils: Kato, who had been his chief of staff at Tsushima, was chief of the General Staff, and was to become Minister of the Navy; Shimamura then became chief of the General Staff in his place. Togo continued to direct the education of the Prince Imperial. In October, 1915, he accompanied his pupil on board a cruiser of the First Squadron to be present at a gunnery-training exercise. The Imperial Fleet shelled an old battleship which was being used as a target: she was the *Iki*. Togo stared thoughtfully at the target, for she was an old acquaintance—at Tsushima she had been called the *Nicholas I*. Now, once again, Japanese shells were exploding against her hull. With the smell of the sea wind and of guncotton in his nostrils, Togo might well imagine that presently the three flags of the signal X G H would be run up her mast again —*I ask to negotiate*. But the only signal ratings aboard the *Nicholas I* now were ghosts. Time had passed, and life does not begin again.

In 1920 the Prince attained his majority, and his schooling was officially over. The future Emperor Hirohito was going to England. Togo paid a visit to the palace at Hayama, where the mikado was in residence, and there, as ceremoniously as he had read his report on the war with Russia, read the emperor his report on the prince's education. From there he made his way to the Shrine of Meiji, in the suburbs of Tokyo, to thank Heaven for having allowed him to bring his last task to a successful conclusion.

We are entitled to be curious concerning his children. Hyo, Togo's eldest son, did not inherit his father's naval vocation. Like his father, he went to England, but to study Western agricultural methods. He returned to Japan in 1916, married, and in due course presented Togo with two grandsons. Togo's other son, Minorou, was a naval officer. He married, had one son, was in no way favored because of the magical name he bore, and had an honorable but not particularly distinguished career. Finally, his surviving daughter married a naval officer and had one son.

Togo had reached the age of seventy-three. He withdrew from public life. He spent his time at his house in Kajima-Machi, often in his garden, clad in the traditional costume of his people, busy with his books, his flowers, his dwarf trees, and with his grandchildren. To the public character, Admiral Togo, succeeded another, not less popular: representatives of Japanese and foreign newspapers came to photograph "Grandfather" Togo, white-haired and white-bearded among a bevy of jet-haired, smiling children. With his hair clipped short and in his long robe, Togo resembled an aged bonze.

In 1922 an earthquake devastated Tokyo and the surrounding country; innumerable houses of wood and paper were destroyed by fire. Togo and his whole family, helped by the neighbors, had to fight a fire in his own house. In due course the damage done was repaired and life was resumed as before. From time to time, on the occasion of a national event or ceremony, Togo would emerge from his retirement in full-dress uniform, including the Collar which had been added to his Grand Cordon of the Order of the Chrysanthemum and was the highest honor in his country's gift, shared only with the Prince Imperial. Thus attired and decorated, and cheered wherever he showed himself, Togo was the personification of the national ideal. He was patriotism incarnate, Bushido in the shape of a living man. An association called Togo's Boys was founded, and joined by tens of thousands of schoolboys who took an oath to shape their lives by the admiral's example. His admirers presented him with a statuette of Nelson, carved out of a piece of wood from the *Victory*.

On May 27, 1934, Togo was not present at the Tsushima Anniversary celebration. He was bed-ridden, suffering from cancer of the pharynx. The disease had been diagnosed five months before; none of the treatments prescribed had had any effect. Togo had no illusions about his condition, and awaited death with a tranquil spirit. The Countess, his wife, suffering from neuritis, lay sick in another room.

Friends and kinsmen came to call upon the sick man that day; now, at the precise moment when, as he knew, the emperor would be showing himself to the assembled multitude, and before anyone could foresee Togo's intention, he rose from his bed and knelt on the floor of his room.

On the following day his condition had deteriorated. In the afternoon a messenger came from the palace bearing an imperial decree creating Togo a marquis. His wife was carried into his room so that she could be present at the ceremony. Those who watched could scarcely restrain their tears when the husband and wife, who had lived fifty-three years together, sharing the best and the worst, decided that now was the moment to take their last leave of each other. Tetsuko died seven months later.

As for the admiral, he died on May 30th at half-past six in the morning, having been fifteen hours in a coma. For thirty-six hours the radio broadcast bulletins on his condition every hour. During all that time a crowd stood still and silent in the street before his house, praying in the rain, day and night.

The funeral took place on June 5th. For the first time a national funeral was accorded to a man who had not been a prince of the blood. It lasted from dawn till dusk. Every minute during all that day came the dull thud of a big gun, from the direction of the naval anchorage. Seaplanes of the Imperial Fleet flew above the long funeral procession. The coffin, covered with white silk, was placed upon a gun carriage drawn by sailors. A multitude, bowed in grief, lined the last long road which Togo traveled to lie beside the Mikado Taisho in Tama cemetery, thirty-five miles from Tokyo.

The admiral had spoken his last words on April 29th at noon. And it is possible that they were in fact what they were reported to be. They reveal no secret; yet it seems to me that for us they may serve as a sign; and that they bring that silent, reserved and often, to us, enigmatic Japanese, a little nearer. For me, at least, his last words enable me to leave him not quite as we leave a stranger, a foreigner:

"I desire only to rest until the end. My thoughts turn to my emperor"—a sigh—"and to roses."

·